1976

This book may be kept

FOURTEEN DAYS

THE DIVINE SCIENCE

NUMBER 151 OF THE
COLUMBIA UNIVERSITY STUDIES IN
ENGLISH AND COMPARATIVE
LITERATURE

THE DIVINE SCIENCE

THE AESTHETIC
OF SOME REPRESENTATIVE
SEVENTEENTH-CENTURY
ENGLISH POETS

By LEAH JONAS

OCTAGON BOOKS

A DIVISION OF FARRAR, STRAUS AND GIROUX

New York   1973

Copyright 1940 by Columbia University Press

Reprinted 1973
by special arrangement with Columbia University Press

OCTAGON BOOKS
A DIVISION OF FARRAR, STRAUS & GIROUX, INC.
19 Union Square West
New York, N. Y. 10003

Library of Congress Cataloging in Publication Data

Jonas, Leah, 1907—
    The divine science.

        Original ed. issued as no. 151 of Columbia University studies in
        English and comparative literature.

        Originally presented as the author's thesis, Columbia.

        CONTENTS: The theory of English poetry about 1600.—Ben
        Jonson.—Michael Drayton. [etc.]
        1. English poetry—Early modern (to 1700)—History and criti-
        cism. I. Title. II. Series: Columbia University studies in Eng-
        lish and comparative literature, no. 151.

PR541.J6   1973   821'.3'09   73-1886
ISBN 0-374-94270-6

Printed in USA by
Thomson-Shore, Inc.
Dexter, Michigan

To all whose hope has been my help

ACKNOWLEDGMENTS

THE AUTHOR of a book such as this one has good cause to be grateful to those few experts who both can and will give assistance. Tribute of thanks I gladly bring first to Professor Frank Allen Patterson, under whose careful supervision I laid the groundwork and wrote the early drafts of this study. For his ungrudging patience and labor I remain his debtor. During Professor Patterson's absence from the university I came under the guidance of Professor Oscar James Campbell who brought the benefit of his fresh viewpoint and inexhaustible vitality to the later stages of the work. Finally it would be impossible for me to overestimate the help of Dr. Henry Willis Wells. He "from the first was present" and to the last was active, a continuing and most creative critic.

These acknowledgments would be incomplete without the name of Adele Borgo Mendelsohn, to whom I am indebted not only for her efficient preparation of the typescript, a task shared by Eleanor Jaqua, but also for a decade of unfailing kindness and encouragement.

L. J.

New York
October, 1940

CONTENTS

It is more Praise worthy in noble and excellent Things to know something, though little, than in mean and ignoble Matters to have a perfect Knowledge. Amongst all those rare Ornaments the Mind of Man, Poesy hath had a most eminent Place, and been in high Esteem, not only at one Time and in one Climate, but during all Times, and through all those Parts of the World, where any Ray of Humanity and Civility hath shined. So that she hath not unworthily deserved the Name of the Mistress of Humane Life, the Height of Eloquence, the Quintessence of Knowledge, the loud Trumpet of Fame, the language of the Gods. There is not anything endureth longer: Homer's Troy hath out-lived many Republicks, and both the Roman and Grecian monarchies; she subsisteth by her self; and after one Demeanor and Continuance her Beauty appeareth to all Ages. In vain have some Men of late (Transformers of every Thing) consulted upon her Reformation and endeavoured to abstract her to Metaphysical Ideas and Scholastical Quiddities, denuding her of her own Habits and those Ornaments with which she hath amused the World some Thousand Years. Poesy is not a Thing that is yet in the finding and search, or which may be otherwise found out, being already condescended upon by all Nations, Italians, French, Spaniards. Neither do I think that a good Piece of Poesy, which Homer, Virgil, Ovid, Petrarch, Bartas, Ronsard, Boscan, Garcilasso (if they were alive, and had that Language) could not understand, and reach the Sense of the Writer. . . . What is not like and the Ancients and conform to those Rules which hath been agreed unto by all Times, may (indeed) be something like unto Poesy, but is no more Poesy than a Monster is a Man.

WILLIAM DRUMMOND, *Works*, 1711, PAGE 143

It is not without grief and indignation that I behold that Divine Science employing all her inexhaustible riches of Wit and Eloquence, either in the wicked and beggarly Flattery of great persons, or the unmanly Idolizing of Foolish Women, or the wretched affectation of scurril Laughter, or at best on confused antiquated Dreams of sense-less Fables and Metamorphoses.

ABRAHAM COWLEY, *Poems*, EDITED BY A. R. WALLER

INTRODUCTION

THE CHARACTER of English poetry changed radically during the seventeenth century. The opening of that period found poetic achievement richly imaginative, strangely conceited, diversified in tone, and extraordinary in range; the close found it restrained, clear, rational, and limited in scope by an Augustan ideal. The change was not, however, a steady and simple narrowing. Indeed, the forces operating were so complex that the student can never hope for a convenient general term by which to indicate broadly the quality of the period. There is a consequent tendency to regard this difficult age in terms of its neighbor eras, to consider it a decadence of the Elizabethan glory, a disintegration prior to a new integrated cycle.[1] Hitherto the main aids to study have been certain partial classifications that call attention to the diversity of movements in poetry rather than to the general trend of the century. The much used division into the "schools" of Jonson, of Donne, and of Spenser stresses differences in style and personality, but tends to minimize points of resemblance. It has the further disadvantage of being incomplete. It makes no allowance for the tremendous influence of Sidney. There are poets like Carew, who was a disciple of both Jonson and Donne; and those who, like Wither, served a very short imitative apprenticeship before breaking away from all models. Thus the schools, although valuable for dividing the century into manageable units, are neither comprehensive nor mutually exclusive. This weakness is inherent in the fact that the criterion for each school is some one aspect, usually style or subject matter. But the choice of both subject matter and style is affected by a writer's theory of poetry. There is the possibility, hitherto overlooked, that the theory underlying the work of representative poets can be traced and used to obtain a broader understanding of seventeenth century poetic evolution.

Ideally, a study of literary theory would base itself on the critics and supplement their work by reference to such poets as have made

[1] Wendell, *The Temper of the Seventeenth Century in Literature.*

more or less extended comments on their art. The problem of reconstructing the theories that prevailed in England during the first half of the seventeenth century cannot be approached in this way because there was so little contemporary criticism. Spingarn's collection of critical essays shows that from 1602, when Daniel published his *Defence of Rime*, to 1668, when Dryden wrote his *Essay of Dramatick Poesie*, there was no whole work whose purpose was purely critical.[2] Thus little help can be expected from that quarter. It is possible, however, to derive the theories of seventeenth-century poetry from other available materials. Many of the poets, realizing that their works would raise certain questions in the minds of an audience, took the precaution of writing an explanatory preface or notes. They frequently anticipated and attempted to forestall adverse criticism or, failing that, answered it. The nature of a man's work and any opinions expressed in the course of it are additional sources of information. If to a consideration of the type of work done by a given writer there is added a sifting and compiling of all his references to poetry, the result will be a picture of his theory of poetry more or less complete in proportion to the data supplied. The object of this study is to examine the theories of certain representative poets with a view to demonstrating what beliefs were common concerning the nature, the purpose, and the practice of their art; to view the mural of seventeenth-century poetic development as it appeared to the men who were engaged in painting it.

[2] Spingarn, *Critical Essays of the Seventeenth Century*. I am excepting from consideration as too narrowly specialized the *Mythomystes* of Henry Reynolds.

CHAPTER I

THE THEORY OF ENGLISH POETRY
ABOUT 1600

THE SEVENTEENTH-CENTURY English poet inherited many ideas from the critics of the Renaissance and, in particular, was aware of the English writers who digested and reëxpressed the most active of the traditions. As few, however, if any of these native critics constructed a complete theory of poetry, it is hardly strange that the seventeenth-century poet had to go further afield in search of authoritative solutions to some of the problems of his art. When forced to show cause why poetry should be countenanced by sober and thoughtful persons, when eager to rally to its defense every possible witness to its good character, noble achievements, and glorious possibilities, the English poet, following the lead of Sidney, naturally turned to the critics of the Italian Renaissance who had succeeded in developing a rich body of theory that covered almost all the ethical and esthetic problems that could confront the champions of poetry.

BEFORE 1600

The close of the sixteenth century found English poetry just past the danger of following the false light of classical meters, but facing another serious crisis. Guy A. Thompson, in his *Elizabethan Criticism of Poetry,* has made a composite picture of the poetic situation as it seemed to the leading Elizabethan critics. His survey of critical opinion finds the writers, though far from unanimous in details, strongly convinced that the state of English poetry was unsatisfactory. From this general sense of dissatisfaction they were led to search for reasons and remedies.

One reason why poetry had fallen into disrepute was a growing tide of Puritanism that regarded the whole art of poetry with a suspicion not entirely unwarranted. Many persons were so disgusted by ribald comedy, vicious satire, and lascivious love strains that they caught eagerly at Plato's suggestion that poetry should be banished from his commonwealth. If allowed to remain, poetry should, in their opinion, be branded as a gross and wanton pastime. "Religion," says Grierson, "and the desire to be amused are . . . two of the strongest passions of the human mind, each at times threatening to displace the other." [1] Such displacement was in progress. The very power of poetry to entertain rendered it suspect. And poetry, coming from the court to the country at large, felt the insistence of the less sophisticated audience's request that it justify itself in some practical fashion. In answer to the attacks of the moralists, the defenders of poetry had first to admit the evidence, and second to demonstrate that the practices complained of all represented abuses rather than legitimate uses of poetry. Plato had banished such poetry, true, but he had at the same time used the poetic device of feigning dialogues to further his own teaching. And far from being a dealer in disreputable trifles, the poet had from earliest days been associated with the loftiest duties. He had in pagan times been the prophet, as the word *vates* with its dual meaning of bard and seer testified. He could be historically proved a figure of the highest social and national significance. As to any incompatability between poetry and religion, that was easy to confute by the example of David, in the Old Testament, and of Jesus, teaching by fiction in the New. Sidney argued along these lines and to bear out his conclusions wrote metrical translations of the Psalms and recommended a wider use of the religious lyric. Yet unquestionably the bulk of poetry derived its inspiration, in thought as well as in art, from pagan rather than from orthodox religious sources and was therefore open to attack during an era of strong religious feeling. The Reformation, with its insistence on a sharp distinction between matters secular and religious and its consignment of all secular art to an inferior rank, constituted, as Grierson shows, a cross current that strongly affected the humanistic trend in literature. [2] To counter the charges of the Puritans, the poetical standard would have to be raised to such a height that even the most severe censor must honor the art. Every type of poetry would have to be defended, or, to the extent that it could not justify

[1] Grierson, *Cross Currents in English Literature of the XVIIth Century*, p. 63.
[2] *Cross Currents*, p. 33.

its existence as socially desirable, condemned. A complete theory of art required a delicate balance of pleasurable and profitable elements, a balance not wholly determined by artistic considerations.

But it was not only the Puritans who made the mistake of treating all verse as poetry. The number of properly trained readers was small. At the opposite extreme from the Puritan faction, which had a general objection to all secular poetry, was an equally undiscriminating group who accepted almost anything that rimed and fell within their limited comprehension. This was the "uncapable Multitude," who knew nothing of the true virtue of art and were unable to distinguish between rime and poetry. Plainly there was a great need for education here.

The abuses of poetry were largely perpetrated by a group that Thompson, following Gabriel Harvey, labels the "Rakehelly Rout," irresponsible poetasters who, scribbling for a wretched pittance or for fashion's sake, had no true concept of their art but wrote all manner of vile trash. To avoid being confused with these cheap versifiers, the true poet took every opportunity of distinguishing himself from them and of pouring a full measure of contempt upon them. The poets united with the Puritans in considering this base riming

> such a sinne
> As I thinke that brings dearth, and Spaniards in.[3]

If England was ever to obtain her patriotic desire and have a poetry comparable to that of ancient Rome or Renaissance Italy, she required poets of ample learning and proper training, men who would inevitably despise the "poet-apes" by whom their profession was disgraced.

The great problem of the seventeenth-century poet was to establish and maintain a desirable attitude toward poetry, among both the public and the imitative or commercial writers. This attitude did not have to be created; the tradition had existed in classical times, it had been taught to Italy by the Renaissance critics, it had spread to France and was guiding the minds of the Pléiade, it was present in England among the Areopagites, and had already pro-

---

[3] Donne, *Complete Poetry and Selected Prose of John Donne,* ed. by Hayward, p. 124.

duced a Spenser when Sidney drew on it heavily to defend English poetry against the attack of Gosson.

The richest source of traditional poetic theory available in 1600 was the writings of the Renaissance Italians. As Spingarn shows, from 1527 to 1600 there were twenty-five important critical works published by Italians, as compared to twelve written by the French and twelve by the English.[4] Upon the Italian theorists, as the eldest heirs of the classical principles, first fell the task of combining the Horatian and the Aristotelian dicta,[5] and the more difficult problem of reconciling, as far as possible, pagan art with Christian theology. The particular questions most under discussion and the suggested solutions are thoroughly set forth in Spingarn's invaluable study, *Literary Criticism in the Renaissance*. Some notion of the complexity and detail of Renaissance theory may be gathered from the fact that Scaliger's *Poetics* filled seven volumes.[6] A glance at the *Poetics* will serve to establish the Renaissance basis of much seventeenth-century theory. In his writings, Scaliger succeeded to some extent in securing an integrated theory by blending the Greek and Roman tradition and adding certain concepts of his own. According to his definition

The poetical art is a science, that is, it is a habit of production in accordance with those laws which underlie that symmetrical fashioning known as poetry. So it has three elements—the material [subject], the form [type], and the execution [style]. In the higher criticism, a fourth element is recognized, the end, that is imitation, or the ulterior end, instruction.[7]

To Scaliger as to Horace, excellence of verse is a more practical criterion of poetry than the broad concept of imitation, which he treats as the purpose rather than the nature of poetry. Scaliger was far more exact than Horace in his differentiation of types. Ranking poems in the order of excellence, he lists

1. Hymns, paeans
2. Songs, odes, scolia sung in praise of brave men
3. Epics, in which are both heroes and lesser men
4. Tragedies, comedies

[4] *Literary Criticism in the Renaissance*, pp. 312–13.   [5] *Ibid.*, p. 23.
[6] Scaliger, *Poetices libri septem*, [Heidelberg?], 1594.
[7] Padelford, *Select Translations from Scaliger's Poetics*, p. 18.

5. Satires, exodia, interludes, jests, nuptial songs, elegies, mono-
dies, incantations, epigrams
  6. Pastorals [8]

This is obviously listing the types in order of the excellence of the
subject matter. A spirit of integration manifests itself when he recog-
nizes the epic as "the chiefest of all forms" because of its catholicity
of range. Since the epic is all-embracing in its scope, he considers
it the norm or standard from which other types of poetry should
receive regulative principles, according to their distinctive subject
matter and nature.[9] Scaliger established in full detail the subject
and treatment proper to each of the types mentioned, subdividing
each for consideration when the historical development warranted
it, for instance comedy, old, middle, and new. Yet all poetry, he
insisted, is characterized by planned unity, variety in expression,
forcefulness of language tempered by grace, and a master aim of
pleasing persuasion.

In considering the fourth element of aim, Scaliger explained that
the poet, like the philosopher and orator, who also use the art of
language, seeks to persuade. He quotes Euripides to the effect that
the major merit of a poet is "the ability to impress adroitly upon
citizens the need of being better men."[10] The poet's art is similar
to that of the historian, but superior in that he is not confined to
the representation of things as they were and are, but may go on
to the more god-like task of creating things which are not. Like the
philosopher, the orator, and the historian, the poet seeks to persuade
men to right living: "The poet teaches mental disposition through
action, so that we embrace the good and imitate it in our conduct
and reject the evil and abstain from that."[11] He surpasses his fellows
in the scope and attractiveness of his means of persuasion, wherefore
it seemed to Scaliger that poetry was the master science,[12] or, as
Cowley was later to call it, the divine science: "Through poetry,
indeed, the spirit is turned back upon itself, and it draws forth from
its inner sanctuary, which is, indeed, an inexhaustible spring, that
which inheres therein from the divine life."[13]

[8] *Ibid.*, p. 20.
[10] *Ibid.*, pp. 2, 3.
[12] *Ibid.*, p. 8.

[9] *Ibid.*, p. 54.
[11] *Ibid.*, p. 83.
[13] *Ibid.*, p. 13.

In his discussion of poetic inspiration, Scaliger goes beyond Horace in that he not only acknowledges the necessity for special talent in the poet, but also defines that special talent as a peculiar ability to transcend the ordinary realization of that which is divine. Having mentioned the class of poets to whom divine power comes with no effort other than simple invocation, he goes on to speak, without derogatory comment, of those poets who require the aid of wine to stimulate their imaginations.

As far as the seventeenth-century English poet was concerned, the most significant contribution of the Renaissance critics was their concept of the purpose of poetry. By means of it they had solved the vital problem of justifying "imaginative literature in a way to satisfy non-literary criteria." [14] In Italy, although Castelvetro maintained what he considered to be the Aristotelian thesis that the end of poetry was delight, Cinthio, Minturno, and Scaliger went further and interpreted the aim of poetry as delightful teaching, particularly the inculcation of virtue through delightful example. To quote the conclusion of Spingarn:

it was as an effective guide to life that poetry was chiefly valued. Even when delight was admitted as an end, it was simply because of its usefulness in effecting the ethical aim.[15]

The conclusions of the Renaissance critics concerning poetry were, moreover, reinforced and vitalized by their harmony with the philosophical trend of the time. Basil Willey, in his study of the seventeenth-century background, has noted the growing desire to control natural forces for the increasing happiness of men.[16] He has to some extent considered the responses of heroic poetry to the changing "climates of opinion." But the analysis may be carried much further, until most seventeenth-century major poetry in satisfying the Renaissance requirements is also consonant with the practical Baconian philosophy: [17]

Therefore, because the Acts or Events of true Historie have not that Magnitude which satisfieth the minde of Man, Poesie faineth Acts and Events Greater and more Heroicall; because true Historie propoundeth the successes

---

[14] Spingarn, *Literary Criticism*, p. 3.   [15] *Ibid.*, p. 58.
[16] *The Seventeenth Century Background*, p. 6.
[17] Spingarn, *Critical Essays of the Seventeenth Century*, I, ix.

and issues of actions not so agreable to the merits of Vertue and Vice, therefore Poesie faines them more just in Retribution and more according to Revealed Providence; because true Historie representeth Actions and Events more ordinarie and less interchanged, therefore Poesie endueth them with more Rarenesse and more unexpected and alternative Variations: So as it appeareth that Poesie serveth and conferreth to Magnanimitie, Moralitie, and to delectation.[18]

It is noteworthy that Italian theorists concentrated their attention for the most part on the higher kinds of poetry. They gave but scant notice to the pastoral and quite ignored the nonclassical Petrarchan sonnet. About the middle of the century there began a French critical literature, which reinforced the effect of the Italian influence upon contemporary English tradition [19] and which emphasized the sonnet and imitative pastoral as desirable types of the *genres inférieurs*. Certainly, as J. B. Fletcher indicates, the Areopagus group was close to the spirit of the Pléiade in its desire to harmonize the native medieval with the classic tradition, in its attempt to defend poetry against the accusation that it was a wanton, deceitful art, in its effort to restore the poet to his ancient elevation, in its consideration of vocabulary, of metrics, and of types.

Although a young English poet would be thoroughly dominated by classical and Continental forces, he would also be somewhat affected by the native tradition, now two hundred years old. He would render homage to Chaucer, who had most completely and successfully naturalized the European tradition for the British. And although it was hard to reconcile *Piers Plowman* or such rattling satire as the *Bowge of Court* with the European esthetic, yet Englishmen never entirely lost sight of the unique and powerful figures of Langland and Skelton. There was a spirit evinced in such poems that met with their complete approval, for, as Spingarn has shown, the English critics always sought a didactic core in poetry, whether they held to the medieval belief that the poet, afraid to teach directly, deemed it safer to hide his meaning within a seemingly light fable; [20] or advanced to the Renaissance belief that the poet, eager

[18] *Ibid.*, I, 6.
[19] J. B. Fletcher, "Areopagus and Pleiade," *Journal of Germanic Philology*, II (1898–99), 429–53.
[20] Spingarn, *Literary Criticism*, p. 262.

to secure his audience, had deemed it desirable to cloak his teaching under a pleasing exterior. Finally, the English were most eager to retain in the canon of proper poetry the versified historical chronicles that had slight artistic merit, but fed their patriotism and desire to gain political perspective.

The English theory was most fully stated by Sidney in his *Defense of Poesie,* which is largely a digest of Italian theory. Sidney avoided basing his argument on the divine origin of poetry and made no mention of *poeticus furor.* Plato, he said, "attributeth to poesy more than myself do, namely to be a very inspiring of a divine force, far above man's wit." He himself concentrated rather on justifying poetry as the superlative mortal means of teaching virtue. He was careful to define his art by its noble function rather than by attributes that might be misapplied. He demonstrated that men became poets when they used feigning to enter into the "gates of popular judgment" and taught by delighting the hearer. Verse, though usual in poetry, was not essential; teaching by imitation of life was. He eulogized the poetic office and defended the poet's imaginative power. The poet had the privilege of creating beyond nature, of inventing fictitious monsters or ideal heroes. Sidney held that a feigned example was as good as a real one; it might even be better than a real one for purposes of delightful instruction. He, too, divided poetry into several categories: the pastoral type (elegiac); two kinds of satire, bitter and playful; drama, comic and tragic; the lyric; and the heroic type. He felt that although the poet must have inborn talent, it devolved upon him as a duty to increase that original endowment by art, imitation of approved models, and exercise. He thought that the lyric could be well employed in praising God and ought not to be solely devoted to unconvincing love songs. He advised that the best art seemed natural and did not try to flaunt itself. Finally, he praised English as a language specially adapted to poetry.

At the close of the sixteenth century this accumulation of tradition was vitalized by the fact that Spenser, in his unfinished masterpiece, had achieved, though in fragmentary fashion, a great English epic. He had realized the promise of the Renaissance theory by writing a poem of amazing virtuosity, depicting action and employing religious, moral, and national themes. He had undergone the recommended period of early training; he had followed approved models; he had exercised himself in pastorals, in satire, in love poetry, and in drama. Apparently, then, Renaissance theory was feasible for English poets and the way to the heights of poetry was clearly charted.

AFTER 1600

In the seventeenth century the influence of the Reformation cross current reinforced the Renaissance sense of relative values, which had created a hierarchy of types. Purpose and form, considered jointly, were used to establish a range of values. The amount of pleasure and profit in each recognized type of poetry was noted and the types were accordingly assigned to their places. Not all poets accepted the same classification, but generally the epic, the ode, and the tragedy were recognized as the most exalted types of poetry. Of these, the epic received the most theoretical attention. Should it be classical or romantic, or neither? Should the subject be historical or religious? What metrical scheme should be employed? The only unanimity was found in the opinion that the epic should have high seriousness of purpose. Theories in regard to the ode were even more liberal. Should it be Horatian or Pindaric? If Pindaric, should it follow the form or the spirit of Pindar? Should it be religious, personal, national? Equal to the epic and ode, or only slightly less in rank, came the drama. The lofty position of tragedy was undisputed. Comedy was variously considered, but when it was rated high its function was invariably didactic. According to Campbell, "the belief of the Renaissance critics was that where no social correction is administered, no real comedy exists." [21] Here again the problem was one of models. Should the dramatist imitate Greek or Roman forerunners, should he desert the classics to work along more romantic lines, alter the formula so as to work along satiric lines, or should he write chronicle plays?

At the other extreme of the hierarchy were the love lyric and the pastoral. These "low" forms were pleasing but not profitable; they were valued chiefly for the technical exercise they afforded the poet. It was quite correct for them to be highly imitative. The son-

[21] O. J. Campbell, *Comicall Satyre and Shakespeare's Troilus and Cressida*, p. 13.

nets particularly tended to be largely borrowed from the Italian and the French. Almost all critics united to minimize the pastoral and the sonnet. In order to include them in a theory of poetry it was necessary to consider that they had a preparatory value for the higher types of work, or to claim boldly that there was an intrinsic merit in sheer delight.

Under the general heading of satire were grouped two very different kinds of poetry: the burlesque, beginning with the mock heroic, which the epic engenders as its antitype (the pendulum swinging from an *Iliad* to a *Batracho-myo-Machia*); and the more common variety, sprung from the drama, which is a reaction to life rather than to literature. In a century so concerned as the seventeenth with improving life by means of poetry, it was the satire dealing in criticism and comment on life which received the predominant emphasis. In view of its reforming purpose, this type clearly ranked above the merely pleasing forms of verse, but except where satire was employed within the framework of the epic or the drama, it was usually classified as "low." It had didactic value, but inasmuch as it dealt with specific and, it was to be hoped, transient abuses, no great effort was made to perpetuate it beyond the life of the circumstance that had given it birth; the style was consciously rough and unfinished. It aimed at a limited and direct profit and it wasted almost no effort on pleasing. Even if it was artistically done, it could not rise above intermediate rank, since it did not set positive examples of virtue but impelled the reader toward right living by holding up to ridicule examples of foolishness and vice. Here again the question of the best model was unsettled. Should satire be toothless or fanged? Was it to follow urbane Horace or harsh Juvenal or epigrammatic Martial? Should the Englishman adopt the nonclassical tone of Chaucer's *Sir Thopas* or the rapid riming of Skelton? Could satirical comedy be used to perform the functions of the prohibited satire? The only general rule was that satire should not become an instrument for venting personal spite; it should not be directed against recognizable individuals.

Thus the English poet of 1600 possessed a basic theory and a variety of examples from which he might choose his own mode of applying it. Unless a man had far more ability in one kind of work than in another, the choice was a difficult one, for whatever he rejected was also valuable. It is small wonder that a serious student, like Milton, who insisted on examining all possibilities before holding fast to the best, found himself long-choosing. It is even less singular, when one considers the implications of Renaissance theory, that he found himself long-preparing.

In view of the lofty duties which the full-fledged poet was to fulfill, it was understood that he must be well qualified for his exacting office. Not only was a special talent required, but also a fundamental excellence of character. He must be a good man, sensitive to the responsibility that lay upon him. He must be willing to devote himself to mastering the rules of his art and to exercising his gift constantly, so that it should improve. Although he would almost certainly acquire his technique by early practice in the lower types, he was to be ever conscious of the ultimate goal. Only a base and unworthy spirit would be content to waste or prostitute so vital a talent. With an eye to his great task as a teacher of men, he must dedicate himself to intensive study to acquire the knowledge he intended to communicate. Finally, he must be proudly aware that his place in the scheme of things was an exalted one, outstripping as he did orator, historian, philosopher, soldier, or divine, in his power to enlighten and advance civilization. His work, too, comes nearer than any of theirs to the divine attributes of creation and immortality. Despite Sidney's jesting reference to it, the Renaissance poet was inclined to take rather seriously the concept of poetic immorality: [22]

> Exegi monumentum aere perennius.

That monument, or pillar, or pyramid became a commonplace of later-day theory, a solace to poets, an inducement to patrons, and in some cases, notably those of Drayton and Herrick, a force determining the nature of their work. It was an age when the poet felt himself an earthborn child of Jove, sure of his own immortality in the light of his heroic accomplishment; he was a Hercules that could strangle snakes in his cradle and move on to mightier labors for the welfare of mankind.

[22] Elton, "Literary Fame: A Renaissance Study," *Otia Merseiana*, IV (1904), 24–52.

The concept of the poet as the controller of a great didactic and moral force led to a growing emphasis on the nobler functions of his art and a continuing exaltation of the more difficult and sustained kind of poetry, the grand subject treated in the lofty style. Consequently a group of writers emerged whose primary interest was the writing of lofty poetry in the established tradition, and who, in accordance with that tradition, were willing to serve a suitable apprenticeship to their art. Usually such poets ran the whole course from the "low" forms of pastoral, sonnet, and satire, to the "high" epic, gathering power by more or less imitative exercises, and gradually approaching an ultimate heroic poem as their technique grew surer.

The extraordinary complexity and variety of seventeenth-century lyric poetry is largely attributable to a group of poets who did not attempt to realize so comprehensive an ideal. In most cases they wrote for a limited and sympathetic audience, an audience that could be reached by circulating the work in manuscript. Their concern with poetry was slighter, more casual. They were, by pressure of circumstance or peculiarity of talent, not desirous of essaying heroic composition, and they turned to other forms perfectible with less elaborate preparation, notably the lyric. Thus there arose a group of poets unusually free from the necessity of pleasing a wide audience, free, too, from the concept of disciplinary preparation and the weight of an impressive body of theory, their main problem being to satisfy a personal aim within the brief compass of a few stanzas.

For a consideration of seventeenth-century poetic theory, it is helpful to distinguish between these two principal groups by using the terms major and minor poets. The distinction is by no means an attempt to evaluate achievement; it is made rather to indicate a difference in aim. The poets of the major group were motivated by the desire eventually to write an opus, to use their art on a great work that should teach mankind delightfully, a sort of landmark of poetry comparable to the *Aeneid* or the *Faerie Queene*. The primary aim of the minor poet was to perfect each brief work as a separate entity.

It is not, however, to be supposed that because of their broad agreement on didactic purpose the major poets manifested any striking similarity in the details of their poetic theory. Even when seeking the same objective, they showed considerable divergence on questions of the material and style of their nobly dedicated efforts. The important virtue of patriotism is taught by such different methods as Drayton's laborious inventory in *Poly-Olbion*, Browne's slight story and satirical digressions in *Britannia's Pastorals*, and Wither's forthright contemporary warning in *Britain's Remembrancer*. Whereas most of the major poets placed the emphasis on extolling virtue, Jonson utilized the principles of comedy and satire and taught by ridiculing vice. The struggle of reason and virtue against desire and vice is furthered by allegories as different as the Spenserian *Purple Island* and the neoclassic *Gondibert*. The Old Testament yields heroic protagonists for Cowley's Vergilian epic of David and for Milton's Greek tragedy of Samson. Perfect Christian heroism, as exemplified in Christ, is celebrated with Spenserian richness by Giles Fletcher and with severe concentration by Milton. Milton, too, creates the greatest study of the attributes to be overcome, in his full epic portrait of the eternal antagonist. But however the individual poet chose to reach the common goal, that goal remained the education of England and the development of its inhabitants to the highest degree of Christian perfection. Unfinished works and noble failures speak of a century in which idealism and enthusiasm led many beyond their power, in the effort to clothe virtue in the richest dress of art and lead her forth to the fullest delight and profit of mankind.

The major poets practiced the various forms of "low" poetry as necessary preparation for the larger and loftier measures they should one day attempt, but obviously, from their very attitude toward "low" poetry, they could hardly be expected materially to forward its development. It is to the group whose practice was limited to the shorter types that the seventeenth century owes much of its striking development in lyric theory. Within the minor group were many who were fascinated by an art that even in its smallest divisions seemed to bear the seeds of immortality. It was evident that the attractive power of poetry was inherent in the form, rather than in the subject matter or purpose; there was a mysterious charm for humanity in the music of "numbers," aside from all question of the worth of the thought conveyed. Men continued to explore the possibilities of the minor poem and to concentrate on the perfection of the lyrical element. Ben Jonson gave fresh impetus to this movement by directing attention to minor classical poetry. He demonstrated that not all forms of minor poetry had been exploited as practice material by the major poets; he reminded English poets that there was sound classical precedent for epistles and songs, lyrics that excelled the rigid sonnet in virtuosity and were better suited to the needs of the English writer. Herrick and Carew were quick to adopt his Roman technique of smooth, brief stanzas. Their emphasis on style led to a high degree of imitation, whereas a concentration of interest on subject matter was frequently accompanied by new developments in technique. Donne, trying to crowd his scholastic erudition and overwrought passion into brief compass, lost smoothness and clarity, but added, as Carew realized, the power of intensity. Following Donne, later religious poets found in the short poem an ideal medium for the fitting expression of their emotion. Originality was characteristic of these writers, who were indifferent to their earthly immortality, and, being independent of an audience, might depart from tradition with impunity.

Minor religious poetry reached its height in the works of Herbert, Crashaw, and Vaughan, and died out gradually as the preoccupation with style and classical imitation turned lyric writers toward other subject matter at the dawn of the Augustan age.

But the triumph of classical theory in the minor poetry of Denham and Waller was as sterile as the triumph of the classical epic in Cowley. As the powerful stimuli of patriotism and religion died down and personal passion was moderated to conform to a classic ideal, the quality of both epic and lyric began to decay. The way was left clear for an era of translations and for the rise and maximum development of that hitherto undervalued form, the satire. This was now given full recognition as an artistic type worthy of careful and brilliant writing. It could be used for subjective expression, it had classical precedent, and it was capable of being expanded to epic proportions. Finally, it was thoroughly acceptable as, in the last quarter of the seventeenth century, emphasis began to be laid not on the enduring value of poetry but on its capacity to attract contemporary interest.

The picture of seventeenth-century poetic evolution that emerges from the theories of representative poets is complex but by no means confused. Through the century passes a dominant group of major poets, those who run the whole gamut of their art and stress the delightful teaching of mankind as the divine purpose of poetry. But there are also two groups of minor poets who practice the very forms and emphasize the very attributes of their art that the major poets regard as secondary. These groups are concerned primarily with the religious or purely artistic values of poetry. The general theory is based on didacticism, but it is broad enough to include partial theories devoted to the extremes of piety and pleasure.

CHAPTER II

BEN JONSON

BETWEEN Sidney's *Defense of Poesie* (written *c.* 1583) and Dryden's *Essay of Dramatick Poesie* there was written an essay on poetic theory that probably outstripped even these masterpieces in merit and interest. It was composed by Ben Jonson as a preface to his translation of Horace's *Art of Poetry* and it presented an English theory derived from Horace and Aristotle. Jonson referred to this essay several times and read from it on his visit to Drummond. He had, he said, written an art of English poetry twenty years before, but he had not desired to print it. This early draft, which would be dated about 1598, was probably set down principally to crystallize his own thought; in 1605 he decided to publish it and referred the reader to it as a volume immediately forthcoming;[1] but the expectation was not fulfilled and as late as 1614 he revised his work to include an apology for *Bartholomew Fair*.[2] The new draft was written in dialogue form with Dr. Donne cast in the role of Criticus. In addition to expounding Jonson's principles of the drama, it contained arguments against the poetic theories of Campion and Daniel. This remarkable book, which had remained unprinted so long, was left in manuscript for five years more and then perished in the fire that destroyed Jonson's library in 1623.

This discourse did not, however, vanish without leaving a few helpful traces. The very fact that such a book once existed makes it a simpler task to assemble Jonson's theory of poetry, for, having once formulated and recorded a complete code, he exhibited a tendency to reiterate and expound it in various ways. Thus his poetic creed dominates the record of his conversations with Drummond; it fills his *Discoveries;* more remarkable is the fact that it obtrudes itself to an unusual degree in his plays. The material, though loose

[1] Jonson, Introduction to *Sejanus,* The Complete Plays of Ben Jonson, introduction by Schelling, I, 308.

[2] *Conversations with Drummond,* Herford and Simpson, Ben Jonson: the Man and His Work, I, 134.

and scattered, is evidently part of a fund of precepts carefully derived and steadily maintained. As the beliefs are sorted out and arranged, one begins to grasp the homogeneity of the scheme, to feel the central unity that determined every detail of his complete concept of poetry.

A haphazard collection of fragments from Jonson's basic doctrine is to be found in the famous commonplace book in which he set down the choicest fruits of his wide reading, principally passages from his favorite classical authors that expressed his own deepest convictions. Many an apt statement was translated or digested into English and set down among his *Explorata*, or *Discoveries*. Nor were these ideas forgotten, but appeared, sometimes more than once, in his works. He adopted them completely and felt them his because he had selected them as being in harmony with his own belief. For this reason it is of little concern to a student of Jonson's literary theory that *Discoveries* is being steadily proved less and less original.[3] It is still valid as a source of his artistic theory and general philosophy because it presents thoughts to which he strongly and enthusiastically subscribed and to which he frequently alluded in his other writings.

Jonson's definitions of his art, whether adopted or original, all tend to exalt and magnify poetry, which he finds in the concise phrasing of *Explorata* "the queen of arts, which had her original from heaven, received thence from the Hebrews and had in prime estimation with the Greeks, transmitted to the Latins and all nations that professed civility." [4] Like Tennyson's flower in the crannied wall, this statement provides a key to much of seventeenth-century poetic theory if we can but capture all its implication. It implies three points that will be repeated in most discussions on poetry during this period: (1) the heavenly origin of poetry, (2) the priority of poetry among the arts and sciences, (3) the coincidence of poetry and civilization. The great poets of the age were deeply concerned with these ideas, which were an important part of their Renaissance heritage.

---

[3] Castelain, *Discoveries*, pp. xv–xvii.

[4] *Discoveries*, The Works of Ben Jonson, ed. by Whalley, VII, 147. Cf. Complete Plays, I, 241.

Jonson's ranking of poetry foremost among the arts is illustrated by a comparison between poetry and painting, based on Plutarch's remark that poetry is a speaking picture and a picture, mute poesy. Both, Jonson explains, concern themselves with imitation,

both invent, feign, and devise many things, and accommodate all they invent to the use and service of nature. Yet of the two, the pen is more noble than the pencil; for that can speak to the understanding; the other but to the sense. They both behold pleasure and profit as their common object.[5]

Jonson recurred to this theory in his printed volume of the masques, explaining, in the kind of statement that must have infuriated Inigo Jones, that long after the splendor of the spectacle had vanished, the libretto would have meaning and beauty. The preface to *Hymenaei* echoes *Discoveries* and then goes further:

It is a noble and just advantage that the things subjected to understanding have of those which are objected to sense; that the one sort are but momentary, and merely taking; the other impressing and lasting.[6]

Poetry of all the arts can best appeal to the understanding as well as to the senses. It is this unique power that elevates poetry to primacy among the arts, for the true poet writes not only to please but to instruct. In the general opinion of the wise, true poetry has the merit of forming manners and of being conducive to virtue; it leads delightfully to nobility of thought and action:

And whereas they entitle philosophy to be a rigid and austere poesy; they have, on the contrary stiled poesy a dulcet and gentle philosophy, which leads on and guides us by the hand to action, with a ravishing delight and incredible sweetness.[7]

It is noted in *Discoveries* that Cicero had expatiated on the value of poetry and Aristotle had maintained that the study of poetry offered a "pattern of living well and happily, disposing us to all civil offices of society." [8] In short, there is no merit that Jonson fails to claim for poetry, no power that he denies to the true poet:

I could never think the study of wisdom confined only to the philosopher; or of piety to the divine; or of state to the politick. But that he which can feign a commonwealth (which is the poet) can govern it with counsels,

---

[5] *Discoveries,* Works, ed. by Whalley, VII, 118.
[6] The Works of Ben Jonson, ed. by Gifford, VII, 45.
[7] *Discoveries,* Works, ed. by Whalley, VII, 147.
[8] *Ibid.*

strengthen it with laws, correct it with judgments, inform it with religion and morals, is all these.[9]

Since to Jonson the great attribute of poetry was its ability to reach the understanding, we may expect to find him ranking matter before manner. What he really desired in a poet was the ideal combination of both, but if forced to choose, he invariably placed content above form:

Of the two (if either were to be wished) I would rather have a plain downright wisdom, than a foolish and affected eloquence. For what is so furious and Bethlem like, as a vain sound of chosen and excellent words, without any subject of sentence or science mixed.[10]

The fundamental value of words is that they serve to formulate ideas; they convey a thought:

The sense is, as the life and soul of language, without which all words are dead.[11]

Not only the emphasis on subject matter but the nature of that subject matter is clarified by subsequent statements:

A poet is that which by the Greek is called a maker, or a feigner; his art, an art of imitation or feigning; expressing the life of man in fit measure, numbers, and harmony, according to Aristotle. . . . Hence he is called a poet, not he which writeth in measure only, but that feigneth and formeth a fable, and writes things like the truth.[12]

The conceits of the mind are the pictures of things, and the tongue is the interpreter of those pictures. The order of God's creatures in themselves is not only admirable and glorious, but eloquent: then he who could apprehend the consequences of things in their truth, and utter his apprehensions as truly, were the best writer or speaker.[13]

The highest eloquence would be a straightforward conveyance from one human mind to another of a complete understanding of the universe. In lieu of this theoretical perfection, the practical ideal becomes a clear and attractive statement of some part of the wisdom of a well-stocked mind. Even more impressive than the control of expression that Jonson expected in a poet is what he considered necessary by way of control of matter. The poet ought to have as wide a general knowledge as possible; yet since complete comprehensive information is impossible, the actual requirement is a good

[9] *Ibid.*, p. 103. [10] *Ibid.*, p. 81. [11] *Ibid.*, p. 131.
[12] *Ibid.*, p. 145. Cf. p. 147. [13] *Ibid.*, p. 138.

mastery of those fields of which he intends to write. Thus Jonson himself, in addition to his full preparation in his own art, professed and possessed a working control over the principles of alchemy, heraldry, cookery, medicine, fencing, civil prudence, law, and cosmetics; and he utilized these branches of knowledge in his writing. Whatever can be obtained by hard study, the poet should know; he must, however, take care not to bog down in a marsh of details.

Jonson places one noteworthy restriction upon the matter, or "sense," that the poet is to use his words to convey: it is to be entirely secular. Truth is the only immortal thing which mankind may properly make the subject of inquiry. Too much curiosity concerning God, even on the part of a divine, is inadvisable:

For to utter truth of God (but as he thinks only) may be dangerous; who is best known by our not knowing.[14]

Men should learn those truths concerning God which he himself has chosen to reveal; for the rest, let them busy their conception about the myriad finite problems: "Sense is wrought out of experience, the knowledge of human life and actions, or of the liberal arts." [15] As might be expected from this Baconian attitude, Jonson's religious poetry is slight and by no means outstanding.

The proper study of the poet is man, both as an individual and as a member of society. His responsibility as a factor in civil life is very heavy. "He must have civil prudence and eloquence, and that whole." [16] He must have full, first-hand information on matters of government. In a monarchy his function is to guide and support the ruler, out of the knowledge that he has gained under that ruler's aegis. Poet and prince benefit and support each other:

Learning needs rest: sovereignity gives it. Sovereignity needs counsel: learning affords it. There is such a consociation of offices between the prince and whom his favour breeds, that they help to sustain his power, as he their knowledge.[17]

The counsellor must show due respect to his sovereign and yet not compromise with truth. He must never allow himself the vicious luxury of promoting his own interests through base flattery.[18]

The ability to advise presupposes a vast amount of knowledge

14 *Discoveries*, Works, ed. by Whalley, VII, 87.   15 *Ibid.*, p. 131.   16 *Ibid.*, p. 152.
17 *Ibid.*, p. 72. Cf. *ibid.*, p. 110.   18 *Ibid.*, p. 105.

in the adviser, particularly knowledge of human nature. It is not sufficient to have a mere agglomeration of learning. There must also be the power to distinguish, sort out, and present separately the human characteristic requiring consideration in any given problem:

In being able to counsel others, a man must be furnished with an universal store in himself, the knowledge of all nature: that is the matter and seed plot; there are the seats of all argument and invention. But especially you must be cunning in the nature of man: there is the variety of things which are as the elements, and letters, which his art and wisdom must rank, and order to the present occasion. For we see not all letters in single words: nor all places in particular discourses. That cause seldom happens, wherein a man will use all arguments.[19]

The particular problem of isolating certain elements in human nature for complete analysis is that which Jonson solved in comedy by the use of "humours" as a key to analysis and a method of characterization, thereby fulfilling his own most difficult requirement for the true poet, who is to give both profit and delight:

We do not require in him mere elocution, or an excellent faculty in verse, but the exact knowledge of all virtues, and their contraries with ability to render the one loved, the other hated, by his proper embatteling them.[20]

Like many of his contemporaries, Jonson believed that God had provided poetic power to aid the progress of civilization by leading men into the paths of knowledge and virtue. As Herford and Simpson point out, Jonson's emphasis on the doctrinal aspect in his esthetic was not unique, although it was extreme:

The Jonsonian attitude of *corrector morum* was the characteristic fashion of a "quick spirited age" when, as Barnabe Rich said, "many excellent wittes are endeavouring by their pennes to set upp lightes & to give the world new eyes to see into deformities." [21]

Swinburne revealed the crux of the matter when he wrote, "Jonson would be the noblest of poets if criticism of life were the essence or end of poetry." [22] If we consider that Jonson felt amply justified in his criticism of life, felt that by such analysis and demonstration as he practiced folly could be put down and virtue elevated, all with the delight of the beneficiaries ever duly held in mind, we begin

[19] *Ibid.*, p. 72.
[20] *Ibid.*, p. 103.
[21] Herford and Simpson, Ben Jonson, I, 11.
[22] *A Study of Ben Jonson*, p. 165.

to realize why he set himself up as a criterion, why he arrogated a monopoly of correct judgment and successfully ruled an empire of wit in which he was self-elected sovereign—or not quite self-elected, but, as Milton might have termed it, monarch by merit. For he was a true poet under the terms of his own very exacting definition. All about him was a plague of poetasters. There were some few fellow poets, not one of whom, however, measured up as well as he did to his standards, although some exceeded him in certain respects. Thus despite his deep admiration for Shakespeare, Jonson felt that more careful revision would have resulted in even greater work; Daniel was a good man but no poet; Sidney had not observed decorum; Drummond had no feeling for the spirit of his own day; and even the mighty Dr. Donne had grown obscure and drifted into strange courses.

Because Jonson believed so deeply in the didactic purpose of poetry, nothing can exceed the scorn he felt for the poetasters, those vile creatures who by writing their wretched stuff in verse, or the outward form of poetry, brought the whole art into disrepute. Over and over again he fulminated against the unworthy "parcel-poets," the "poetic apes" who, to get a name for wit or to earn money, would prostitute whatever verbal facility they possessed and then dare to call themselves poets. They were men who could not boast with him,

> Here is rhime, not empty of reason.
> This we were bid to credit from our poet,
> Whose true scope, if you would know it,
> In all his poems still hath been this measure,
> To mix profit with your pleasure.[23]

The true poet must employ his talents for some worthy end, in sharp contrast to the poetaster, who meanly uses his skill to advance himself. The true poet must be willing to labor for the best interests of mankind without reward [24] and without fear of consequences. He must be

One whom no servile hope of gain, or frosty apprehension of danger, can make to be a parasite, either to time, place, or opinion.[25]

---

[23] *Volpone*, Complete Plays, Prologue, I, 403.
[24] *Every Man out of His Humour*, Complete Plays, I, 224.   [25] *Ibid.*, p. 59.

Both in prose and in poetry Jonson strenuously maintained the thesis, which will not be heard of again until Milton reaffirms it, that if the poet was to teach virtue, he must himself be a good man. The contemptible Crispinus, by identifying himself as a poet, brings down the wrath of Caesar:

> O, that profaned name!
> O, who shall follow Virtue and embrace her,
>
> .   .   .   .
>
> Who shall, with greater comforts comprehend
> Her unseen being and her excellence;
> When you, that teach and should eternise her,
> Live as she were no law unto your lives,
> Nor lived herself, but with your idle breaths? [26]

The preface to *Volpone* cries aloud at the injustice of damning poetry because of the lowness of some of those that profess it, since the true poet must in the very nature of his art be a man of the highest mental and spiritual order:

the too much license of poetasters in this time hath deformed their mistress: but for their petulancy, it were an act of the greatest injustice, either to let the learned suffer, or so divine a skill (which indeed should not be attempted with unclean hands) to fall under the least contempt. For, if men will impartially and not asquint, look toward the offices and functions of a poet, they will easily conclude to themselves the impossibility of any man's being a good poet, without first being a good man. He that is said to be able to inform young men to all good disciplines, inflame grown men to all great virtues, keep old men in their best and supreme state; . . . that comes forth the interpreter and arbiter of nature, a teacher of things divine no less than human, a master in manners, and can alone, or with a few, effect the business of mankind: this, I take him, is no subject for pride and ignorance to exercise their railing rhetoric upon.[27]

The prologue to *The Staple of News* carries a similar plea:

> . . . make a difference 'twixt poetic elves,
> And poets: all that dabble in the ink,
> And defile quills, are not those few can think,
> Conceive, express, and steer the souls of men,
> As with a rudder, round thus, with their pen.
> He must be one that can instruct your youth,

---

[26] *The Poetaster,* Complete Plays, I, 276.
[27] Complete Plays, I, 400. Cf. *Every Man in His Humour,* Complete Plays, I, 56.

And keep your acme in a state of truth,
Must enterprise this work.[28]

The Poetaster is largely given over to exemplifying the difference between true and false poets. Ovid's opening soliloquy to poetry bemoans

> the abuse
> Of thy great powers in adulterate brains.[29]

The critics of poetry should not, in fairness, judge it by the output of the poetasters, for the poetaster, with his narrow and shallow aim, not only fails to transmit knowledge, but also, in many cases, fails even to possess it. Caesar is careful to explain the type of poetry that he praises so highly. Poetry is of all the faculties on earth,

> The most abstract and perfect; if she be
> True-born, and nursed with all the sciences.[30]

Vergil represents the poetic ideal; a supreme master of technique, he is also a fount of wisdom; he has left a memorable comment on almost every serious point in life.[31]

In addition to grave deficiencies in proper purpose and background, the poetaster usually had very little by way of technique. He was a mere copier—if not a plagiarist. He was unaware of or indifferent to the great proven principles of his art. Nothing in Jonson's emphasis on subject matter must be construed to argue an indifference to technique. Rather, the emphasis on content enhanced the importance of technique as the means by which the wisdom of the poet was to be effectively disseminated. A long and arduous preparation was needed to master his art of feigning:

I would lead you to the knowledge of our poet by a perfect information what he is or should be by nature, by exercise, by imitation, by study, and so bring him down through the disciplines of grammar, logick, rhetorick, and the ethicks, adding somewhat out of all, peculiar to himself and worthy of your admittance or reception.[32]

The first requirement and the basic one is "a goodness of natural wit." Jonson is not setting out to make bricks without straw. The poet is born, not made.[33] *Discoveries* is full of practical hints and

---

[28] Complete Plays, II, 349. Cf. *The Poetaster*, Complete Plays, I, 241.

[29] *Ibid.*, I, 241.   [30] *The Poetaster*, Complete Plays, I, 282.

[31] *Ibid.*, p. 284.   [32] *Discoveries*, Works, ed. by Whalley, VII, 147.

[33] *Ibid.*, p. 119.

suggestions, but through it, like a recurring chorus, runs the refrain, "There is no doctrine will do good where nature is wanting." [34] When Jonson expounds this natural or inborn requirement of the poet in more detail, he equates it with the "instinct to pour out the treasure of his mind," [35] a progressive excitement or rapture that seizes the poet and carries him above normal pitch.

Such basic poetic genius, though indispensable, is not sufficient. To it must be added frequent exercise, patient practice. It is easy to versify, but hard to write immortal poetry. Jonson distrusts bursts of speed. He advises frequent pauses for reconsideration and revision, especially if the writer has been working rapidly in a fit of inspiration. The only kind of facility he values is that which comes from long discipline in careful writing.

By way of discipline for a youthful poet, Jonson prescribes imitating the work of some established writer. He does not mean to recommend slavish and indiscriminate mimicry, but he does desire the would-be poet to study one model thoroughly, absorb that master's practices, and convert them to his own use.[36]

The most significant requirement that Jonson makes of the fledgling poet is "an exactness of style and multiplicity of reading." His style must be clear and appropriate; it must never represent mere mannerism. Jonson passes in review certain examples of what to avoid. There is the ostentatious style, in which all the effort is expended on the surface, none on the substance. There is the deliberately rough and broken style, designed to seem rugged and striking. What Jonson thought of that may be gathered from the following statement:

A man should so deliver himself to the nature of the subject whereof he speaks, that his hearer may take knowledge of his discipline with some delight: and so apparel fair and good matter, that the studious of elegancy be not defrauded; redeem arts from their rough and brakey seats, where they lay hid and overgrown with thorns, to a pure, open, and flowry light.[37]

At the other end of the scale from roughhewn composition is the sweet kind of versifying that says nothing:

[34] *Ibid.*, p. 92. Cf. *ibid.*, pp. 127, 151.
[35] *Ibid.*, p. 148.   [36] *Ibid.*, pp. 150, 98.
[37] *Ibid.*, p. 74.

Others there are that have no composition at all; but a kind of tuning and rhiming fall in what they write. It runs and slides, and only makes a sound.[38]

Style should reflect the ripeness of a mind enriched by wide study; yet there are authors who quote from their reading indiscriminately, even to the extent of quoting conflicting opinions; they exercise no power of selection. Some plagiarize, and some mock at all learning and art, relying merely on their own talent.[39] Finally some compose huge tomes by writing down far more than is needed. The poet must never forget that the purpose of his composition is to convey valuable matter in attractive form. Sweetness and decoration have no intrinsic value; harshness presents a challenge and not an invitation to the reader; writers without learning or with undigested learning cannot very well enlighten their readers. Careful selection and proper planning are essential elements of composition: ". . . the learned use ever election and a mean; they look back to what they intended at first, and make all an even and proportioned body." [40]

To all of these—nature, exercise, imitation, and study—must be added art, if the poet is to achieve full perfection. For this requisite, he must consult the acknowledged masters of theory, above all, the two foremost critics, Horace and Aristotle. In asserting the authority of Aristotle, Jonson manifests no desire to circumscribe the poet by any hard and fast set of rules. His point is not that one must obey the laws outlined in the *Poetics,* but that those laws represent the most direct route to right procedure, inasmuch as they have been scientifically worked out:

But whatsoever nature at any time dictated to the most happy, or long exercise to the most laborious, that the wisdom and learning of Aristotle hath brought into an art, because he understood the causes of things: and what other men did by chance or custom, he doth by reason; and not only found out the way not to err, but the short way we should take not to err.[41]

Jonson was too much the admirer of Bacon [42] to be fanatical in his reverence of Aristotle. He merely wanted a hearing for the past, fair play and decent respect for a great philosopher. If, under equitable

38 *Discoveries,* Works, ed. by Whalley, VII, 93.
39 *Ibid.,* p. 94.   40 *Ibid.,* p. 95.
41 *Ibid.,* p. 153.   42 *Ibid.,* pp. 99, 100. Cf. also p. 103.

circumstances, Aristotle still lost ground, Jonson was very willing to welcome such new excellence as had rightly displaced the ancient judgment.[43] He was as eager as any true conservative to progress in a direction he could recognize as better, but he had the characteristic conservative distrust of mistaking novelty for improvement. He stood for recognition of truths, both old and new, without prejudice either for or against their antiquity:

I know nothing can conduce more to letters, than to examine the writings of the ancients, and not to rest in their sole authority, or take all upon trust from them; provided the plagues of judging and pronouncing against them be away; such as are envy, bitterness, precipitation, impudence, and scurril scoffing. For to all the observations of the ancients, we have our own experience; which if we will use and apply, we have better means to pronounce. It is true they opened the gates and went before us; but as guides, not commanders. Truth lies open to all; it is no man's several.[44]

From the careful study of the past and the calm evaluation of it in the light of more recent knowledge, Jonson expected his disciples to draw their own conclusions as to which theory had produced the best results and to form their style accordingly:

Then make exact animadversion where stile hath degenerated, where flourished and thrived in choiceness of phrase, round and clean composition of sentence, sweet falling of the clause, varying illustration by tropes and figures, weight of matter, worth of subject, soundness of argument, life of invention, and depth of judgment.[45]

The phrases in the above quotation are by no means a haphazard collection. Every point that appears there has been treated by Jonson in some detail. The word, the phrase, the sentence, each properly used could illumine the thought; or carelessly used, obscure it.

On the point of vocabulary Jonson is most emphatic. "Pure and neat language I love, yet plain and customary." [46] He presents strong arguments against the two extremes of excessive innovation and affected employment of obsolete expressions. The use of a new word is a dangerous business, Jonson warns. And since the chief requirement of writing is to be understood, he advises against the frequent use of archaic language. Granted that old words add an element of majesty and delight to a style, nevertheless their strange-

---

[43] *Ibid.*, p. 137.
[45] *Ibid.*, p. 138.
[44] *Ibid.*, p. 74.
[46] *Ibid.*, p. 130.

ness conflicts with "the chief virtue of a style . . . perspicuity."
The extensive use of obsolete forms is inexcusable. He scores the
English fad of "Chaucerisms." [47] He has ever in mind the mistake
of Spenser, whose subject matter was excellent but who, "in affect-
ing the ancients, writ no language." [48]

Jonson is equally conservative in the matter of figurative and
metaphorical expression, which he terms *translation*. Herein lies
the opportunity for elegance and propriety. But Jonson does not
counsel the use of figurative speech, except when no simple term is
available or when the simple term is for some reason not as suit-
able. [49] The metaphor must always be a help and not a hindrance
to understanding. It must not be far-fetched or affected or taken
from an inappropriate source. There is danger, too, of mixed meta-
phors or hyperbole so exaggerated as to be ridiculous. Carlo Buffone
in *Every Man out of His Humour* dramatically emphasizes Jonson's
views on figurative speech. A fondness for vulgar display causes him
to break his jests in "adulterate similes" [50] until his mouth is sealed
up by the injured and aroused Puntovarlo. All things considered,
Jonson advised a very sparing employment of figures of speech:

> But why do men depart at all from the right and natural ways of speaking?
> Sometimes for necessity when we are driven, or think it fitter to speak that
> in obscure words, or by circumstance, which uttered plainly would offend
> the hearers. Or to avoid obsceneness, or sometimes for pleasure, and variety,
> as travellers turn out of the highway, drawn either by the commodity of a
> foot-path, or the delicacy or freshness of the fields. [51]

What Jonson particularly wanted to assail was the prevalent popu-
lar confusion between affectation and wit, the idea that naturalness
and simplicity were hardly characteristics of great writing:

> But now nothing is good that is natural: right and natural language seems
> to have least of wit in it; that which is writhed and tortured, is counted the
> more exquisite. . . . All must be affected and preposterous. [52]

The abuse of words, though perhaps the smallest sin of the poet-
asters, was one that Jonson loved to attack. He was a consummate
master of English speech, for, unlike most poets of his day, who

---

[47] *Discoveries*, Works, ed. by Whalley, VII, 133. [48] *Ibid.*, p. 128.
[49] *Ibid.*, p. 131. [50] Complete Plays, I, 66.
[51] *Discoveries*, Works, ed. by Whalley, VII, 135.
[52] *Ibid.*, p. 88. Cf. *ibid.*, p. 95.

busied themselves about Italian or French, Jonson lavished his time on his native tongue. He knew its dialects and its professional patter, its grammar and derivation. He chose from his wide range of vocabulary with loving precision,[53] and the loose or idle employment of a term caused him acute irritation. The failure to suit speech to character, to maintain a proper decorum, annoyed him in writers of pastorals. Lack of realism or appropriateness was an even worse fault in a type of writing that aimed to imitate life, and Jonson tried hard to reform comedy in this respect.[54] He was going to use no "foot and half-foot words" but "language such as men do use." [55] He did not attempt to reproduce everyday speech, but he did assign to special types of characters certain phrases or tricks of language natural to them. The particular kind of attraction that a strange word exercised over a mind less disciplined than his own was laughable to him:

She is like one of your ignorant poetasters . . . who when they have got acquainted with a strange word, never rest till they have wrung it in, though it loosen the whole fabric of their sense.[56]

He burlesques with gusto the worship of words in *The New Inn*, *The Case Is Altered*, and *The Poetaster*. The use of a word simply because it fascinates the author violates the basic principle of Jonson's literary art, which he has Vergil state for the instruction of Crispinus:

But let your matter run before your words.[57]

To explain various manners of using words, Jonson employs an elaborate comparison with the human body. A fleshy style is marked by many periphrases and by circumlocution. A good, full-blooded style has apt, sweet-sounding words; the phrases are neat and well chosen. A style that is full-blooded but very direct (our nervous style), he calls sinewy.[58] He considered redundancy a lesser evil than bareness, in that it was more easily remedied.[59] But the perfect style expresses thought readily and fully, not profusely. "A strict and

---

[53] Wells, "Ben Jonson, Patriarch of Speech Study," *Shakespeare Association Bulletin*, XIII (Jan., 1938), 54–62.
[54] *Discoveries*, Works, ed. by Whalley, VII, 133.
[55] *Every Man in His Humour*, Complete Plays, I, 560. Cf. *The Poetaster, ibid.*, p. 261.
[56] *The Poetaster, ibid.*, p. 172.   [57] *The Poetaster, ibid.*, p. 297.
[58] *Discoveries*, Works, ed. by Whalley, VII, 137, *passim*.   [59] *Ibid.*, p. 127.

succint style is that, where you can take away nothing without loss, and that loss to be manifest."

It was Jonson's belief that "Language most shews a man," that speech reflects accurately the mind whence it springs. If language is to be analyzed completely, the student must consider the "greatness, aptness, sound, structure, and harmony of it." He distinguishes four important classifications: high, low, middle, and vicious:

Some language is high and great. Then the words are chosen, their sound ample, the composition full, the absolution plenteous, and poured out, all grave, sinewy, and strong.[60]

In humble and low speech, the words are poor and flat, the members and periods are thin and weak, without knitting or number. Middle language is "plain and pleasing; even without stopping, round without swelling; all well-torned, composed elegant and accurate." Vicious language is vast, gaping, swelling, and irregular.[61] Jonson's strong distaste for turgid and inflated rhetoric was given full expression during his quarrel with Marston. The result is the famous regurgitation scene of *The Poetaster*, in which Crispinus is purged of his offending words. Not so pungent, but more widely applicable is the withering satire with which Pennyboy Canter exposes the professional bombast of various types of men.

But these styles must be applied to proper subject matter if their names are to be valid. Thus a high style applied to a petty subject would become poor, and a suitable style for an ordinary topic would become ridiculous if applied to a lofty theme. Greatness and aptness must be considered simultaneously:

For a man to write well, there are required three necessaries: to read the best authors, observe the best speakers, and much exercise of his own stile. In stile to consider what ought to be written, and after what manner; he must first think and excogitate his matter, then choose his words and examine the weight of either. Then take care in placing and ranking both matter and words, that the composition be comely, and to do this with diligence and often.[62]

A further consideration is the nature of the sentences. Jonson recognizes two main types, one characterized by short, succinct

[60] *Discoveries*, Works, ed. by Whalley, VII, 135.   [61] *Ibid.*, pp. 135, 136.
[62] *Ibid.*, p. 124.

periods, numerous and polished; the other, by equal and strong parts, everywhere answerable and weighed, i. e., our balanced sentence. As for the general flow of style, he requires a "well-joining, cementing and coagmentation of words," probably meaning much what we today call clear reference and smooth transition. He prefers the fairly short, clear sentence: "We should speak what we can the nearest way, so as we keep our gait, not leap; for too short may as well be not let into the memory, as too long not kept in." [63]

The central principle of Jonson's theory of style is that style must never be developed as an end in itself, but always with regard to its purpose—the transmission of thought; it is therefore to be strictly ordered and disciplined, to the end that it may have maximum efficiency.

Jonson's insistence on the subordinate position to be occupied by style left its mark on his attitude toward rime and stanzas. We know that his "discourse of poesie" was directed against Campion and more particularly against Daniel. In speaking to Drummond of a projected epic poem, Jonson specified that it was to be all in couplets "for he detesteth all other Rimes." [64] His lost discourse "proves couplets to be the bravest sort of Verses, especially when they are broken, like Hexameters" and that "crosse Rimes and Stanzaes (because the purpose would lead him beyond 8 lines to conclude) were all forced." [65] He had no love for the parceling off of a lengthy thought development into stanzas. Neither did he care for the long Alexandrine nor the fourteener. Jonson, like Milton, resented any bondage of sense to rime, and, when rime was desirable, sought the type that offered him most freedom. It is not surprising to find him cursing Petrarch "for redacting Verses to Sonets, which he said were like that Tirrants bed, wher some who were too short were racked, others too long cut short," [66] nor to find him asserting that "Spencers stanzaes pleased him not." [67] This attitude is all the more interesting since no one would accuse Jonson of rebelling against the tyranny of rime because he lacked the skill to create verses. Nothing could refute such an idea more swiftly than his

[63] *Discoveries,* Works, ed. by Whalley, VII, 134.
[64] *Conversations with Drummond,* Herford and Simpson, Ben Jonson, I, 132.
[65] *Ibid.*   [66] *Ibid.,* p. 133.
[67] *Ibid.,* p. 132.

"Fit of Rhime against Rhime." The paradox of the poem is a perfect
reflection of the paradox in Jonson's evaluation of stanzas. Rime
was a bane if it dominated the poet, but there was a certain exalta-
tion in conquering this refractory element and adding its strength
to the force of an argument; for again, the main ground of Jonson's
aversion is that rime spoils sense.[68]

Esther C. Dunn, in her book on *Ben Jonson's Art,* thinks that
Jonson overstated the importance of the material of poetry because
he found too little content and too much form in the elaborate verse
of the time.[69] So jealous was Jonson of the possible triumph of verse
over sense that he wrote all his work first in prose. Drummond
records, under his guest's opinion of verses, "That Verses stood by
sense without Colours or accent, which yett other tymes he de-
nied." [70] Perhaps the explanation of this apparent contradiction is
Jonson's belief that the primary poetic requirement is to convey
sense, but that the choice of a certain stanza by a poet imposes addi-
tional subordinate requirements peculiar to that stanza. He cen-
sured Donne, whose wit he greatly admired, "for not keeping of
the accent," [71] for electing to work within a pattern, yet refusing
to abide by its limitations. He had no love of "running verses,"
greatly preferring that an author observe the natural pause at the
end of a line. Certainly Jonson had no use for empty sweetness of
the type produced by the "women's poets," [72] or for the mere jingling
of related sounds:

> How it chimes, and cries tink in the close, divinely.[73]

> In rhime! fine tinkling rhime! and flowand verse!
> With now and then some sense! [74]

Jonson treated with outright scorn the anagrams, acrostics, palin-
dromes, and picture-forming verses that were so unaccountably
popular in his day.[75] With the attitude apparent in the "Conversa-
tions" thus confirmed by passages from the plays, it is evident that

[68] *Underwoods,* Works, ed. by Whalley, VI, 386. [69] Page 90.
[70] *Conversations,* Herford and Simpson, Ben Jonson, I, 143. [71] *Ibid.,* p. 133.
[72] In Works, ed. by Gifford, VII, 340.
[73] *The Silent Woman,* in Complete Plays, I, 503.
[74] *The Fortunate Isles,* in Works, ed. by Whalley, VI, 192.
[75] *Underwoods,* Works, ed. by Whalley, VI, 405.

for Jonson rime was never an essential and not always a *desideratum* of poetry.

From the scattered general theory of poetry in the first part of *Discoveries*, Jonson progresses at the end to a more collected and detailed study of two special types of composition that he held highest, the drama and the epic. He finds the composition of the fable similar in both. It is "the imitation of one entire and perfect action, whose parts are so joined and knit together, as nothing in the structure can be changed, or taken away, without impairing or troubling the whole, of which there is a proportionable magnitude in the members." [76] The main difference between an epic and a dramatic poem is the difference in size.

Jonson did not exemplify his theory of the epic, although one of the first things he told Drummond was that "he had ane intention to perfect ane Epick poem intitled Heroologia of the Worthies of his Country, rowsed by fame, and was to dedicate it to his Country." [77] Herford and Simpson have an interesting idea as to what this epic would have been like.[78] From Jonson's statement that Arthurian material was the best groundwork for a heroic poem, they assume that his epic would have had somewhat the tone of the Arthurian passages of the masques. Jonson censured Drayton for having departed from his declared purpose in *Poly-Olbion* "to write the deads of all ye Worthies," [79] for such a work would have served to inculcate virtue by the direct way of example.

Although he chose to follow the comic muse, Jonson did not feel that he was operating on an inferior poetic plane. His dramatic theory was unique, in that he held the comic poet in great esteem. He considered him to be very like an orator "because in moving the minds of men, and stirring of affections . . . he chiefly excells." [80] The laughter-provoking quality of comedy was not its chief merit; the value lay in the power of ridicule and caricature so to portray vices as to make them hated. The primary purpose of comedy, of tragedy, of all true poetry was the same. The theory expounded at

[76] *Discoveries,* Works, ed. by Whalley, VII, 156.
[77] *Conversations,* Herford and Simpson, Ben Jonson, I, 132.
[78] *Ibid.,* p. 74.
[79] *Ibid.,* p. 132.
[80] *Discoveries,* Works, ed. by Whalley, VII, 152.

the beginning of *The Silent Woman* is the theory that concludes *The Staple of News* over twenty years later:

> The ends of all, who for the scene do write,
> Are, or should be, to profit and delight.[81]

> Thus have you seen the maker's double scope
> To profit and delight.[82]

Jonson turned to the classics for dramatic formulas that would best combine delight with instruction. *Every Man in His Humour* is typical of the New Comedy as understood by Renaissance critics; it observes the unities, has the stock characters and the conventional tissue of cleverly involved situations. But although greatly indebted to the Plautian theory of comedy, Jonson in no wise held himself bound to accept it completely. In *Every Man out of His Humour*, as Oscar James Campbell has shown,[83] Jonson's desire to find a substitute for the prohibited satire led him back to the *vetus comoedia* from which, as many Renaissance critics held, formal satire had originally been derived. His comical satires merged the attributes of formal satire with the dramatic technique of the Old Comedy, omitting only the element of personal detraction, outlawed by Renaissance theory. His greatest plays explored the tremendous possibilities of "humour" as a basis for characterization, displayed with maximum effectiveness by a thorough development of protasis, epitasis, catastasis, and catastrophe, and particular care in the management of mass scenes.[84]

The useful Cordatus tries to prepare the public for the shift from the accustomed Plautian and Terentian formula to the satirical comedy by explaining that the so-called laws of comedy are not binding upon a playwright; they merely represent the successful practices of his predecessors, not necessarily the only successful practices. Comedy has a long history of development:

every man in the dignity of his spirit and judgment supplied something. . . . I see not then, but we should enjoy the same license, or free power to

---

[81] *The Silent Woman*, Complete Plays, I, 490.
[82] *The Staple of News*, Complete Plays, II, 425.
[83] *Comicall Satyre and Shakespeare's Troilus and Cressida*, p. 54.
[84] Knowlton, "The Plots of Ben Jonson," *Modern Language Notes*, No. 44 (Feb., 1929), pp. 77–86. Cf. *The Magnetic Lady*, Complete Plays, II, 519.

illustrate and heighten our invention, as they did; and not be tied to those strict and regular forms which the niceness of a few, who are nothing but form, would thrust upon us.[85]

To the question *Quid sit comoedia?* Jonson answers that Cicero's definition will serve until someone proposes a better. Comedy is an *"imitatio vitae, speculum consuetudinis, imago veritatis;* a thing throughout pleasant and ridiculous, and accommodated to the correction of manners." [86] The *speculum consuetudinis* of Jonson was not by any means the Shakespearean mirror held to the face of nature and reflecting various men and moods in all their complexity. The mirror of Jonson was a highly selective one that concentrated its beams on peculiarities, deformities, vices, affectations—all those deviations from normal and desirable behavior that Jonson classed as "humours." This mirror of comedy distorts and isolates certain elements in order to deal with them more effectively.[87]

The proper characters for the comic poet to exercise his didactic art upon were obviously those exhibiting some imperfection. Those who were out of humor could be brought into proper humor, or their humors could be reconciled, or, if incorrigible, punished, a practice which Jonson defended in the preface to *Volpone.* Accordingly we find Jonson passing in critical review "Waiting-women, parasites, knights, captains, courtiers, lawyers," [88] bawds, cheats, misers, prodigals, poetasters, Puritans, gulls, sharpers, and a host of minor humors. So accurate were these pictures that he was accused of indulging in personal satire, a charge which he repeatedly denied.

Satire of a certain kind was an essential in Jonson's type of didactic comedy. The poet's method of turning his audience against vice was to ridicule the improprieties of behavior that he portrayed in his characters. Jonson therefore insisted vigorously that the poet retain the privilege of satirizing evils, provided his satire was general and not particular. The rule that satire is excellent, as long as the poet attacks vices and not persons, is stated first by Asper in one of those famous colloquies that Jonson inserted for the instruction of his audience.[89] Next Vergil, in *The Poetaster,* maintains the value of

---

[85] *Every Man out of His Humour,* Complete Plays, I, 65.   [86] *Ibid.,* p. 105.
[87] *Ibid.,* p. 63.   [88] *The Magnetic Lady,* Complete Plays, II, 505.
[89] *Every Man out of His Humour,* Complete Plays, I, 61. Cf. *The Poetaster,* Complete Plays, pp. 302, 304.

broad satire and indicates that perfectly proper satire can be rendered harmful by a vicious interpreter who will make it seem to have a personal application:

> 'Tis not the wholesome sharp morality,
> Or modest anger of a satiric spirit,
> That hurts or wounds the body of the state;
> But the sinister application
> Of the malicous, ignorant, and base
> Interpreter; who will distort and strain
> The general scope and purpose of an author
> To his particular and private spleen.[90]

Jonson protested repeatedly that in those comedies which he had written alone, with certain recognized and justifiable exceptions, he had never directed his sharpness at individuals. That was libel; that was the sort of filth in which the poetasters dealt.[91] He assured his critics that it was not a writer's business to deal with truth, but with "things, like truths, well feign'd." [92]

> We yet adventure here to . . .
> . . . shew you common follies, and so known,
> That though they are not truths, the innocent Muse,
> Hath made so like, as phant'sy could them state,
> Or poetry, without scandal, imitate.[93]

Besides those of his readers who considered that he was lampooning individuals, there were those who represented him as assailing certain types; and, finally, there were those who, too ignorant to understand his satiric comedy, considered all he wrote mere railing.[94] Captain Tucca represents this last group ably:

I would fain come with my cockatrice one day, and see a play, if I knew when there was a good bawdy one; but they say you have nothing but Humours, Revels, and Satires, that gird and f—t at the time.[95]

In *The Staple of News* he tried to defend himself against the charge of ridiculing certain professions. Pennyboy Canter rebukes his son for having chosen companions so badly. Why had he not sought out

[90] *The Poetaster*, Complete Plays, p. 289. [91] *Volpone*, Complete Plays, I, 401.
[92] *The Silent Woman*, Complete Plays, p. 490.
[93] *The Staple of News*, Complete Plays, II, 350.
[94] *Apologetical Dialogue*, Complete Plays, I, 306.
[95] *The Poetaster*, Complete Plays, I, 362.

Just as sense of the lofty function of poetry made him undervalue the lyric, so it made him reject the romance. This type, to him, embodied fiction running wild, sweetness that brought no corresponding light. There is no grain of knowledge in such chaff.[114] In reproaching Vulcan for having destroyed his works, Jonson asks why the fire did not first consume the dross of poetry:

> . . . the whole sum
> Of errant knighthood, with the dames and dwarfs;
> The charmed boats, and the inchanted wharfs,
> The Tristans, Lanc'lots, Turpins, and the Peers
> All the mad Rolands, and sweet Olivers.[115]

One of his loftiest characters, Lovel, explains at length that his education in virtue proceeded from right studies: no romances—Arthurs, Rosicleers, knights of the sun, Amadis de Ĝauls, Primalions, Pantagruels, public nothings:

> Abortives of the fabulous dark cloyster,
> Sent out to poison courts and infest manners.[116]

Instead of these, Homer and Vergil gave him "examples of heroic virtue." It was not the material itself, but the wrong use of it that Jonson rejected. He had acknowledged the prime value of the Arthurian story for an epic and had utilized Arthur in *Prince Henry's Barriers*. The distinction is very similar to that which he made in comedy: he condemned the use of fools and devils when their function was merely to raise an empty laugh; yet he used a devil himself to point a moral.

Certainly the only romance material that he favored was the English story of Arthur. Baskervill speaks with good reason of the "fundamental inclination of the man toward an intense Anglicism." [117] Despite Jonson's wide classical learning (he informed Drummond that "he was better Versed & knew more in Greek and Latin than all the Poets in England"), he never felt any desire to write in the classical tongues. From the beginning his whole effort was to adapt the classical lore to the needs of his own day and locality.

---

[114] *The Silent Woman*, Complete Plays, I, 525.

[115] *Underwoods*, Works, ed. by Whalley, VI, 405.

[116] *The New Inn*, Complete Plays, II, 441.

[117] "English Elements in Jonson's Early Comedy," *Bulletin of the University of Texas*, No. 178 (1911), p. 33.

The first effect of this on his writing is the revision of *Every Man in His Humour*. Jonson had decided to drive the lesson home. What an English audience could lightly dismiss as the follies of an Italian group, became inescapable when the names and scenes were made English. The prologue to *The Alchemist* proclaims clearly that it intends to teach Englishmen by English examples, of which there are, alas, enough:

> Our scene is London, 'cause we would make known,
> No country's mirth is better than our own;
> No clime breeds better matter for your whore,
> Bawd, squire, imposter, many persons more,
> Whose manners, now call'd humours, feed the stage.[118]

The masques frequently drew on English material, obviously in *Prince Henry's Barriers, The Irish Masque, For the Honour of Wales;* and more subtly in several of the others, notably *The Masque of Queens, Mercury Vindicated,* and *Love Restored. The Sad Shepherd* confined itself strictly to English matter and openly set out to rival the classics in doing so.

Jonson, conscious that he was breaking new ground and deeply convinced of the merit of his innovations, divided the world around him (exclusive of the poetasters, his and poetry's arch enemies) into four significant groups. There was first and highest the learned group that realized and appreciated what he was doing. Second came the rank and file, the vulgar, the ordinary spectators or readers. The unassuming members of this group had many honest prejudices and little real knowledge. Third came the gallants who pretended to some knowledge, but were likely to be amateur critics of the most shallow sort. Fourth, there were the other poets, especially the fledgling poets. Each of these groups required and received different treatment at his hands.

The learned and appreciative group was rewarded by receiving a permanent form of commendation. Jonson set forth their names in epigrams or dedications. Much of his praise was heaped on the king, and Jonson had every reason to honor James as his lawful monarch, his patron, and a man of no mean learning. Then came the many notables of the court: the Earl of Pembroke, Lady Mary Wroth,

[118] Complete Plays, II, 2.

Lucy, Countess of Bedford, Lord Aubigny, and others who had
earned his regard.

To the noble and courtly audience Jonson did not have to justify
his art, but he was not content with having pleased only them.[119]
A playwright should please the general public. He soon found that
the taste of the lower class of theatergoer ran to the customary.
Unlike the court, which delighted in novelty, the common folk
wanted endless repetition of the old satisfying pattern. Jonson did
not want to follow that pattern and so he undertook the heroic task
of educating public opinion to the point where it could enjoy his
different and better kind of play. He had, in some way, to explain
these comedies that carried so much more than mere mirth.

To reach the public directly and yet dramatically, Jonson made
very effective use of the prologue and induction. He also experi-
mented with a much more remarkable device, suggested in part by
the Greek chorus [120] and in part by the requirements of formal
satire: [121] the use of a group of extra characters who, appearing at
the beginning of the play and between the acts, served to guide the
reaction of the audience. Thus Asper, in the earliest of these didactic
dialogues, explains the primary tenets of the Jonsonian creed, the
true function of the poet, and the proper attitude of his audience:

Asper: . . . my strict hand
            Was made to seize on vice, and with a gripe
            Squeeze out the humour of such spongy souls,
            As lick up every idle vanity.
Cordatus: Why, this is right *furor poeticus!*
Asper: And I will mix with you in industry
            To please: but whom? attentive auditors,
            Such as will join their profit with their pleasures,
            And come to feed their understanding parts.[122]

Throughout *Every Man out of His Humour*, Mitis raises objections
which Cordatus patiently answers, explaining quite frankly that
all this is a device of the author to satisfy the audience on those very
points.[123] Brilliantly, in *The Staple of News*, he presents four ladies,

---

[119] *The Silent Woman*, Complete Plays, I, 490.   [120] Symonds, *Ben Jonson*, p. 27.
[121] O. J. Campbell, *Comicall Satyre*, p. 52.
[122] *Every Man out of His Humour*, Complete Plays, I, 63, 64.
[123] Complete Plays, I, 87.

the gossips Mirth, Tattle, Expectation,[124] and Curiosity, who repre-
sent the attitudes that he must overcome. By means of these dialogues
Jonson waged war on whatever militated against a fair reception
of his plays.

The greatest difficulty, however, lay in combating the rising cult
of criticism among the young gallants. Jonson made a special effort to
reëducate these "plush and velvet" [125] critics. True wit did not neces-
sarily consist in damning plays, but rather in finding the excellences
of them.[126] At the same time, Jonson tried to wean the public away
from too great dependence on the opinion of these gallants.[127] After
many years of teaching the public, Jonson seemed to feel that he
had gained his points:

> He that hath feasted you these forty years,
> And fitted fables for your finer ears,
> Although at first he scarce could hit the bore;
> Yet you with patience harkening more and more,
> At length have grown up to him, and make known
> The working of his pen is now your own.[128]

Jonson carried on an even more direct campaign to educate the
readers of his plays. The reader in some ways provided a superior
public because his attention was not so distracted as that of the play-
goer.[129] For the benefit of the reader, the poet recast portions of his
commonplace book as prefatory material.[130]

Not the least reason for the complete triumph of the classical
tradition at the end of the century was the deliberate effort on Jon-
son's part to disseminate his beliefs among the promising wits of the
age. The poet laureate was interested in spreading his theory of
poetry by direct teaching as well as by example. He was not a
secluded and retired figure, but a rare good fellow who held con-
vivial court in "the Apollo of the Old Devil Tavern, Temple-Bar;
that being his Club-Room." [131] There gathered many of the brilliant

---

[124] *The New Inn*, Complete Plays, II, 429. Cf. *The Magnetic Lady*, Complete Plays,
II, 518.
[125] *The Magnetic Lady*, Complete Plays, II, 506.
[126] *Ibid.*, p. 531.
[127] *The New Inn*, Complete Plays, II, 426.
[128] *The Sad Shepherd*, Complete Plays, II, 637.
[129] *The Staple of News*, Complete Plays, II, 349.
[130] *The Alchemist*, Complete Plays, II, 1.   [131] Works, ed. by Whalley, VII, 291.

and tuneful young men of London, the "sons of Ben" who were to carry out the patriarch's doctrine, each in his own way. Fortunately for them, this great man to whom they listened was not only an inspired poet but a careful scholar and a gifted teacher. To his followers, as to himself, Ben Jonson seemed a rock of the true and original poetic faith, and it was this attitude that led his admiring disciple Herrick to write:

> When I a Verse shall make,
> Know I have praid thee,
> For old Religions sake,
> Saint Ben to aide me.

Once a play had been presented or published, Jonson fully recognized the right of any person to criticize it. What he did not grant was the validity of everyone's judgment. Ordinary critics revealed their own limitations and not the author's. To the average reader Jonson said plainly:

Neither praise nor dispraise from you can affect me. . . . The commendation of good things may fall within a many, the approbation but in a few; for the most commend out of affection, self-tickling, an easiness or imitation; but men judge only out of knowledge.[132]

Obviously very few persons would be competent to judge of an art so complex as Jonson's art of poetry. Only an exceptional poet could qualify as an informed critic.[133] The favorable judgment of a true critic was something Jonson greatly desired for his muse:

> The garland that she wears, their hands must twine,
> Who can both censure, understand, define
> What merit is: then cast those piercing rays,
> Round as a crown, instead of honour'd bays,
> About his poesy. . . .[134]

His epigram "To the Learned Critick" repeats his belief that only such a judge can award bays worth the having.

Drawn by the similarity of scholarly background and independent spirit, Jonson himself turned for contemporary critical opinion to John Donne.[135] Some of Donne's early poetry seemed to Jonson

---

[132] *Catiline*, Complete Plays, II, 91.
[133] *Discoveries*, Works, ed. by Whalley, VII, 153.
[134] *Cynthia's Revels*, Complete Plays, I, 154.
[135] *Epigrams*, Works, ed by Whalley, VI, 260.

the best he had ever read. The later affectation of harshness and obscurity were points to be condemned, but Donne still ranked high enough as a conscious artist to be designated as the Criticus of the *Art of Poetry*. Both men were opposed to the Spenserian style; both were satirically inclined. But a wide gulf separated them. Donne wrote in the contemporary vocabulary, with a sinewy forcefulness akin to Jonson's power, but he, more than Spenser, soon became guilty of writing no language that could conceivably reach a wide audience. Nor did he profess such a motive or make any effort to publish his work. He wrote on the very themes of love and personal passion that supplied subjects to the sonneteers, even though he wore his passion with a difference. At least once Jonson found him blasphemous.

Peculiarly enough, Jonson in certain important critical principles was nearer to Spenser, whom he disparaged so readily, than to Donne, whom he so greatly admired. Both Jonson and Spenser held that it was the function of the poet to delight and to instruct, "to impress adroitly upon citizens the need of being better men." Theirs was the dedication to the more arduous undertaking, the avowal of the loftier, more socially conscious attitude of the major poet. To the end that he might teach delightfully, each strove to perfect his technique by embodying the best principles of previous ages. Spenser was the heir of Vergil via Ariosto and Tasso; Jonson saw Vergil in the terms of Horace and Aristotle. Both men were vitally interested in the history of their mother tongue; both were well-grounded in Chaucer. Spenser's interest led him back toward archaisms; Jonson's led him to the tradition that was to prevail—a rigorous standard of pure contemporary style. Jonson, in his fight against the empty and sensuous delights of decadent romanticism, seems to have misunderstood the intent of this great Renaissance figure. A later lover of the classics was to see with clearer eyes that Spenser, too, was a great moral allegorist and was to give him deserved credit as "a sage and serious teacher." Certainly the combined strength of both Jonson and Spenser nurtures the great seventeenth-century belief that the highest function of the poet is to enrich his nation by the elevating and moral force of poetry, and the corollary that the highest form of his art would be that most effective for this purpose.

CHAPTER III

MICHAEL DRAYTON

BEN JONSON'S emphasis on the didactic force of his art found expression in an enlargement of the theory of comedy to suit his requirements. The deep conviction that poetry had a vital role to play in the development of the English nation found a more typical expression in the work of Michael Drayton, a poet equal to Jonson in his constant awareness of the theory of his art. It is a pity that Drayton did not yield to the temptation that assailed him in several of his prefaces and write a complete manual of poetic art. In the preface to his *Legends* he says, "To particularize the Lawes of this Poeme, were to teach the making of a Poeme; a Worke for a Volume, not an Epistle," [1] thus revealing that he had formulated or adopted a large body of "lawes" by which he guided his own writing. The language of his address to the honorable gentlemen of England, true favorers of Poesie, implies his possession of very definite and satisfactory poetic standards, since he berates those whose dull eyes are "so over-clowded with mistie ignorance as never able to look into the celestiall secrets of divine Poesie, thereby to discerne the right and true method of a perfect and exquisite Poeme." [2] In his "Skeltoniad" Drayton toys with a miniature "Ars Poetica" and drops some hints as to the "right and true method":

> The Muse should be sprightly,
> Yet not handling lightly
> Things grave; as much loath,
> Things that be slight to cloath
> Curiously: To retayne
> The comelinesse in meane
> Is true Knowledge and Wit.
> Neyther each ryming Slave
> Deserves the Name to have
> Of Poet:
> My resolution such,

---

[1] Drayton, *Legends* (1619), Works of Michael Drayton, ed. by Hebel, II, 382.
[2] *Matilda* (1594), Works, I, 211.

How well, and not how much
To write.[3]

The same Horatian flavor pervades his more specific advice to the writer of the epic, and, in the second stanza, to the dramatist:

Or if the deeds of *Heroes* ye rehearse,
Let them be sung in so well-ord'red Verse
    That each word have his weight,
    Yet runne with pleasure;
    Holding one stately height,
    In so brave measure
That they may make the stiffest Storme seeme weake.

And if yee list to exercise your Vayne,
Or in the Sock, or in the Buskin'd Strayne,
    Let Art and Nature goe
    One with the other;
    Yet so, that Art may show
    Nature her Mother.[4]

In Song II of *Poly-Olbion* he repeats and elaborates these ideas that look back to Horace and forward to Pope.[5]

The most general of Drayton's critical comments occurs in his preface to the *Pastorals* of 1619:

The chiefe Law of Pastorals is the same which is of all Poesie, and of all wise carriage, to wit, *Decorum*, and that not to be exceeded without leave, or without at least faire warning.[6]

That is, a shepherd should talk like a shepherd unless he warns the reader that, inspired by love, he is about to transcend the usual limits of pastoral poetry; or aroused by instances of folly or vice, he is about to be satiric. More generally, each type of poetry has its appropriate subject matter and style which should be maintained, except for an occasional conscious and careful digression. Thus he rebukes his muse for being satirical in an elegiac epistle,[7] and conversely checks an extravagant burst in a plain-spoken satire.[8]

It is possible to glean from his works and set in order certain vital principles of his theory of poetry. In several passages he expresses his conviction that poetry is clearly of divine origin. It is "the delight of

---

[3] *Odes. With other Lyrick Poesies* (1619), Works, II, 370.   [4] *Ibid.*, p. 358.
[5] Works, IV, 29.   [6] *Poems Lyric and Pastoral* (1606), Works, II, 517.
[7] *Englands Heroicall Epistles* (1597), Works, II, 239–40.   [8] *Ibid.*, p. 293.

Blessed soules, and the language of Angels." [9] After detailing the nine orders of angels he continues:

> From these the Muses onely are derived,
> Which of the Angels were in nine contrived;
> These heaven-inspired Babes of memorie,
> Which by a like attracting Sympathy
> Apollos Prophets in theyr furies wrought,
> And in theyr spirit inchaunting numbers taught,
> To teach such as at Poesie repine,
> That it is onely heavenly and divine,
> And manifest her intellectual parts,
> Sucking the purest of the purest Arts.[10]

In Drayton's esthetic the distinguishing attribute of poetry is "inchaunting numbers," an element so mysterious and so powerful as to be inexplicable unless attributed to heavenly inspiration. The shade of Cromwell, invoking strength for his poet-defendant, calls on the aid of "powerfull Number" and "the high Divinitie in sound." [11] Reverence for the power of verse and willingness to toil patiently toward mastery of that subtle force characterize Drayton's work. Good verse should be smooth,[12] flowing,[13] and tunable.[14] In a prayer for increased poetic power he asks that his thought may be "Wrap'd up in Numbers flowing," adding,

> And in my choise Composures
> The soft and easie Closures
> So amorously shall meet;
>
> That ev'ry lively Ceasure
> Shall tread a perfect measure,
> Set on so equall feet.[15]

That he was careful to develop his facility in numbers by unintermitted exercise is evident in "An Ode Written in the Peake":

> This while we are abroad
> Shall we not touch our Lyre?
> Shall we not sing an Ode?
> Shall that holy fire,
> In us that strongly glow'd

[9] *Battaille of Agincourt* (1619), Works, III, 2. Cf. p. 176.
[10] *Endimion and Phœbe* (1594), Works, I, 152.
[11] *Legends* (1619), Works, II, 452.   [12] *Elegies*, Works, III, 216.
[13] *Ibid.*, p. 225.   [14] *The Moone-Calfe*, Works, III, 176.
[15] *Odes. With other Lyrick Poesies* (1619), Works, II, 351.

> In this cold Ayre expire?
>
> No sport our Houres shall breake
>   To exercise our Vaine.[16]

He did not, however, overemphasize the importance of number,
nor did he consider it more than an element of the much higher
term, poetry. *Poetry* seems to have meant to Drayton the fanciful
and striking expression of a thought that is born of the limitations
and license of verse; whereas *number* applies not to the poet's imagi-
nation, but to his gift of expressing himself through an instinct for
the right sounds and words. *Rime* is a similar term including both
measure and recurrent end sound. This distinction between the proc-
esses of conception and expression is epitomized in Drayton's re-
quirements for a writer of odes. He must have both

> the trick
> of Ryming, with Invention quick.[17]

Of these two indispensable elements, Drayton held that rime yields
first place to invention. At the conclusion of a careful evaluation
of the merit of various types of stanzas he remarks, "but generally,
all Stanzas are in my opinion but Tyrants and Torturers, when they
make Invention obey their number, which sometimes would other-
wise scantle it selfe." [18] Since invention is the more important ele-
ment, he vindicates all verse that provides a responsive medium for
the poet's thoughts:

> To those that with despight
> Shall term these Numbers slight,
>   Tell them their Judgement's blind
> Much erring from the right,
>   It is a Noble kind.
>
> Nor is't the verse doth make,
> That giveth, or doth take,
>   'Tis possible to clyme,
> To kindle, or to slake
>   Although in Skelton's Ryme.[19]

Theoretically, poetry notable for its invention may be found in any
type of verse. But in general practice Drayton gave great attention

---

[16] *Odes. With other Lyrick Poesies* (1619), Works, II, 365.   [17] *Ibid.*, p. 344.
[18] *To the Reader of the Barons Warres*, Works, II, 3.   [19] *Ibid.*, p. 349.

to the selection of a suitable measure; for though the type of rime
has nothing to do with the value of the thought expressed, it strongly
affects the projection of that thought, the scope and duration of its
appeal:

> The Ryme nor marres, nor makes,
> Nor addeth it, nor takes,
>   From that which we propose;
> Things imaginarie
> Doe so strangely varie,
>   That quickly we them lose.
>
> And what's quickly begot,
> As soone againe is not,
>   This doe I truly know:
> Yea, and what's borne with paine,
> That Sense doth long'st retaine
>   Gone with a greater Flow.[20]

The primary problem of poetry is to fix the imaginative creation
in verse before it vanishes; but the poet who tries to keep pace with
his imagination will write too rapidly for permanence. Drayton
sought a solution of this dilemma in revision. As he gained in power,
he went back, carefully improved, and in some cases completely
altered the pastorals, sonnets, satires, legends, and *Mortimeriados*.
He took pains to "augment and polish" an early version of *Piers
Gaveston* and *Matilda*, which he termed "unformed and indigested,
like a Beare whelpe before it is lickt by the Dam"; [21] and he con-
scientiously changed from a stanza of seven lines to one of eight in
The Barons Warres, because, as his preliminary discussion shows, the
eight-line stanza "hath in it, Majestie, Perfection, and Solidity." [22]

Conspicuous in Drayton's theory is his exalted view of the poetic
office. In *Endimion and Phœbe* he considered poets as only twice re-
moved in the line of descent from angels. In the *Heroicall Epistles*
he places them next to the angels or gods (he shifts religious systems
most disconcertingly). The following lines, spoken by Henry How-
ard, are substantially Drayton's own theory; they reveal the concept
behind Drayton's exaltation of poetry and its creators:

[20] *Odes. With other Lyrick Poesies* (1619), Works, II, 366.
[21] *The Tragicall Legend of Robert, Duke of Normandy* (1596), Works, I, 251.
[22] *To the Reader of the Barons Warres*, Works, II, 3.

> When Heav'n would strive to doe the best it can
> And put an Angels Spirit into a Man,
> The utmost pow'r it hath, it then doth spend,
> When to the World a Poet it doth intend.
> That little diff'rence 'twixt the Gods and us,
> (By them confirm'd) distinguished onely thus:
> Whom they, in Birth, ordaine to happy dayes,
> The Gods commit their glory to our prayse;
> T'eternall Life when they dissolve their breath,
> We likewise share a second Pow'r by Death.
> When Time shall turne those Amber Lockes to Gray,
> My Verse againe shall guild and make them gay,

> .   .   .   .

> If *Florence* once should lose her old renowne,
> As famous *Athens*, now a Fisher-Towne
> My lines for thee a *Florence* shall erect,
> Which great Apollo ever shall protect,
> And with the Numbers from my Penne that falls,
> Bring Marble Mines to re-erect those Walls.[23]

The poet is the most god-like of men because to him is entrusted the power of conferring glory in life and immortality in death. The turn that such a theory will give to Drayton's love poetry is clearly indicated, and the prediction made concerning Florence is the one he fulfilled for England in *Poly-Olbion*. Drayton again expresses his noble view of the poet's function and power in a passage filled with scathing denunciation of such poets as prostitute their gift for worldly advancement:

> Those rare Promethii, fetching fire from Heaven;
> To whom the Functions of the Gods are given,
> Raising fraile dust with their redouble flame,
> Mounted with Hymnes upon the wings of Fame;
> Ordain'd by Nature (Truch-men for the great)
> To fire their Noble hearts with glorious heat.
> You Sun-bred Ayerie, whose immortall Birth,
> Beares you aloft, beyond the sight of Earth,
> But who their great Profession can protect,
> That rob themselves of their owne due respect?
> For they whose Minds should be exhal'd and hie,
> As Free and Noble as cleere Poesie,

---

[23] 1597. *Works*, II, 280.

In the slight favour of some Lord to come,
Basely doe crouch to his attending Groome.
Immortall gift that art not bought with Gold,
That thou to Peasants should be basely sold! [24]

Drayton insists on the "purity" of the poet; he must be free espe-
cially from the necessity of praising any particular person, an almost
impossible condition at court, where patronage was to be secured
only by adulation.[25] The ode "To Himselfe and the Harpe" main-
tains that Apollo forbids his shrine to no one who is born a poet and
whose hands are pure.[26] The true poet must consider himself pri-
marily an instrument of the gods, and must be careful to exercise
properly his power to confer undying fame.

Why was Drayton so concerned with the immortalizing power of
poetry, which many other poets have recognized, but few have
accorded equal prominence? Because he saw in this aspect of his art
a force which might be used to further individual and national
virtue. Obviously virtue was sometimes rather badly treated by fate.
It could not be exempt from the vicissitudes of fortune as that would
imply a limitation of God's power,[27] but the seeming injustice of such
an arrangement is counteracted by the poet, who rewards virtue
here on earth with fame and immortality. Drayton made clear his
feeling concerning fame, fortune, virtue, and immortality in *The
Tragicall Legend of Robert, Duke of Normandy*. This is a "vision"
poem in which the poet appears and speaks in his own proper person.
Before him come the figures of Fame and Fortune, who compete for
supremacy over Robert, the type of the deserving but ill-fated man.[28]
Fortune states the situation:

Behold this Duke of *Normandy,* quoth she,

. . . . .

Appealing to be justifie'd by Thee [i. e., Fame]
(Whose Tragedy, this Poet must compile).[29]

There follows a debate between Fortune and Fame, each in a long
harangue averring herself superior, each insisting that she was glori-

[24] *The Owle* (1604), Works, II, 497.   [25] *Heroicall Epistles*, Works, II, 291.
[26] *Odes. With other Lyrick Poesies*, Works, II, 347.
[27] *Heroicall Epistles*, Works, II, 234. Cf. *Legends, ibid.*, p. 382.
[28] Works, II, 382.   [29] *Ibid.*, p. 386.

fied by "th' old Poets." Drayton acknowledges the necessity as well as the power of Fortune in her argument, but the most significant lines are those of Fame:

> I am alone the Vanquisher of Time:
> Bearing those Sweets, which cure death's bitternesse.[30]

Thus the poet by his power to confer undying fame becomes an important factor in the promotion of virtue. Accordingly, no position was too high for the true poet, as for instance, the passage describing the two books of Fame:

> That; the faire booke of heavenly memory,
> Th'other, the black scrowle of infamy:
> One stuff'd with Poets Saints, and Conquerors,
> Th'other with Atheists, Tyrants, Usurers.[31]

In boasting of the poet's control over fame, Drayton was not being original. Horace, himself copying Pindar, had done it centuries before, and, as Oliver Elton has shown in his article on the subject, the concept of literary fame was extremely popular during the Renaissance.[32] To be sure, the Renaissance vaunt of poetic immortality was often purely conventional, but there were a number of poets who were deeply convinced of the perpetuating power of their art. Spenser, and later Drayton, felt the broadest implications of the theory, felt the combat of fame against time and the great role of the poet therein. It is the poet

> from whose Sacred Rage
> Flowes the full Glorie of each plenteous Age.[33]

Certainly no one took more seriously than Drayton the responsibility of the poet in the fight of all earthly things against oblivion. The distinctive peculiarity of his theory is that he insisted more and more upon turning a common Renaissance claim into an active principle of his work.

His strong interest in the concept of poetic fame manifests itself first in conventional ways. In his love poetry the theme of fame predominates; Drayton does not ask the lady to pity or to return his

---

[30] *Legends*, p. 391.
[31] *The Tragicall Legend of Robert, Duke of Normandy*, Works, I, 256. Cf. *ibid.*, II, 385.
[32] *Otia Merseiana*, IV (1904), 24–52.   [33] *The Owle*, Works, II, 497.

passion half so feelingly as he implores her to look upon the lasting memorial he has built for her. Consider the first Amour:

> Receave the incense which I offer heere,
> By my strong fayth ascending to thy fame,
> My zeale, my hope, my vowes, my praise, my prayer,
> My soules oblations to thy sacred name.
> Which name my Muse to highest heaven shal raise,
> By chast desire, true love, and vertues praise.[34]

In the lovely fourth Amour he acknowledges her as his inspiration and concludes, as the most important result of her power,

> Thus from thy selfe the cause is thus derived
> That by thy fame all fame shall be survived.[35]

It is easy to multiply examples.[36] One of the best quatorzains in the revised and expanded group of sonnets shows how his preoccupation with the idea of poetic fame developed:

> How many paltry, foolish, painted things,
> That now in Coaches trouble ev'ry Street,
> Shall be forgotten, whom no Poet sings,
> Ere they be well wrap'd in their winding Sheet?
> Where I to thee Eternitie shall give,
> When nothing else remayneth of these dayes,
> And Queens hereafter shall be glad to live
> Upon the Almes of thy superfluous prayse;
>
> .   .   .   .   .
>
> So shalt thou flye above the vulgar Throng,
> Still to survive in my immortall Song.[37]

In Sonnet 47 Drayton touches also upon another type of fame, the pursuit of which he says he has abandoned, the fame conferred on the poet by his works.[38] But in a previous sonnet, 44, he draws a truer picture of the situation and recognizes that he has achieved immortality not only for his lady but, by the same token, for himself:

> Whilst thus my Pen strives to eternize thee,
> Age rules my Lines with Wrinkles in my Face.
>
> .   .   .   .   .

---

[34] *Ideas Mirrour*, Works, I, 98.   [35] *Ibid.*, p. 99.

[36] *Ibid.*, p. 100. Cf. pp. 110, 117 (i. e., *Amours* 6, 23, 28).

[37] *Idea*, Works, II, 313. Cf. *Elegies*, Works, III, 220; *Odes*, Works, II, 352.

[38] *Ibid.*, p. 334.

> Medea-like, I make thee young againe
> Proudly thou scornest my World-out-wearing Rimes,
> And though in youth, my Youth untimely perish,
> To keep Thee from Oblivion and the Grave
> Ensuing Ages yet my Rimes shall cherish,
>
> .   .   .   .
>
> And though this Earthly Body fade and die,
> My Name shall mount upon Eternitie.[39]

His consciousness of the poet's own right to immortality is clearly seen in his pastoral lament for Elphin:

> Oh Elphin, Elphin, though thou hence be gone,
> In spight of death, yet shalt thou live for aye,
> Thy Poesie is garlanded with Bay.[40]

Again in the preface to his revised *Eglogues* he says: "Master *Edmund Spenser* had done enough for the immortalitie of his Name, had he only given us his Shepheards Kalendar. . . ." [41] Ultimately, in Drayton's theory of poetry, the principle of poetic fame grew far beyond its conventional boundaries and became of paramount importance.

According to the principle of decorum, Drayton recognized several types of poetry, each with a suitable style and subject matter. What were the values of these various types and where did each find its place in a theory of poetry whose principal tenet was a serious view of poetic responsiblity, which took specific form as a high-minded resolve to use the attractive power of poetry to eternize worthy subjects?

Drayton's first publication was wholly didactic in purpose; it was a poetical paraphrase of certain songs of the Bible, an undertaking which may have been suggested by the experiment of the Sidneys with the Psalms of David. While this book, *The Harmonie of the Church* (1591), should perhaps be considered as merely an exercise in translation, there are two passages in it of interest to the student of literary theory because they express an abnegation, that he was soon forced to retract, of certain devices for procuring delight. In the preface to Lady Jane Devoreaux, he begs her to measure the

---

[39] *Idea*, Works, II, 332.
[40] *Idea The Shepheards Garland*, Works, I, 64. Cf. p. 62; and *Pastorals. Contayning Eglogues* (1619), Works, II, 549.
[41] *Pastorals. Contayning Eglogues* (1619), Works, II, 518.

poems "not by my abilitie but by their authoritie: not as Poems of Poets, but praiers of Prophets." In the accompanying address to the reader, Drayton is even more explicit:

Gentle Reader, my meaning is not with the varietie of verse to feede any vaine humour, neither to trouble thee with devises of mine owne invention, as carieng an overweening of mine own wit: but here I present thee with these Psalmes or Songes of praise, so exactly translated as the prose would permit, or sence would in any way suffer me: which (if thou shalt be the same in hart thou art in name, I mean a Christian) I doubt not but thou wilt take as great delight in these as in any Poetical fiction. I speak not of Mars, the god of Wars, nor of Venus, the goddesse of love, but of the Lord of Hostes, that made heaven and earth: Not of Toyes in Mount Ida, but of triumphes in Mount Sion: Not of Vanitie but of Veritie: not of Tales, but of Truethes.[42]

He seems uneasily aware, as he urges the comparison between the usual formula for poetic delight and his own more salutary offering, that the reader will miss the variety of verse, devices, classical mythology, the "Toyes" of the pastoral, the predominance of fiction, all of which he had temporarily rejected in his effort to disseminate pure truth.

But Drayton's desire to be a poet of "Truethes" received a severe setback in the harsh reception accorded *The Harmonie of the Church*. His next publication came more into line with the prevailing taste in poetry when, following Spenser and in the classical tradition, he produced *Idea The Shepheards Garland* (1593). This sudden *démarche* into a most artificial type of poetry did not mean that Drayton had abandoned his desire to write of truth. What had happened was that his first book had taught him the extreme difficulty of writing effective poetry while concentrating too completely on any other objective, however worthy in itself. He would need much more control over the element of poetic delight if he wished to make his poetry serve any weighty purpose and still remain attractive. In his second attempt, therefore, he picked a type far better suited to a beginner, one which a later preface characterizes thus:

Pastorals, as they are a Species of Poesie, signify fained Dialogues, or other speeches in Verse, fathered upon Heardsmen . . . who are ordinarie persons in this kind of Poeme, worthily therefore to be called base or low. . . .

---

[42] *The Harmonie of the Church* (1591), Works, I, 3.

The subject of Pastorals, as the language of it ought to be poor, silly, and of the coursest Woofe in appearance.

Lowly characters, opportunity for variety in meter, simple subject matter, all made the pastoral an ideal incubator for a fledgling poet. Pastorals, of course, might be used to shadow more worthy things; but Drayton did not attempt to incorporate a deeper meaning, since he very consciously regarded this type as merely preparatory to his more serious writing:

But he who has almost nothing Pastorall in his Pastoralls, but the name (which is my Case) deales more plainly, because *detracto velamine* he speakes of most weightie things. . . . Spenser is the prime Pastoralist of England. My Pastorals bold upon a new straine, must speake for themselves.[43]

As might be expected, he placed a very low intrinsic value on this type of poetry, although allowing it to be delightsome to the young. In Eglog II, the old poet Wynken disrelishes the sweet, but slight verses of his youth.[44] That pastoral poetry was an apprentice stage is evident in Eglog III. Perkin, disgusted with the ribald or fulsomely flattering poets that are gaining attention, urges Rowland to attempt a poem in praise of Elizabeth, but Rowland replies that such poetry is above the reach of his limited skill. To sing "of worthies deede" is the task of a developed poet; he is not yet ready, like "learned Collin," to abandon his pipes for a higher lay.[45]

But if Drayton felt himself too weak as yet to follow Spenser, there were passages in the pastorals in which he felt that he was improving and achieving a higher type of poetry. When writing of love he seemed to strike a loftier strain, and Eglog V announces itself as an essay on this level:

> This lustie swayne his lowly quill,
>   to higher notes doth rayse
> And in Ideas person paynts
>   his lovely lasses prayse.[46]

---

[43] *Pastorals. Contayning Eglogues* (1619), Works, II, 517. Apparently Drayton had no high opinion of the meaningful *Bucolics*, for he refuses to pass judgment on Vergil as a pastoral poet, although he pays him honor as a prophet of Christ.

[44] *Idea The Shepheards Garland*, Works, I, 51.

[45] *Ibid.*, p. 55.   [46] *Ibid.*, p. 65.

But love poetry was not the highest type, for a little later Rowland "sore repents what he before missaide," i. e., that he had "lewdly feigned" love to be almost divine. The next step is indicated by Motto, who, after listening to Rowland's song in Idea's praise, says:

> Cease shepheard cease, reserve thy Muses store,
> Till after time shall teach thy Oaten reede
> Aloft in ayre with Egles wings to sore,
> And sing in honor of some worthies deede,
> To serve Idea in some better steede.[47]

Even higher in value than direct praise of Idea would be a notable poem dedicated to her. Although Drayton needed more skill and power before attempting heroic subjects,[48] the time had come for him to quit the pastoral. He was so feelingly aware of the glaring absurdities of this form that he incorporated a brilliant burlesque, the Rime of Dowsabell, as part of his *Shepheards Garland*.

Although not his next publication, it is very likely that *Ideas Mirrour* (1594) was his next piece of writing, since the preliminary sonnet,[49] probably by Drayton himself, mentions him merely as a pastoral poet who had sung in praise of Elizabeth. These sonnets, though declaring their freedom from French and Italian models,[50] reflect very strongly the influence of Sidney (*Astrophel and Stella*, 1591) and *Daniel* (*Delia*, 1592), and were probably written at intervals from 1591 on, as they form no sequence but merely a collection.

The internal evidence all seems to indicate that these quatorzains were exercises, rather than the result of a powerful emotion.[51] Perhaps the best proof of this is obtained by comparing the first edition with the much revised and enlarged *Amours* of 1605. The order of the early sonnets has been greatly changed, and the interpolations are so frequent as to show that there was no significance in the original arrangement. Three lines in Amour 28 definitely state that those who think he is depicting real feelings for a mistress disguised under the name of *Idea* are wrong:

[47] *Ibid.*, p. 69. [48] *Ibid.*, p. 66. Cf. p. 84.
[49] *Ibid.*, p. 93. [50] *Ideas Mirrour*, Works, I, 96
[51] *Idea*, Works, II, 324, No. 28. *Ideas Mirrour*, Works, I, 119, No. 41.

> Some who reach not the height of my conceite,
> They say, (as Poets doe) I use to fayne,
> And in bare words paynt out my passions payne.[52]

Whether the "Height of his conceite" means that *Idea* should be interpreted platonically,[53] or merely that the whole thing is an imaginative exercise, the quotation indicates that these sonnets had an artistic rather than a passionate origin. Drayton prefaced the revised version of *Idea* (1619) with some lines that should completely dispel any notion other than that he found a sonnet collection based on love congenial to his muse.

To the Reader of These Sonnets

> Into these Loves who but for Passion lookes,
> At his first sight, here let him lay them by,
> And seeke else-where, in turning other Bookes,
> Which better may his labour satisfie.
> No farre-fetch'd Sigh shall ever wound my Brest,
> Love from mine Eye a teare shall never wring,
> Nor in *Ah-mees* my whyning Sonnets drest,
> (A Libertine) fantastickly I sing:
> My verse is the true image of my Mind,
> Ever in motion, still desiring change;
> And as thus to Varietie inclin'd,
> So in all Humors sportively I range:
>   My Muse is rightly of the English Straine,
>   That cannot long one Fashion intertaine.[54]

Although within the collection he ingeniously attempts, as a competent sonneteer should, to attribute both his humorous, forthright, unadorned style [55] and his strange wresting of invention and "giddy Metaphors" [56] to the effects of passion, the true explanation of these extremes brings us back to Drayton, the journeyman poet. Drayton was not primarily concerned with the sonnet *per se*, but with the sonnet as a means of advancing toward the lofty style which he considered a necessary part of a heroic poet's technique. This remote objective came near to ruining the effectiveness of the series. Drum-

---

[52] *Ideas Mirrour*, Works, I, 112.
[53] This is unlikely, since Drayton sets himself apart from "the humorous Platonist." *Poly-Olbion*, Works, IV, 101, l. 178.
[54] Works, II, 310.   [55] *Idea* (1619), Works, II, 322.
[56] *Ibid.*, p. 315. Cf. *To the Criticke*, Works, II, 326.

mond's comment on the sonnets, and Drummond was a great admirer of Drayton's other works, touches this weakness:

Drayton seemeth rather to have loved his Muse than his Mistress; by I know not what artificial Similes, this sheweth well his mind but not the Passion.[57]

Drayton realized that he had a natural genius in the simple style, the talent which shows delightfully in the *Odes* and *Nimphidia,* and indeed, in all the pieces written in relaxation for diversion. His early and serious efforts were devoted to acquiring a more elevated manner. He consciously overelaborated and overformalized his style until he had corrected the deficiency. Amour 21 ruefully contrasts the effectiveness of his natural spontaneity with that of his careful procedure. He tells how he had dashed off a sonnet for a "witless gallant"

> As fast as e'r my Penne could trot,
> Powr'd out what first from quicke Invention came;
> Nor never stood one word thereof to blot.

The gallant was successful;

> But see, for you to Heav'n for Phraze I runne,
> And ransacke all Apollo's golden Treasure;
>
> .   .   .   .
>
> And I lose you for all my Wit and Paines.[58]

In 1594 Drayton, experimenting with another type of poetry, produced *Endimion and Phœbe.* He had by this time published two of his *Legends,* and that he should turn back from his announced goal of heroic narrative, in which his patriotism and his love for history and fact received an outlet, to the lower level of an Ovidian love story seems strange until we see the sort of treatment he gave his theme. That he should have pitched upon a myth at all is easily explained. His interest in Greek fable was of long standing, and traces of it pervade all his earlier work. Drayton, moreover, was always keen to observe and eager to utilize the prevailing trend of taste. Just at this time the expanded Greek myth, as represented by *Venus and Adonis* and *Hero and Leander,* was enjoying an enormous

[57] Laing, ed., *Conversation between Drummond and Jonson,* "Shakespeare Society Publications," Nos. 8–10, p. 50.
[58] *Idea,* Works, II, 321.

popularity, which Drayton had already noted in the first stanza of *Matilda*. But he, unlike Shakespeare and Marlowe, was not satisfied to retell the tale elaborately, but instead attempted to stuff it with all sorts of informative matter. His poem is an amazing miscellany, held together at first strongly, but later very feebly by the Endymion story, and employing such stock devices of classical epics as the catalogues and the detailed descriptions of characters, superhuman beings, and supernatural events. Tiring of these, Drayton explores all sorts of themes that interest him; little disquisitions on melancholy, passion, astronomy, and numbers appear. Lodge, in his *Fig for Momus*, praised Drayton for this attempt, and scored all poetry that had not a high moral purpose, but the author, worn out by aimless meandering among various topics, finally broke off in an abrupt couplet:

> And what in vision there to him befell,
> My weary Muse some other time shall tell.

Drayton's satire, *The Owl* (1606), though very poor of its kind, sheds light on his evaluation of this particular form. He evidently considered it a retrogression from his recent work in the heroic vein:

> Our Pen late steep'd in English Barons wounds,
> Sent War-like accents to your tunefull Eare.
> Our active Muse, to gentler Morals dight
> Her slight conceits in humbler tunes doth sing.[59]

But why write this type of poetry at all if it is admittedly inferior? To answer that point he lines up great writers who have set a precedent—Homer, Vergil, and Vida—yet acknowledges that satire is "By how much immateriall, so much the more difficult to handle with an encomiastick defence or passionate comparison." [60] It is true that it is an inferior kind of poetry but it is also a difficult kind to write well. The Owl enunciates what Drayton would have liked to believe:

> Mightie, said he, though my plaine homely words,
> Have not that grace that elegance affords;
> Truth of itselfe is of sufficient worth,
> Nor needs it glosse of Arte to set it forth.[61]

---

[59] Works, II, 477.   [60] *The Barons Warres*, Works, II, 79.
[61] *The Owle*, Works, II, 488.

Yet *The Owle* is studded with allusions to the loves of Jove and all the other tales of the *Metamorphoses*. The basic allegory was inspired by the tale of Ascallaphus.[62] Drayton, who had learned how necessary to the propagation of truth was the gloss of art, was again attempting to combine the morals of the Mantuan with the grace of Ovid.[63] In fact, the artist in Drayton frequently got the upper hand. He would begin to embellish until he thought he had gone too far for a satire and then he would check himself:

> But whither wandreth my high-ravisht Muse? [64]

Later on, disillusioned in regard to James and disgusted with the state of poetry in England, he found even more merit in satire. The Tenth Nimphall has the following introduction:

> A Satyre on Elizium lights
> Whose ugly shape the Nimphes affrights
> Yet when they heare his just complaint
> They make him an Elizian saint.[65]

In the *Nimphalls* and again in *Poly-Olbion* he stressed the moral purpose of satire, which compensates for its crudity. It is

> the Satyres use
> To taxe the guilty times and raile upon abuse.[66]

He was strongly tempted to introduce satire into *Poly-Olbion,* but refrained in accordance with the rule of decorum.[67]

In 1606 Drayton tried a little-explored field of poetry in his *Odes with Other Lyrick Poesies.* He had evidently experimented with short-lined verses in a spirit of artistic curiosity and recreation —"New they are, and the worke of playing Houres," [68]—and, getting obviously satisfactory results, had decided to publish them. As befits a poet consciously working in a light vein, the arguments of his poems represent a pleasant miscellany. There are excellent love verses, a poem "To the Virginian Voyage," and keen discussions of poetic theory which have been quoted freely in the early

---

62 *Ibid.,* p. 482.   63 *Ibid.,* p. 497. Cf. *Heroicall Epistles.*
64 *Ibid.,* p. 492. Cf. p. 493.
65 *The Muses Elizium* (1630), Works, III, 321. Cf. *ibid.,* p. 322.
66 *Poly-Olbion,* Works, IV, 315.   67 *Ibid.,* p. 322, ll. 359–62.
68 *Odes,* Works, II, 345.

part of this chapter. That even these recreational verses were governed by his strong sense of form and decorum is apparent from the careful preface to the reader in the edition of 1619, justifying his use of the title *Odes*:

Odes I have called these my few Poems; which how happie soever they prove, yet Criticisme it selfe cannot say, that the Name is wrongfully usurped: For (not to begin with Definitions against the prescript Rule of Poetrie in a Poeticall Argument, . . .) an Ode is knowne to have been properly a Song, moduled to the ancient Harpe, and neither too short-breathed, as hasting to the end, nor composed of the longest Verses, as unfit for the sudden Turnes and loftie Tricks with which Apollo used to manage it. . . . Of a mixed kind were Horaces. Such are Drayton's, little partaking of the high Dialect of Pindar nor altogether of Anacreon, the Arguments being Amorous, Morall, or what the Muse pleaseth.[69]

Drayton shows an understanding of the theory and history of the ode, a deep respect for its successful creators, but few or no signs of having been directly influenced by them. His meter was not a popular contemporary type, but a rhythm inspired by an influence which figured strongly in Drayton's writing, his Cambro-Britannic interest. These pieces are such that

> They may become John Hewes his lyre,
> Which oft at Powlsworth by the fire
> Hath made us gravely merry.

> Th'old British bards
> To stirre their youth to Warlike Rage

> .   .   .   .

> In these loose Numbers sung.[70]

It was a meter also attributable in part to Skelton, whose facility and vigor and compact line were very congenial to Drayton.

For his shorter pieces he does not solicit commendation from the public, although he assures his patron in the dedicatory poem that it takes no mean degree of skill to compose a lyric, but for the last and longest of the odes, the "Ballad of Agincourt," he seems most eager to secure general favor:

. . . what I thinke above the rest, of the last Ode of this Number, or if thou wilt, Ballad in my Booke: for both the great Master of Italian Rymes,

---

[69] *Odes*, Works, II, 345.   [70] *Ibid.*, p. 344.

Petrarch, and our Chaucer, and other of the upper House of the Muses, have thought their Canzons honored in the title of a Ballad; which, for that I labour to meet truely therein with the old English Garbe, I hope as able to justifie, as the learned Colin Clout his Roundelay.[71]

Drayton is very desirous that no one think the worse of this poem because in accordance with its antique spirit he has called it a ballad. But why the singling out and stressing of one particular ode? The other poems in the collection are delightful, meritorious; no one appreciated the metrical victory they represented more than their author; but the "Ballad of Agincourt" alone of all the odes satisfies his major purpose of poetic commemoration:

> O when shall English Men
> With such Acts fill a Pen,
> Or England breed again
>   Such a King Harry? [72]

Here, in concentrated form, is the very spirit that prompts a *Poly-Olbion*, a spirit of commemorative singing derived in great measure from the old British bards and dedicated to stimulating patriotism.

Thus again in the odes Drayton's idea of relative values in poetry shows itself, serious subject matter being accounted the more worthy, although other subjects were occasionally imperative:

> And when I reach
> At Morall Things
> And that my Strings
> Gravely should strike
> Straight some mislike
> Blotteth mine Ode
>
> .   .   .   .
>
> So to your prayse
> I turn ever.[73]

In spite of his dominant interest in poetry dedicated to a worthy subject, Drayton never wholly deserted the service of his lighter muse, and, as the spirit of the new era became manifest, developed it with the judgment and adaptability that served him instead of a more original genius. In his revised pastorals (1619) he comments:

[71] *Ibid.*, p. 345.   [72] *Ibid.*, p. 378.   [73] *Ibid.*, p. 361.

> Nor as 'twas wont, now Rurall be our Rimes,
> Shepheards of late are waxed wondrous neate.
> Though they were richer in the former Times
> We be inraged with the more kindly heate.[74]

In *The Legend of Cromwell*, Drayton, speaking of Cromwell's songs, before the Pope, justifies an occasional lapse from loftiness:

> Light humours, them when judgement doth direct,
> .Even of the Wise winne plausible respect.[75]

The major function of poetry, however, was didactic:

> But Muse . . .
>   Leave not . . . Posteritie to doubt,
>   That to the World obscured else may bee,
>   If in this place revealed not by Thee.[76]

Concurrently with his progress through the conventional forms, in which he was emphasizing the element of poetic delight, Drayton put forth a succession of historical works which should more fully realize his aim of profit through pleasure. As Professor Lily B. Campbell has shown, the Elizabethan mind regarded history as a series of repeated patterns, and greatly valued the guidance supplied by the past.[77] Three of Drayton's main sources, Hall, Holinshed, and Daniel, believed in the importance of recognizing and utilizing the theory that history repeats itself. To Drayton, as to many of the historians, poetry and history seemed to have a striking community of aim.[78] Both fought against oblivion, both embodied the past experience of the race, especially for the leaders of men, both showed the fickleness of fortune, both were branches of rhetoric, but poetry had the inestimable advantage of a more universal appeal. In 1593, Drayton, having found a suitable model in Daniel's *Rosamund*, attempted his first historical poem *Peirs Gaveston*. The subject was most timely, for to the Elizabethan the name Piers Gaveston typified the current fear of the danger involved when any sovereign

[74] *Pastorals, Works*, II, 532. Cf. *The Shepheards Sirena, Works*, III, 159.
[75] *Legends, Works*, II, 456.   [76] *Ibid.*, p. 467.
[77] Lily B. Campbell, "The Use of Historical Patterns in the Reign of Elizabeth," *Huntington Library Quarterly*, I (Jan., 1938), 135–67.
[78] Lily B. Campbell, typescript of speech, lent me through the courtesy of Professor O. J. Campbell.

was influenced too greatly by favorites.[79] The atmosphere of social consciousness in the poem is enhanced by a long passage referring to *The Vision of Piers Plowman*.[80] It is likely that Drayton had already finished his early sonnets and had been, perhaps, about to polish them when he determined to try a historical poem instead; for, in dedicating the sonnets to Cavendish, he calls them "rude unpolish'd rymes" and speaks of them as having "slept long in sable night." Furthermore, in *Peirs Gaveston* the spirit of Peirs praises this man who,

> To tell my cares hath layde his owne to sleepe.[81]

Apparently in the midst of his work on the sonnets, he felt strong enough to follow the advice of his character Motto and serve Idea, not by the direct praise of a love lyric, but by the higher offering of excellent poetry that her inspiration had created. Idea is very well remembered at the end of the poem, and Drayton was evidently not trying to make a sharp transition from one type of work to the other. He felt the continuity of his development as a poet. His last lines show his realization that this is but a partially successful first essay at "Chanting Heroique Angel-tuned notes," that he has not left the "humble Pastor's Nectar-filled lines" far behind him; he begs indulgence for

> This same babe my Muse hath now brought forth
> Till shee present thee with some lines of worth.[82]

In 1594 he tried heroic narrative again with the story of *Matilda*. The next year Daniel published the first four books of his *Civil Wars*, and Drayton followed his lead in 1596 by publishing *Mortimeriados*, which bore as subtitle *The Lamentable Civill Warres of Edward II and the Barrons*. He used the same stanza as Daniel. This was Drayton's first book-length effort in his chosen branch of heroic poetry.

His next poem, *The Tragicall Legend of Robert, Duke of Normandy*, was the first to bear the special title of "legend." In the preface to the revised work of 1619, Drayton gave very specific definitions for the benefit of the reader who might fail to appreciate this type of poetry because he did not understand its purpose:

[79] *Huntington Library Quarterly*, I, 157.
[81] *Peirs Gaveston*, Works, I, 159.
[80] *Legends*, Works, II, 470.
[82] *Ibid.*, p. 206.

But the principall is, that being a Species of an Epick or Heroick Poeme, it eminently describeth the act or acts of some one or other eminent Person; not with too much labour, compasse, or extension, but roundly rather, and by way of Briefe, or Compendium.[83]

In 1597 Drayton, who had been strengthening his facility in verse and exercising his imagination by writing pastorals, sonnets, and Ovidian myths, effected, in *Englands Heroicall Epistles,* a perfect fusion of the elements that composed his theory of poetry. He had learned that intrinsic merit of subject matter was insufficient, that mere versified truths and chronicles were dull stuff. On the other hand, the tribunal of the public, in whose hands the immortality of a poem lay, showed an insatiable appetite for brilliance of style, for the theme of love, for allusions to myths, for dramatic form. The historical epistle, as practiced by his sure guide Daniel, offered scope for all of these. It was only necessary to unite the worthy subject to the welcome style. His thorough acquaintance with Ovid was now made to bear golden fruit by grafting upon it his knowledge of English history. In the foreword to the reader, Drayton reveals his theory of poetry more completely than in any previous work. The title is explained by the fact that this is an imitation of Ovid's use of the word "heroicall . . . as meaning a great Person." He then treats of the reason for the notes:

because the Wirk might in truth be judged Braynish, if nothing but amorous Humor were handled therein, I have inter-woven Matters Historicall, which unexplained might defraud the Mind of much content.[84]

After the first Epistle, which is his old legend of Matilda treated far more competently, there occurs the following apologetic note:

This Epistle of King John to Matilda is much more Poeticall than Historicall, making no mention at all of the Occurents of the Time, or State, touching only his love to her, and the extremities of his Passions.[85]

Drayton is keenly aware that poetry, in the sense of the fictitious element, and history are likely to pull his work in opposite directions. Yet in order to achieve his ideal of poetry, he tries as hard as possible to make his fictions carry their due share of fact to the reader. When he cannot, he notes sadly, "This Epistle containeth no particular

---

[83] *Legends*, Works, II, 382.   [84] *Ibid.*, p. 130.   [85] Works, II, 152.

points of History," [86] an omission which can be condoned only after an explanation. There is a long note in which he discusses with great generosity the foreign treatment of truth and fiction. He condemns the general practice "rather to fail sometime in the truth of Circumstance, than to forgoe the grace of their Conceit," but adds

Yet may Bandello be very well excused, as being a stranger, whose errors in the truth of our Historie, are not so materiall, that they should need an Invective, lest his Wit should be defrauded of any part of his due, which were not the lesse, were every part a Fiction.[87]

In the *Heroicall Epistles* the artist in Drayton triumphed over the teacher, to the extent that the teacher is confined rather straitly to the footnotes. He could even relinquish an opportunity for chronicling if such chronicling had no artistic justification:

This Epistle of Edward to Mistress Shore, and of hers to him, being of unlawfull Affection, ministreth small occasion of Historicall Notes; for had he mentioned the many Battels betwixt the Lancastrian faction and him, or other warlike dangers, it had beene more like to Plautus boasting Souldier then a Kingly courtier. Notwithstanding, it shall not be amisse to annexe a Line or two.[88]

In several of his notes appears that worship of truth and accuracy which came near to undoing him as a poet. He considers the following simple substitution worth a footnote: "Isis is here used for Themesis by a Synecdochicall kind of speech, or by a Poeticall libertie, in using one for another." [89] The introduction of a magic device seems to demand justification:

Howbeit, as those . . . Arts are but illusions: so in honor of so rare a Gentleman as this Earle (and therewithall so noble a Poet; a qualitie, by which his other Titles receive their greatest lustre) Invention may make somewhat bolde . . . above the barren truth.[90]

In 1603, after a long interval spent as a collaborator in chronicle plays, Drayton tried to attract the notice of the new monarch by a poem of welcome, but was unsuccessful. His next poem, *The Barons Warres* is really a thorough revision of *Mortimeriados*. It is preceded by a long and detailed address to the reader, which tells how the dignity and magnitude of this topic had first attracted Drayton.

[86] *Ibid.*, p. 158.   [87] *Ibid.*, p. 181.   [88] *Ibid.*, p. 252.
[89] *Ibid.*, p. 259.   [90] *Ibid.*, p. 284.

He is revising the poem because recent printings have been careless. His long explanation of the change in stanza proves him a careful student of the mechanics of verse. He also refers learnedly to the authorities for dividing his poem into sections and designating those sections cantos. He seems to be harried by the idea of unfavorable criticism and eager to perfect his defenses.

As has already been noted, the *Odes* of 1606 contained as their masterpiece Drayton's historical "Ballad of Agincourt," a brief and brilliant commemorative song. In 1598 Drayton had projected and begun his great commemorative masterpiece *Poly-Olbion*. Fifteen years later appeared the first eighteen songs of *Poly-Olbion,* which Drummond most extravagantly lauded as "the only epic poem England hath to be proud of." Since Drayton's great work resembles neither Vergil nor Spenser, Drummond apparently used the term epic, as was common in the seventeeth century,[91] to denote the qualities of heroic proportion, tremendous scope, and complete devotion to preserving the national glory. But the author himself preferred to distinguish his undertaking in form, though not in purpose, from the usual concept of the epic: "My Poem is genuine and first in this kind." [92] He more properly characterized his work as "a Chorographicall Description . . . Digested into a Poem."

Drayton was for the most part in thorough accord with the general principles of Renaissance poetic theory about epic poetry. His ultimate purpose was to create a great poem that should have high didactic value. He began with the accepted heroic formula: "But the principall is, that being a Species of an Epick or Heroick Poeme, it eminently describeth the act or acts of some one or other eminent Person." But he almost never succeeded in constructing his poems upon a basis of action. The unifying element in the legends was personality; they became biographical sketches. The *Heroicall Epistles* were integrated only by a similarity in the formula employed and by the fact that all of the characters were drawn from English history. *Mortimeriados* and its revised form *The Barons Warres* came the

[91] Ball, "The Background of the Minor English Renaissance Epics," *Journal of English Literary History,* I (April, 1934), 63–89.
[92] "Dedication to Prince Henry," *Poly-Olbion,* Works, IV, 111.

nearest to centering in a pervasive struggle, but it was Edward II rather than Drayton who so arranged it. In *Poly-Olbion* Drayton finally broke completely with the formula by relegating characters as well as action to a very incidental role; he left, too, the subject matter of history, which had automatically supplied character and true actions. His antiquarian and "chorographical" interests were allowed to predominate, with the result that the poem became not an epic but a monumental gazetteer. Drayton was conscious that he was using his poetry as a medium for transmitting a tremendous mass of facts, that he was overweighting *Poly-Olbion* heavily on the teaching side. In the *Moone-Calfe* he defended not his art but his research; he claimed credit for having sought, found, vitalized, and perpetuated his country's glories. The ignorant critic did, however,

> Dare with a desperate boldnesse roughly passe
> His censure on those Bookes, which the poore Asse
> Can never reach to, things from darknesse sought,
> That to the light with blood and sweat were brought.[93]

Such would be Drayton's studies in Speed, Holinshed, and Hall,[94] Powel's *Historie of Cambria*,[95] and Hakluyt.[96] It was the author's task to offset the aridity of facts thus obtained and reproduced. Drayton enlivened the mass of information by liberal injections of what he considered poetic elements, such as the catalogues and incidental narratives, his peculiar personifications of nature, and his references to the muse. Thus instead of one opening invocation, there is frequent reference to the muse, especially at the opening and conclusion of songs:

> March strongly forth my Muse, whilst yet the temperate air
> Invites us, eas'ly on to hasten our repair.[97]

> When now the wearied Muse her burthen having ply'd
> Herself awhile betakes to bathe her in the Sound.[98]

---

[93] Works, III, 175.

[94] Jenkins, "Sources of Drayton's Battaile of Agincourt," PMLA, XLI (June, 1926), 280–94.

[95] Cawley, "Drayton's Use of Welsh History," *Studies in Philology*, XXII (April, 1925), 234–35.

[96] Cawley, "Drayton and the Voyagers," PMLA, XXXVIII (Sept., 1923), 530.

[97] *Poly-Olbion*, Works, IV, 29.   [98] *Ibid.*, p. 180.

To finish here my Song: the Muse some ease doth ask,
As wearied with the toil in this her serious task.[99]

This constant insistence on the presence of the muse is typical of
Drayton's attempt to avoid the fault which he had found in Daniel
of being "too much historian in verse." [100]

Had Drayton desired to imitate the classical or romantic epic, he
would have been at no loss for a model or material. As early as *The
Shepheards Garland* he had lauded Vergil as the great master of the
epic:

> And who erects the brave *Pyramides*
> Of Monarches or renowned warriours,
> Neede bath his quill for such attempts as these,
> In flowing streames of learned Maros showres.[101]

He deliberately overlooked such splendid subjects as the history
of Brut and the tales of Arthur, concerning whom he wrote:

> That justlie I may charge these ancient Bards of wrong,
> So idly to neglect his glorie in their Song.
> For some abundant braine, ô there had been a storie
> Beyond the Blind-mans might to have inhanc't our glorie.[102]

Despite his maintenance of the truth of these tales,[103] Drayton prob-
ably avoided them as too much clouded in myth and controversy.
The quotation also suggests the first of several reasons that may
have kept him from using the Aristotelian epic tradition: the model
epics were predominantly fiction, arousing national pride and in-
dividual virtue by relating the vicissitudes of a legendary hero. Dray-
ton had never been interested in fiction, except as it could be made
to adorn and preserve truth. But inasmuch as his desire to preserve
facts could be accomplished only by affecting a large audience, he
had always tried to take advantage of the current trend in popular
interest. He had wasted little time in experimenting, simply adopt-
ing the most recently successful work as his model. Spenser's *Faerie
Queene*, the only English epic he might have used, was "caviar to the
general." From the eager reception of maps, itineraries, histories,
chronicle plays, it was obvious that there was a general interest in

---

[99] *Poly-Olbion*, Works, IV, 286.   [100] *Epistle to Reynolds*, Works, III, 229.
[101] *Idea The Shepheards Garland*, Works, I, 85.
[102] *Poly-Olbion*, Works, IV, 58.   [103] *Ibid.*, pp. 207 ff.

all the facts of national identity. Drayton had followed his old leader, Daniel, in writing narratives of civil wars, chronicle plays, legends, and heroical epistles. In all of these he had accomplished to some degree his dominant purpose of reanimating truth through the medium of poetry. Yet all of these ventures had covered but a small portion of that rich national heritage that was every Englishman's birthright. From the reception of *Albion's England* and Camden's *Britannia*, it was apparent that there would be an appreciative audience for a comprehensive, yet attractive, account of the topography and history of his country. Lest any point remain in doubt because of imaginative or necessarily brief treatment, Drayton used the same device that he had employed before in the *Heroicall Epistles* and appended to the first eighteen songs copious notes supplied by Selden.

A third factor possibly influential in determining the type of his greatest work was his appreciation of the Welsh bards. The Cambro-Britons receive very marked attention in *Poly-Olbion* and their poets are paid high reverence. Drayton lauded the tradition of Welsh poetry, which is largely descriptive and expository. He honored whole-heartedly the Druidic practice of perpetuating fact through poetry:

> O memorable Bards of unmixt blood, which still
> Posteritie shall praise for your so wondrous skill,
> That in your noble Songs, the long Descents have kept
> Of your great Heroes, else in Lethe that had slept
>
> How much from time, . . . how bravelie have you gain'd.[104]

In accordance with his extreme patriotism, it is the British authority, not the classical or Italian, that he cites.

Small wonder then, if *Poly-Olbion* to a modern reader seems not to fall within the epic tradition. In Drayton's day, the English epic formula had not been fixed. Spenser had tried one type of long poem; here was another. The instinct of the greater artist proved sound, but the greater masterpiece was written with no truer purpose or more sincere adherence to poetical principle. To Drayton, this work was the categorical imperative of his poetic career. He lost

[104] Works, IV, 118.

the favor of the king and for two years abandoned the whole project, but he had to come back to it. *Poly-Olbion* was his debt to the past and his gift to the future; nothing but that faith could have inspired the patience, energy, loving care, and belief in its worth that pervade the whole. That *Poly-Olbion* was not fully successful is owing in part to the fact that its author, trying to realize a highly didactic purpose, strove to accomplish the impossible, to impart to a work predominantly devoted to preserving fact the charm of a piece of fiction.

In an ideal state, Drayton felt that poets such as he should receive support, or at least honor, from the crown, since they were rendering national service. When James came to England, Drayton, reflecting that he owed little to Elizabeth and might hope for much from a king who was himself a poet (and whom he had celebrated as such in a sonnet as early as 1600), rushed into print with a "gratulatorie Poem" omitting the formality of a funeral poem for Elizabeth, a most significant omission for him. He was fully aware that he was for once setting the pace, instead of following in another's footsteps. In 1604 was published a *Pæan Triumphal*, written for the Society of Goldsmiths to celebrate the entry of James, but apparently this was answered either by silence or by a direct reproof. Drayton tried to accept the situation philosophically, but could never quite realize how a monarch and fellow poet could fail to honor a national poet. The epistle to Sandys reveals a devastating sense of betrayal:

> Yet had not my cleere spirit in Fortunes scorne,
> Me above earth and her afflictions borne;
> He next my God on whom I built my trust,
> Had left me trodden lower then the dust.[105]

From 1604 on, there are no more praises of James, but instead gloomy prognostications, bitter comments, significant omissions, and harsh, thinly disguised allusions. *Poly-Olbion* was ultimately dedicated not to James, but to Prince Charles. In a poem "To my Noble Friend Master William Browne, of the evill time," he decries the neglect of virtue and the elevation to knighthood of men lack-

[105] Works, III, 206.

ing all worth. Such nobles are not at all interested in "vertue's hand-
maid Poesy":

> But to her ruine they shall misse the way
> For tis alone the Monuments of wit,
> Above the rage of Tyrants that doe sit,
> And from their strength, no one himselfe can save,
> But they shall triumph o'r his hated grave.[106]

Despite this ultimate triumph of poetry, Drayton regarded its
present state as one of the worst features of "this beastly Iron
Age." [107] With deliberate ambiguity of phrase, he blames the north-
bred monarch in the preface to his revised poems of 1619:

howsoever they may appear to these more prodigious Dayes, I know not:
but thus much I will say to mine owne disadvantage, (should they hap to
be unwelcome to these Times:) That they were the fruit of that Muse-
nursing Season: before this frosty Boreas (I mean the worlds coldnesse) had
nipt our flowery Tempe; that with his pestilenciall Fogs is like utterly to
poyson the Pierian Spring . . . and, but that as shee [Poetry] is Divine, her
beauties be Immortall, or they had before this blasted her sweetnesse.[108]

Drayton's conviction that poetry had entered a period of temporary
eclipse is evident from the dedication of *The Battaile of Agincourt*
to the noble gentlemen of Great Britain who love neglected Poesy.

This neglect of poetry, which Drayton deplored with increasing
frequency, was largely occasioned by the growth of public interest
in newer kinds of verse. To a poet bred in the grand tradition, the
popularity of work based on less comprehensive and aspiring aims
argued a sad decline of his art. From *The Owle* (1604) to *The Muses
Elizium* (1630), Drayton commented on the degeneration from
worthy purpose and matter. Rarely did some such undertaking as
Britannia's Pastorals move him to vary his gloomy strain by a note of
hope for the resumption of the old way with its gradual progress
from pastoral to epic song.[109] His own failure to secure royal patron-
age was rendered more significant by the rise of a group of poets who
cared nothing for the old heroic vein or for eternizing great and
virtuous native figures in fitting numbers:

---

[106] *Elegies*, Works, III, 240.   [107] *Ibid*., p. 236.   [108] Works, II, 2.
[109] Browne, *The Whole Works of William Browne*, ed. by Hazlitt, prefatory poem.

> those brave numbers are put by for naught,
> Which rarely read, were able to awake,
> Bodyes from graves.[110]

The neglect of heroic poetry placed an awful responsibility on the people

> With whom so many noble spirits then liv'd,
> That were by them of all reward depriv'd.[111]

The effect of the flood of "base Balatry" and "trash" [112] that was being written and read was especially serious for those who could not seek refuge in another language, and thus could not read

> those sinewie Poems writ,
> That are materiall relishing of wit;
> Wise pollicie, Morality, or Story,
> Well purtraying the Ancients and their glory.[113]

Poetry was a source of knowledge, and it was criminal to neglect or debase it.[114]

In the epistle to Sandys, Sandys being then in Virginia, Drayton seemed to feel that a progress of poetry was imminent. He even went so far as to express the hope that his poem would have the honor of being the first to cross the ocean. The preface to *Poly-Olbion* shows that he was well prepared for the cold reception accorded the work which most nearly embodied his theory of poetry:

In such a season, when the Idle Humerous world must heare of nothing, that either savors of Antiquity, or may awake it to seeke after more, than dull and slothfull ignorance may easily reach unto.[115]

He continued to publish *Poly-Olbion*, in spite of its lack of popularity, because of his firm belief that it would be appreciated in a less "barbarous" age.[116]

But although Drayton decried strenuously the neglect of the weighty, significant, heroic poem, he did not object at all to the developments that were taking place within the "lower" types of verse. He liked the new lyricism and smoothness, the variety of meter, and showed himself master of all these tendencies in his last

---

[110] Drayton, *To Master George Sandys*, Works, III, 208.
[111] *To Master William Jeffreys*, Works, III, 241.
[112] *Elegies*, Works, III, 208, 238.   [113] *The Moone-Calfe*, Works, III, 176.
[114] Works, III, 238, 176.   [115] Works, IV, v.   [116] *Ibid.*, p. 391.

work, *The Muses Elizium*. As the title indicated, these verses are purely poetic in intention. They are not, like his earlier pastorals, experiments in technique or revisions of such experiments; neither are they attempts to salvage and preserve some record of virtue. They abound in the elements that Drayton considered essentially poetic, in love (there are more nymphs here than in any other pastorals; so many, in fact, that Drayton names his divisions "Nimphalls"), and in classical atmosphere (the hymn to Apollo and the Muses, the Nimphall on Venus and Cupid). They are typically Caroline with their clever handling of rhythm, their grace and melody, their pleasantness and lack of depth.[117] He frequently reverts to the jocular style and stanza of the rime of Dowsabell. There are only one or two serious reminders that Drayton had taken refuge in *The Muses Elizium* because England was now so bad that even satire could not reach her.[118]

In the epistle to Reynolds Drayton treats "of Poets and Poesie" by tracing the important names in the history of English poetry, from Chaucer down. Three groups are of no interest to him: foreign poets, whom he rejects in favor of the "true native muse"; [119] the numerous host of later dramatists, whom he dismisses; and the "chamber poets," whom he attacks strenuously. The chamber poets were those whose work existed only in manuscript, and, being difficult to obtain, had great vogue. The introduction to *Poly-Olbion* comments on them bitterly:

In publishing my Poem . . . there is this great disadvantage against me; that it cometh out at this time when Verses are wholly deduced to chambers, and nothing esteemed in this lunatic age but what is kept in cabinets and must only pass by transcription.

He suggests letting posterity judge of their merit, implying that unpublished work will hardly reach posterity and thus, from his point of view, is hardly poetry at all. In *Poly-Olbion*, Song XXI,[120] he again attacks this group of "cabinet" poets. Their verse hobbles and they deal in matters unfit for poetry. Despite Hebel's contrary

---

[117] Long, "Drayton's Eighth Nymphal," *Studies in Philology*, XIII (July, 1916), 180–83.
[118] Jenkins, "Drayton's Relation to the School of Donne as Revealed in the Shepheards Sirena," PMLA, XXXVIII (Sept., 1923), 557–87.
[119] *Poly-Olbion*, Works, IV, Introduction, v.   [120] Works, IV, 421.

opinion,[121] Jenkins advances a most plausible theory when he suggests that *The Shepheards Sirena* is an allegorical stand against Donne and his "school." [122] Jenkins interprets Sirena as Drayton's ideal muse and considers the following lines to mean that Drayton had no alternative but to write in a merely pleasing style abandoning all effort to inculcate virtue, or to give up poetry because the type of writing he wished to do no longer had popular appeal:

> Hard the Choise I have to chuse,
> To my selfe if friend I be,
> I must my Sirena loose,
> If not so, shee looseth me.[123]

Jenkins considers that in such poems as *The Battaile of Agincourt* and *The Miseries of Queene Margarite*, Drayton tried to hold to his old ideals; that *The Moone-Calfe* and *Elegies* satirize his enemies; and that *Nimphidia, The Quest of Cynthia,* and *The Muses Elizium* concede to popular taste but combat the poetic principles of the school of Donne. On the other hand, while some animosity against the opposing schools of poets undoubtedly appears, there is not much, and Drayton, having finished his great task, would need no special reason to amuse himself with the short line, sweet melody, and slight theme in which he had always delighted. Except in the case of *Poly-Olbion,* his poems had usually followed the current popular model, a practice which would account for the fairy poems; and it was equally characteristic of him to rework and improve earlier subjects and poems. Finally, he had an excellent Spenserian precedent for poetic relaxation, for the great master himself had not only practiced, but endorsed such measures:

Amoretti LXXX

> After so long a race as I have run
> Through Faery land, which those six books compile,
>
> . . . give leave to me in pleasant mew,
> To sport my muse.

---

[121] "Drayton's Sirena," PMLA, XXXIX (Dec., 1924), 814.

[122] "Drayton's Relation to the School of Donne," PMLA, XXXVIII (Sept., 1923), 557–87. See also "Drayton's Sirena Again," *ibid.*, XLII (March, 1927), 129–39.

[123] Works, III, 158.

Against a background of lesser poets with their shallow or shifting aims, their overcareful or too casual workmanship, their grand but abortive projects or their slight perfected accomplishment, the well-balanced and stalwart figure of Drayton stands out in heroic proportions. His was a simple, straightforward, yet comprehensive theory of poetry. Though he wrote all types of verse, he did not set an equal value on all. If we examine his scale of values, we find emerging that poetical hierarchy in which the lower types are used principally as practice material. The true function of the English poet, as he conceived it, was to preserve the record of national greatness past and thereby stimulate greatness in the present and the future. He proposed to make virtue lovely by awarding to slighted merit the compensation of eternal fame, and he hoped to make his country glorious by immortalizing her history and even her geography. Although he delighted in minor verse and wrote it successfully, poetry was to Drayton not a toy nor a mere personal endowment, but at its highest a great instrument for social and national education.

CHAPTER IV

WILLIAM BROWNE

THE THEORY of William Browne bears eloquent witness to the prevalence and pressure of the magnificent idealism of the seventeenth century. Everything about Browne's work carries the stamp of the dilettante, the gifted amateur writing for his own diversion; yet even his work reflects, though weakly, the great principles that animated his models.

Browne's failure to complete his major work, and his early cessation from almost all poetic activity evidence a certain indifference to his art. He was not interested in the history of forms, metrical experiments, the "laws" of poetry, or the problems of revision, as was Drayton; poetry appealed to Browne not primarily as an art but as a recreation. He respected the phenomenon of poetic talent, but showed no philosophical curiosity as to its source or *raison d'être*. On one occasion he asked divine aid to heighten his art while dealing with an allegory of Truth,[1] but he made no serious assertion that poetry was divinely inspired. He makes but a lukewarm invocation:

> Thrice sacred Powers (if sacred Powers there be
> Whose mild aspect engyrland Poesie)
> Yee happy Sisters of the learned Spring,
>
> .   .   .   .
>
> O be propitious in my Pilgrimage! [2]

According to Browne, poetry might be the careful and polished creation of a gifted artist, or it might be the product of a talented man stimulated by some intense emotion:

> Then if with sacred fire
> A passion ever did a Muse inspire;
> Or if a grief sick heart hath writt a lyne,
> Then Art or Nature could more genuyne
> More full of Accents sad. . . .[3]

---

[1] The Whole Works of William Browne, ed. by Hazlitt, I, 107.
[2] Works, I, 166.   [3] Works, II, 320.

His work was of both varieties. He loved to exercise the sweet gift of song with cunning artistry. On the other hand, his strong feelings: love of friends and country; grief over his wife's death, his friends' deaths; a new love, gave birth to many of his writings. An autobiographical passage in Book II of *Britannia's Pastorals* indicates the origin of some of his lines:

> Sweet soule, thy silent grave
> I give my best verse.[4]

Later, when "the rains are over and gone," there is a more cheerful note. Then it was to Cœlia's beauty that he would attribute all inspiration.[5]

Although Browne had no comment to offer on the source of the poetic gift, he did have a conviction that poets were born with various degrees of power, which did not materially increase or diminish. That he was sure talent was well developed almost as soon as it came of age appears in *Britannia's Pastorals*:

> Here could I spend that spring of Poesie,
> Which not twice ten Sunnes have bestow'd on me;
> And tell the world, the Muses love appeares
> In nonag'd youth as in the length of yeares.[6]

In one of his similes Browne speaks of "daily paines (Arts chiefest due),"[7] from which we may gather that he did not despise the element of practice as an aid to attaining one's fullest power. A poet could not, however, transcend his natural limits by effort.[8] That he chose to classify his own talent as slight, we learn from the comment in one of the epistles:

> The sacred Nyne, . . .
> Were kind in some small measure at my birth.[9]

The conviction of limited possibilities appears again in a poem written in praise of Brooke's play, *The Ghost of Richard the Third*:

> And I would gladly (if the Sisters spring
> Had me inabled) beare a part with thee,
> And, for sweet groves, of brave heroes sing
> But, . . . if fits not my weake melodie.[10]

---

[4] *Ibid.*, p. 127. [5] *Ibid.*, p. 163. [6] Works, I, 127. [7] *Ibid.*, p. 143.
[8] *Ibid.*, p. 75. [9] Works, II, 302. [10] *Ibid.*, p. 357.

It was partly as a result of this belief that he restricted his writing
to what he thought a lowly branch of poetry, one well within the
scope of his talent; and yet, feeling his talent to be full grown, did
not use this type as a stepping-stone, but attempted to elaborate
upon it.

The main reason for Browne's adherence to the pastoral, however,
derives from the purpose of his poetry, which, he repeatedly says,
was to please himself. This statement occurs in varying fashions. At
the end of Book I, it is merely,

> To misse an idle hour, and not for meed,
> With choicest relish shall mine Oaten Reed
> Record their worths.[11]

In another passage, contrasting his objective with that of more
serious and more ambitious poets, he makes it clear that all he ex-
pected from his style of verse was enjoyment.[12] After the death of
his wife the purpose of *Britannia's Pastorals* became not so much
positive pleasure as relief from pain:

> Borne to no other comfort then my teares,
>   Yet rob'd of them by griefes too inly deepe,
> I cannot rightly waile my haplesse yeeres,
> Nor move a passion that for me might weepe.
>   Nature alas too short hath knit
>   My tongue to reach my woe:
>   Nor have I skill sad notes to fit
>   That might my sorrow show.
> And to increase my torments ceaselesse sting,
>   There's no way left to shew my Paines,
>   But by my pen in mournfull straines,
> Which others may perhaps take joy to sing.[13]

Describing the sad fate of Cœlia and Philocel, the old shepherd
suggests that some poet in writing of their sorrow may assuage
his own.[14] In a detailed passage Browne not only states his purpose,
but also enumerates the advantages of poetry over other means of
obtaining pleasure:

[11] *Britannia's Pastorals,* Works, I, 151.
[12] *Ibid.,* p. 190.
[13] Works, II, 46.
[14] *Ibid.,* p. 100.

What now I sing is but to passe away
A tedious houre, as some Musitions play;
Or make another my owne griefes bemone;
Or to be least alone when most alone.
In this can I as oft as I will choose
Hug sweet content by my retired Muse,

    .   .   .

Each man that lives (according to his powre)
On what he loves bestowes an idle houre;
In stead of Hounds. . . .

    .   .   .   .

I like the pleasing cadence of a line

    .   .   .   .

In lieu of Hawkes, the raptures of my soule
Transcend their pitch and baser earths controule.
For courtly dancing I can take more pleasure
To heare a Verse keep time and equal measure.
For winning Riches, seeke the best directions
How I may well subdue mine own affections.
For raising stately piles for heires to come,
Here in this Poem I erect my toombe
And time may be so kinde in these weake lines
To keepe my Name enroll'd past his that shines
In guilded Marble, or in brazen leaves:
Since Verse preserves, when Stone & Brasse deceives.

    .   .   .   .

Such of the Muses are the able powres

    .   .   .   .

         I have oft possest
As much in this as all in all the rest,
And that without expence, when others oft
With their undoings have their pleasures bought.[15]

The fact that he was writing in good part for his own enjoyment is illustrated again in his comments on various themes. He frequently alludes to his preference for certain topics such as pastoral love, rivers, bird songs.[16] After a conscious digression to a subject ill-suited to his poem, but very near to his heart, he apologizes:

        So if to please my selfe I somewhat sing,
        Let it not be to you lesse pleasuring.[17]

---

[15] *Ibid.*, p. 68.   [16] Works, I, 126; *ibid.*, II, 63, 64.   [17] Works, II, 67.

He closes a further justification of digression by a couplet addressed to his audience:

> Yet lest mine own delight might injure you
> (Though loath so soone) I take my Song anew.[18]

Such couplets also indicate that, in addition to pleasing himself, he is desirous of pleasing his readers. There are two types of reader whom he especially mentions. The first is the nobility. In his dedicatory poem to Lord Zouch and again in *Britannia's Pastorals*, he hints that pastoral poetry might not be unacceptable at court.[19] The second portion of the audience to whom he consciously endeavors to appeal is the very element that Drayton held partly responsible for the weakening of poetry—the ladies. Invoking his Muse, Browne asks her to

> Make all the rarest Beauties of our Clyme
>
> .   .   .   .
>
> To linger on each lines enticing graces.[20]

In another part of his poem he pays tribute to the beauteous ladies of his age, who can make a swain "Climbe by his Song where none but soules attaine." [21] He compares his song to Homer's and Spenser's. Although their poems were graced by having the love and beauty of queens as subject matter, his has been heard by more beauties. A little later, excusing a digression on the Golden Age, he exclaims,

> O what a rapture have I gotten now!
> That age of gold, this of the lovely brow
> Have drawne me from my Song! [22]

Certainly the purity of his poetry might well recommend it to the ladies:

> But stay: me thinkes I heare something in me
> That bids me keepe the bounds of modestie;
>
> .   .   .   .
>
> My Maiden Muse flies the lascivious Swaines,
> And scornes to soyle her lines with lustfull straines.[23]

---

18 Works, II, 67.
20 *Ibid.*, p. 166.
22 *Ibid.*, p. 40.

19 Works, I, 3; *ibid.*, p. 151.
21 Works, II, 39.
23 Works, I, 77, 78.

Though Browne's purpose was to please himself and his audience, he was thoroughly aware of that attribute of poetry which had so fascinated Drayton, its preservative power. He mentioned it as one advantage writing poetry had over other forms of recreation. Here again, the emphasis in Browne is on a personal value, the immortality that the poet might acquire through his poetry. In a passage acknowledging his debt to Sidney's *Arcadia* he says:

> And on the Plaines full many a pensive lover
> Shall sing us to their loves, and praising be
> My humble lines: the more, for praising thee.
> Thus we shall live with them, by Rocks, and Springs,
> As well as Homer by the death of Kings.[24]

In one of his odes he expresses more loftily and with more assurance than in Book II [25] the old Horatian idea that through poetry he has built himself a monument *aere perennius*. Heaven has given the poet two lives.[26] In a passage that generalizes this whole concept Browne maintains that

> there is hidden in a Poets name
> A Spell that can command the wings of Fame,
> And maugre all Oblivions hated birth,
> Begin their immortality on earth.[27]

He is careful to note that the fame which confers immortality is not the momentary applause of the multitude, or even the sincere praise of worthy critics, but the fame that the poet knows to be deservedly his. It is such fame that Browne terms in his introduction "The great Rewardresse of a Poets Pen."

Browne offered the usual meed of immortality to his patron, Edward, Lord Zouch:

> (In Lines whose raignes
> In spight of Envy and her restlesse paines:
> Be unconfin'd as blest eternitie:)
> The Vales shall ring
> Thy Honor'd Name; and every Song shall be
> A Pyramis built to thy Memorie.[28]

The poet was expected to exercise his power in favor of those who had fostered and encouraged poetry; on the other hand, Browne

---

[24] Works, II, 9. Cf. *ibid.*, I, 128.   [25] *Vide supra*, p. 68.   [26] Works, II, 279.
[27] *Ibid.*, p. 11.   [28] Works, I, 3. Cf. *ibid.*, II, 167.

would have nothing to do with the base commerce in poetical
flattery:

> My free-born Muse will not like Danae be,
> Won with base drosse to clip with slavery;
> Nor lend her choiser Balme to worthlesse men,
> Whose names would dye but for some hired pen.[29]

The Muses not only confer fame on their favorites, but also, by
withholding their support, condemn their enemies to oblivion.[30]
A similar doom awaits the abusers of poetry; the cheap tobacco-and-
wine inspired verse-makers are powerless to obtain, much less confer,
enduring memory:

> . . . with how much labour these
> Druncke, ritt, and wrongd the learnde Pierides;
> Yet tyme, as soone as ere their workes were done,
> Threwe them and yt into oblivion.[31]

A good part of Browne's later poetry was devoted to the pious
task of preserving the memory of his dead friends in elegiac verses.

Throughout *Britannia's Pastorals* there is an attempt to follow
in the footsteps of Spenser and Drayton and immortalize English
geography and history. The names of Grenville and Drake are men-
tioned at every opportunity. Browne is especially interested in im-
mortalizing his native district of Tavistock, and when the progress
of the poem compels him to leave this undertaking, he promises to
return to it later:

> Ile tune my Reed unto a higher key,
> (And have already cond some of the Lay)
> Wherein (as Mantua by her Virgils birth
> And Thames by him that sung her Nuptiall mirth)
> You [i. e., the Tavy] may be knowne (though not in equall pride)
> As farre as Tiber throwes his swelling Tide.
> And by a Shepherd (feeding on your plaines)
> In humble, lowly, plaine, and ruder straines,
> Heare your worths challenge other floods among,
> To have a period equall with their song.[32]

This promise was never fulfilled. Despite his recognition of the im-
mortalizing power of poetry, Browne evidently considered it an

[29] Works, II, 68.   [30] Ibid., p. 83.
[31] Ibid., p. 132.   [32] Ibid., p. 64.

interesting secondary effect of an art which was for him primarily a means of innocent recreation.

In addition to the concept of poetic fame, Browne accepted without question the current belief in a hierarchy of poetical types, the belief that there were various levels of poetry, determined by a difference in objective, to which corresponded a certain difference in technique. The dedication of the first book of *Britannia's Pastorals* envisions his Muse as growing toward heroic stature:

> When time (that Embrions to perfection brings)
> > Hath taught her straines,
> May better boast their being from the Spring
> Where brave Heroes worths the Sisters sing.[33]

It is surely Drayton's disciple who sings of

> The Muses sitting on the graves of men,
> Singing that Vertue lives and never dyes,
> . . . ever-living Songs,
> With which our Ile was whilome bravely stor'd,[34]

and who suggests in an ambitious moment that he might one day undertake the tale of England's achievements.[35] Throughout his works Browne expresses the greatest admiration for the exponents of this highest type of poetry, for Homer (and Chapman), for Vergil, Spenser, and Drayton. Nor does he limit heroic poetry to the epic. In his Fifth Eglogue he urges Cutty to essay the heights of heroic drama but, except for *The Inner Temple Masque*, he himself made no venture into the field of dramatic poetry, regarding it as beyond his talent. He praised the efforts of his friend Brooke and the works of Jonson. There is some reason to believe that Browne wrote the following couplet, doubtless an allusion to Ben Jonson, in the prefatory lines to a play by Massinger:

> And in the way of Poetry now a dayes,
> Of all that are call'd Workes, the best are plays.[36]

In the middle rank of the hierarchy came poetry devoted to reforming current abuses. Didactic and admonitory verses were to him the variety immediately above the pastoral, and consequently

[33] Works, I, 3.
[34] *Ibid.*, p. 4.
[35] Works, II, 70. Cf. *ibid.*, p. 221.
[36] Works, II, 362.

satire was a type to which a "shepherd" might easily resort if he had occasion:

> Yee English Shepherds, sonnes of Memory,
> For Satyres change your pleasing melody
> For mine owne part although I now commerce
> With lowly Shepherds, in as low a Verse;
> If of my dayes I shall not see an end
> Till more yeares presse me; some few houres Ile spend
> In rough-hewn Satyres, and my busied pen
> Shall ierke to death this infamy of men.[37]

Such expressions as "rough-hewn Satyres" and "harsher straine" indicate his agreement with the conventional idea that the useful message of satire required strong and straightforward style.

Lowest in the scale stands the pastoral cherished for its "pleasing melody" and "sweetned lines." [38] Included in the pastoral is a strong love element, for Browne, like Sidney, took advantage of the lyrical nature of amorous plaints to provide the reader of his long narrative with a welcome change in meter:

> I shall goe on: and first in diffring stripe,
> The floud-Gods speech thus tune on Oaten pipe.[39]

In view of his fondness for the pastoral, his attitude toward the contemporary sonnet is strange. These forms were very similar in their nature; highly artificial, non-didactic, recreational, self-pleasing, frequently used as preliminary *études*; yet Browne does not anywhere praise the sonnets of his favorite poets, Sidney, Spenser, or Drayton. His own sonnets are extremely interesting, in that they are not imitative. Like all his personal expressions of love (notably those addressed to his brother poets), they are simple and sincere. Written after his long works, they do not seem to be exercises. He contrasts them sharply with his pastorals, accounting them less an artistic achievement than a transcript of his emotion:

> You are the subject now, and writing you
> I well may versify, not poetize:
> Here needs no fiction.[40]

> Now could I wish those golden howres unspent,
> Wherein my Fancy led me to the woods,

---

[37] Works, I, 194.
[39] Ibid., p. 55.
[38] Ibid., p. 126.
[40] Sonnets, Works, II, 285.

And tun'd soft layes of rurall merriment,
Of shepherds Loves & never resting Floods:
For had I seen you then, though in a dreame,
   Those songs had slept, and you had bin my Theame.[41]

The most interesting result of Browne's casual adoption of contemporary poetic theory is the hybrid resulting from his choice of a tradition-bound form and his refusal to accept the limitations of that type. He called his chief work *Britannia's Pastorals* and claimed to have chosen this type to suit his new and slender talent, but he was not writing the usual modest eclogue and did not write it until *The Shepheards Pipe;* even then he desired to depart from tradition and make that a series of translations from Occleve. For while Browne pleaded the privileges and immunities of the lowliest poetic style, a slight analysis of *Britannia's Pastorals* will show it to be very unlike the conventional poetic pastoral. Browne seems bent on elevating his pastorals by borrowing the attributes of all the other poetic types. Some of the passages are strongly reminiscent of the pastoral drama; at times the poem digresses suddenly into open satire; at times it approaches an amorphous epic. Certainly it is modeled far more upon the *Arcadia* or *The Faerie Queene* than upon *The Shepheardes Calendar*. The intensely nationalistic Browne changed the locale from Arcadia to the banks of his beloved Tavy,[42] but he retained the basic Sidneian idea of an expanded pastoral.[43] In a passage acknowledging the primary source of his inspiration, Browne says

   Sidney began (and if a wit so Meane
   May taste with him the dewes of Hippocrene)
   I sung the Past'rall next; his Muse, my mover.[44]

To develop his long and professedly pastoral poem, Browne encroached daringly upon the epic technique, borrowing such devices as carefully described allegorical characters, classical catalogues, highly developed similes, a classical cave adorned with panels, and the addition of deities to the dramatis personae. He laid under contribution *The Faerie Queene*, which he held as the consummate achievement of English poetry, "The Muses chiefest glory," [45] to such an extent that his own shepherds and shepherdesses, entangled in all varieties of amorous difficulty, seem like very faint copies of

---

[41] *Ibid.*, p. 289.
[43] Works, II, 8.
[42] *Britannia's Pastorals*, Works, I, 34.
[44] *Ibid.*, p. 9.
[45] Works, I, 190.

Spenser's knights and ladies, minus their armor and wandering in a lesser maze of enchanted sweetness and undeveloped allegory. The continuous meandering story, interspersed with songs, afforded a more variable and inclusive type than the fixed pattern of the classically derived pastoral.

Browne's so-called pastorals differ from the conventional type not only in the attempt at sustained narrative and the borrowing of devices from the romantic and the classical epic, but also in the degree to which he made them a vehicle for reform and violated decorum by introducing unveiled satire and direct appeals to the audience for the correction of current evils. F. W. Moorman has made a thorough study of the moral aspects of Browne's poetry.[46] The pastoral was already a very loose form, in which a poet might practice elegy, eulogy, narrative, lyric, and thinly disguised satire. It was the convention to beg indulgence for excursions into satire, since they infringed so largely on another type. Browne was at first particularly careful in this respect, since he was very conscious of the direct, unassimilated, non-pastoral nature of his satirical interpolations:

> But stay sweet Muse! forbeare this harsher straine,
> Keepe with the Shepherds; leave the Satyres veine.[47]

After a passage bidding England beware of bad bargains in her international traffic, he has the shepherd apologize:

> Excuse me, Thetis, quoth the aged man,
> If passion drew me from the words of Pan.[48]

Similarly, after calling attention to the ships rotting in the river, he says

> Beare with me Shepherds if I doe digresse,
> And speake of what our selves doe not professe.[49]

But Browne was not seriously apologetic for his digressions into matters more befitting other types of poetry. He was consciously bent on enriching the pastoral by this means. He was quite prepared to defend such departures:

> But, here I much digresse, yet pardon, Swaines:
>   .   .   .   .

---

[46] *William Browne, His Britannia's Pastorals and the Pastoral Poetry of the Elizabethan Age,* "Quellen und Forschungen," No. 81 (1897), Chapter III.

[47] *Britannia's Pastorals,* Works, I, 190.   [48] Works, II, 90.   [49] *Ibid.,* p. 66.

> If to wander I am sometimes prest,
> 'Tis for a straine that might adorne the rest.[50]

He justifies digression again by citing the general advantage of variety:

> What Musicke is there in a Shepherds quill
> (Plaid on by him that hath the greatest skill)
> If but a stop or two thereon we spy?
> Musicke is best in her varietie.[51]

In Book III, Browne spoils his fairy passage by using it clumsily to satirize the King of Spain, and returns from some entirely irrelevant lines praising Grenville with no more comment than

> Thus with small things I doe compose the greate.[52]

The influence of both Spenser and Drayton, reinforcing a natural patriotic bent, helps to account for the doubly intense nationalism of Browne's muse. The very title of his main work strikes a note of fervent love of country which is maintained with unflagging insistence. The names of Drake and Grenville occur as often as those of Spenser and Sidney and are accorded equal honor.[53] Browne unhesitatingly interrupts his poem to urge certain reforms, to attack obvious ills, to laud Elizabeth, and to sneer at Philip. The poem is completely insular. Nationalism determined not only its topics, but its medium of expression. Browne never dallied with the idea of a Latin poem. For one thing, he did not regret the limitation of his audience to a British public; for a second, he believed that English, properly handled, was infinitely superior to other languages:

> . . . our Muse . . .
> whose harmonious straine
> Was of such compasse, that no other Nation
> Durst ever venture on a sole Translation;
> Whilst our full language, Musicall and hie,
> Speakes as themselves their best of Poesie.[54]

His nationalism manifested itself, too, in his peculiar emphasis on English sources. He was by no means unaware of or unaffected by the classical past, but under his theory the native tradition was allowed to function in a correspondingly vital fashion. To his active

---

[50] *Britannia's Pastorals*, Works, II, 6.   [51] *Ibid.*, p. 54.   [52] *Ibid.*, p. 149.
[53] *Ibid.*, p. 43.   [54] *To Drayton*, Works, II, 358.

appreciation of English manners and methods may be attributed his experiments in "vision" poetry and his tendency in *Britannia's Pastorals* to teach by means of allegory. Browne's interest in tradesfolk and farmers had medieval precedent in the work of Chaucer and Langland. His didacticism and satire preserve the naïve, ingenuous quality of the early English moralists. *Britannia's Pastorals* includes a brief passage reviewing the Seven Deadly Sins.[55] Perhaps the most notable instance of medieval influence on Browne appears in his attempt to popularize Occleve by printing, as the first eclogue of *The Shepheards Pipe*, a modernized version of one of Occleve's tales. He was strongly attracted to the long-winded moralizing narrative of his predecessors:

> 'Tis a song, not many Swaines
> Singen can, and though it be
> Not so deckt with nycetee
> Of sweet words full neatly chused
> As are now by Shepheards used.
>
> Yet if well you sound the sence,
> And the morals excellence,
> You shal finde it quit the while,
> And excuse the homely stile.

In Browne's attitude toward Drayton is revealed the strange duality of interest that reached a precarious balance in his theory. He admired the elder poet's lofty purpose and prolific industry; he hailed him as the last and not the least of the Elizabethans, a great poet in petty times:

> To My Honor'd Friend Mr. Drayton
>
> Englands brave Genius, raise thy head, and see,
> We have a Muse in this mortalitie
> Of Vertue yet survives.
>
> .   .   .   .
>
> Then why lives Drayton, when the Times refuse,
> Both Meanes to live, and Matter for a Muse? [56]

But it was the poet's power to please and to delight that was emphasized by Browne in *Britannia's Pastorals:*

---

[55] *Britannia's Pastorals*, Works, I, 113.   [56] Works, II, 358.

Our second Ovid, the most pleasing Muse
That heav'n did ere in mortals braine infuse,
All-loved Draiton, in soul-raping straines,
A genuine noat, of all the Nimphish traines
Began to tune. . . .[57]

Browne felt no special sense of dedication to poetry, no duty toward his gift other than the moral obligation not to employ it for licentious description or flattery. It was a talent given to him primarily for his own use, not for the world's. He knew that he was not, like Spenser, a man with the power to write a national epic. He did not feel, like Drayton, that the real purpose of his gift was to preserve the past; nor yet, like Wither, that it was to forecast the future. Rather, like Sidney, he desired to lighten his sorrows by song and story. For the most part he attempted to use fiction as a means of recreation and yet make it the vehicle for a certain amount of truth by interrupting his story whenever he desired to teach. Though *Britannia's Pastorals* reflects clearly his primary purpose of diverting himself, it mirrors with equal fidelity the fact that, driven by the spirit of his age he frequently concerns himself with moral and patriotic problems.

The most important similarity between Browne and the next poet to be discussed, Wither, whom Browne termed "my songs chief mate," [58] is the way in which their personal interests are acknowledged and consciously included as part of their theory of poetry. Hitherto the main personal value stressed by major poets had been their opportunity for earthly immortality. Browne and Wither were not oblivious to this aspect of their art, though Wither in his later days desired prophetic rather than poetic fame; but, in addition to this uncertain benefit, they emphasized another reward of the poet, the pleasure he derived from the exercise of his art. In their theory, the author is recognized as the person most vitally affected by his work of art. This is, of course, a principle commonly enunciated in lyric poetry, but relatively rare in longer works. The poems of these two authors seem highly subjective when compared with the long works of Drayton and Giles Fletcher—or even those of Phineas

[57] *Britannia's Pastorals*, Works, II, 10.
[58] *Ibid.*, p. 36.

Fletcher, who has personal references in his pastoral introduction—
and of Cowley, who acknowledged that he wrote to get away from
the cares of the world. With Browne and Wither, the reader begins
to discern a strong subjective strain in major poetry, a tendency that
reaches its seventeenth-century zenith in *Samson Agonistes,* and in
the eighteenth century, under an altered theory of poetry, produces
such an extended satire as *The Dunciad.*

CHAPTER V

GEORGE WITHER

GEORGE WITHER started his artistic career with ideas and ambitions typical of a seventeenth-century poet. He began conventionally enough with various types of "low" poetry, designed for court consumption: *Prince Henries Obsequies,* satires, epigrams, an epithalamium, verses to the royal family, finally a poem on the model of Browne's pastorals, *The Shepheards Hunting;* and apparently he intended, following the usual procedure, to advance in good time to heroic verses:

> Yet I have learn'd to tune an Oaten Pipe,
> Whereon I'le try what musicke I can make me,
> (Untill Bellona with her Trumpe awake me.) [1]

Had Wither been successful in obtaining royal or noble patronage for his early poems, he would very likely have continued to use the old forms with new ease and simplicity. But the reception of his satire, *Abuses Stript and Whipt,* was unexpectedly severe. The poem which he had hoped would secure him preferment actually effected his imprisonment. By way of contrast, *Wither's Motto,* which had the temper, though not the title, of a satire, was avidly received by the puritanical middle class. His failure to secure favor at court and his easy success with the general public led him to abandon the usual subjects and treatment for matter and methods more suited to his new audience, a group that was not only uncritical, but hostile and suspicious toward the arts. In tracing the theories of Wither, we find first a positive and then a negative attitude toward accepted poetic standards.

Even in his early period, Wither, like Browne, differed from most of the major theorists by assigning a high personal value to his juvenilia, rather than insisting that all his "low" poems were practice work leading up to an ultimate masterpiece of definite social significance. Others might profit by or enjoy his poetry if they would, but

[1] *The Shepheards Hunting,* Works of George Wither, X, 446.

it was written mainly for the profit and pleasure of George Wither. Thus he dedicated *Abuses Stript and Whipt* to himself and, after detailing seven reasons for so peculiar an action, concluded with the following admonition:

Let me advise thee (my deare selfe) then, to make use of this thine own Worke; it will bee better to thee than all the World: for this good it may doe thee, and to this end [to warn himself from future transgressions], I made both it and the Dedication therof to thee.[2]

As for the pleasurable element, Wither even more strongly than Browne emphasized the Muse's power of conferring happiness on her favorite sons. Once again the joy of the creator rather than the pleasure of the reader is brought to the fore:

Wee [poets] in our selves have that shall make us merry:
Which, he that wants, and had the power to know it,
Would give his life that he might die a Poet.[3]

His lines

Come my Muse, if thou disdaine
All my comforts are bereft me,[4]

are justified by the famous passage in which Philarete presents the delights of the Muse:

She doth tell me where to borrow
Comfort in the midst of sorrow;

In my former dayes of blisse,
Her diuine skill taught me this,
That from euery thing I saw,
I could some inuention draw:
And raise pleasure to her height,
Through the meanest obiects sight

From all these and this dull ayre [he was in prison],
A fit object for Despaire,
She hath taught me by her might
To draw comfort and delight.
Therefore thou best earthly blisse,
I will cherish thee for this.
Poesie; thou sweetest content
That e're Heau'n to mortals lent.[5]

---

[2] Works, IX, 11.   [3] *The Shepheards Hunting*, Works, X, 559.
[4] *The Mistresse of Phil'arete*, Works, XI, 747.
[5] *The Shepheards Hunting*, Works, X, 546.

In fact, the writing of poetry gave such pleasure that no one who possessed the talent had ever neglected to use it:

> None ere drunke the Thespian spring
> And knew how, but he did sing.[6]

Wither considered poetry a very satisfying avocation. His enthusiasm for it was the enthusiasm of a man for a beloved hobby. Far from dedicating himself to it, he guarded against lavishing too much time upon it:

> Nor would I wish thee so thy selfe abuse
> As to neglect thy calling for thy Muse.[7]

Neither was he at all interested in perfecting his style; it was the easy spontaneity of his work that made it delightful to him:

> Neither for their [critics'] praises adde
> Ought to mend what they thinke bad:
> Since it never was my fashion,
> To make worke of Recreation.[8]

Throughout his early work, his muse was invoked principally to obtain self-gratification through self-expression.

But as early as the first eclogue of *The Shepheards Hunting*, the theme of personal pleasure began to give place to a strain that later came to dominate, the religious strain. Philarete consoles himself with a sonnet in the sacred vein, causing Willy to remark,

> . . . heer's a Name, and words, that but few swaines
> Have mention'd at their meeting on the Plaines.[9]

Wither, having failed in court poetry, soon turned to a type of religious poetry that was congenial to him and at the same time popular. Probably about 1615 he began his biblical exercises. In pursuing them he drifted further and further from classical and Renaissance influence:

> I find a braue Inuention comming on,
> That scornes to seeke a Muse at Helicon.
> For, know, the Deitie that guides my quill,
> Haunts not Parnassus but faire Sion hill.
> It is the same, who taught the Shepheard King
> To giue his Harpe such curious fingering.[10]

---

[6] *Ibid.*, p. 542. [7] *The Shepheards Hunting*, Works, X, 558.
[8] *Wither's Motto*, Works, XI, 739. [9] Works, X, 505.
[10] *A Preparation to the Psalter*, Works, XXXVII, 151.

Wither had never doubted the heavenly source of his art.[11] As time
went on, the conviction that his verses were divinely inspired
"Sparcklings" of the "great Spirit" [12] grew so strongly upon him
that it resulted in his dedicating his work entirely to the service and
praise of God:

> And if to have these Thoughts, & this Mind known
> Shall spread Gods praise no further then mine own:
> Or if This shall, no more instructive be,
> To others; then it glory is to Me:
> Here let it perish.[13]

By his recognition of poetry as divinely inspired and his shift of
emphasis to religion and social purpose, Wither came into partial
harmony with a well-established trend of seventeenth-century
theory.

His increasing attention to religious poetry was matched by a
steadily decreasing regard for secular work. The preface to *Wither's
Motto* (1618) contains this disparaging comment: "To recreate my
selfe, after some more serious Studies, I tooke occasion to exercise my
Inuention in the illustration of my Motto." [14] When in 1622 he
published *Faire-Virtue, the Mistresse of Phil'arete*, he was careful to
explain that it was an early work and thus excuse it, even though the
poem was entirely inoffensive and pure:

> Never shall my Maiden-Muse,
> So her selfe, and me abuse,
> As to sing what I may feare,
> Will offend the Choisest eare.[15]

From 1619 to 1627 Wither's poetry was controlled by his rapidly
developing interest in religious matters, an interest which culminated
in his sense of ordination as a remembrancer. He began this period by
paraphrasing and explaining certain parts of the Bible, in a shrewd
effort to profit by the growing stress on religion. Soon he came to
believe that God had selected him as a special interpreter and teacher
for those who were still in religious darkness and, to this end, had

---

[11] *Abuses Stript and Whipt*, Works, IX, 292.   [12] *Wither's Motto*, Works, XI, 697.
[13] *Ibid.*, p. 702.   [14] *Wither's Motto*, Works, XI, 625.
[15] *Mistresse of Phil'arete*, Works, XI, 771. Cf. *Preparation to the Psalter*, Works,
XXXVII, 82.

conferred the gift of poetry upon him. God now becomes the "Alpha, and Omega of my Songs." [16] His relationship to God was ineffable,

> And what
> I am to God, it may be guessed at
> But rightly known to none but him and me.[17]

Certainly he had a clear conviction that God had commissioned him for a special service, that God

> this Author did prefer
> To be from him, this Iles Remembrancer.[18]

In the light of this new belief, he interpreted his gift of verse and his previous success as a poet as part of the evidence that God intended him to assume the office of Britain's remembrancer:

> . . . why I pray
> Did he [God] bestow upon thee so much Fame
> For those few childish lines that thou didst frame
> In thy minority?
>
> Beleeve it, he divulgeth not thy Name
> For thine owne honor: But to make the same
> A meanes of spreading his.
>
> Thy Muse he gave thee, not to exercise
> Her pow'r in base and fruitlesse vanities,
> Or to be silenc'd: but to magnifie
> The wondrous workings of his Majesty.
>
> . . . these are Signes which force enough doe carry
> To seale this calling extraordinary.[19]

From 1628 to 1641 Wither produced no poetry except a set of emblems written to order. In 1641 he tried for the last time to interest the public in a book of hymns, this time original hymns of thankfulness for every occasion. After that attempt, he abandoned purely religious verse and concentrated all his efforts on interpreting the divine meaning underlying current natural and political events, terming himself now a premonitor, or *vates*. His position was one of the utmost responsibility, since he felt that by adequate explanation and persuasion he might be able to save men's souls.

[16] *Britain's Remembrancer*, Works, XXVIII, 32, 33.   [17] *Ibid.*, p. 18.
[18] Works, XXIX, 511.   [19] *Britain's Remembrancer*, Works, XXVIII, 200.

In this third period, Wither is an outstanding example in English literature of the poet who regards himself as *vates*. He did not ask for recognition as a poet, but for a hearing as a prophet. The terminology was a matter of indifference:

> . . . and, doubtless, whether I be a Prophet or a Poet (which two words in the Greek, signifie the same thing) I have done the work of a Prophet among them in some measure, and it will have effects upon them at last, for their Good or Evil.[20]

From 1641 on, he held that the "proper errand" of poetry was to be the "Instrument" for sacred things and "Things most pertinent to Man's well being." [21] In his discussion of the types of poetry, Wither recognized three varieties: (1) the fanciful, anagrammatical, conceited kind; (2) necessary truths, couched in parables; (3) plain relation of truths. The first type he considered of no use; the second was helpful to those in the "middle-region of knowledge"; but the third was adapted to both the wisest and the most ignorant.[22] His later poetry was of the third type, making its whole appeal to the intelligence:

> Or though it may want what affects the Sense,
> I hope, that, which affects th'Intelligence
> It shall not want, nor ought, which to that end
> Is needful, whereto, I the same intend.[23]

He had no patience with any poetry, even his own early work, that did not plainly teach the will or glory of God. He says, discussing a burnt sacrifice of useless "paper works,"

> And, griev'd I was not, that, some of mine own
> Must into that refining fire be thrown,
> For though that they might useful be some way,
> Much of them, have (I fear) too much alay.[24]

He was interested only in "useful, sanctifi'd, harmless Peeces." He draws a comparison between his poetry, rich in respect of civil man-

---

[20] *Epistolium-Vagum-Prosa-Metricum* (1659), Works, XII, 15. Cf. *Three Grains of Spirituall Frankincense*, Works, XXII, 4.
[21] *Dark Lantern* (1653), Works, XVI, 41.
[22] *Haleliuah* (1641), Works, XXVI, 15–19.
[23] *Sighs for Pitchers*, Works, XVI, 40.
[24] *Improvement of Imprisonment*, Works, XVI, 57.

ners and pious uses, and poetry "from whence, one sentence, (of such) hardly can be squeas'd." [25]

> Thy Faculties were not confer'd on thee
> For no Imployment; or imployd to bee
> In flattering fools; nor, as at first it was
> To praise the fading beautie of a face:
> Or play with those affections, which infuse
> The vaine expressions that pollute a Muse;
> But, to provoke a vertue: to deter
> From Vice, all chast affections to prefer;
> Gods Judgments to declare; his righteousnesse
> To magnifie; his mercies to confesse. [26]

Inasmuch as Wither's hierarchy was based on progress toward a more morally profitable type of poetry, it approached the theory of his colleagues, but inasmuch as it advocated a recession from all aids to art, ornamentation, fiction, selection, and structure, retaining nothing but the mere "rime and rattle" of unpolished heroic couplets, it was the negation of the prevailing tradition.

Wither's ideas on the nature of poetry varied with his changing concept of the purpose of poetry. In his early days he had ardently championed the poet's privilege of feigning. He was seriously concerned over the insistence of a certain group that anything written in verse was

> Nothing but fables of a lying braine. [27]

He refuted this point most vigorously, arguing that there could be no evil in presenting sacred truths under the guise of fiction, since Jesus had used that method of instruction without blame:

> . . . if that worthy Poets did not teach
> A way beyond their dull conceited reach
> I thinke their shallow wisedome would espy,
> A Parable did differ from a Lie.
> . . . though that kind of teaching some dispraise,
> As there's few good things lik't of now adaies
> Yet I dare say, because the Scriptures show it,
> The best ere taught on earth, taught like a Poet. [28]

---

[25] *Memorandum to London*, Works, XVIII, 7.
[26] *Prosopopoeia Britannica*, Works, XVIII, 113.
[27] *Abuses Stript and Whipt*, Works, IX, 286.
[28] *Ibid.*, p. 287.

But the verse-haters had another string to their bow. Either a poet
is merely fabricating, they said, or he must actually have experi-
enced all that he describes, an inference that would make some of the
poets appear thoroughly villainous. Wither protested against such
nonsense. The very gift of the poet lay in his protean power of as-
suming all shapes convincingly:

> . . . thinke they no man can describe a sin,
> But that which he himselfe hath wallowed in?

> As though that sacred Poesie inspir'd
> No other knowledge than might be acquir'd
> By the dull outward sense; yes this is she,
> That showes us not alone all things that be,
> But by her power layes before our view
> Such wondrous things as Nature never knew.[29]

For this very power of imaginative conception he, like Ben Jonson,
assigned the poet to the highest rank among men:

> For, of all sorts of men here's my beliefe,
> The Poet is most worthy and the chiefe:
> His Science is the absolut'st and best,
> And deserves honour above all the rest
> For tis no humane knowledge gain'd by Art,
> But rather tis inspir'd into the heart
> By *Diuine* meanes.[30]

The evolution of Wither's theories concerning the nature of
poetry may be most easily followed by studying the change in his
attitude toward the more representative poets of his day. From the
first, Wither recognized the difference between his poetry, sparing
of imagery and simple in language, and the traditional type from
which he had deliberately departed. Although he had defended
allegory and claimed to be skillful in fine phrases, he desired to evoke
intellectual rather than sensuous or emotional appreciation. He
prefaced his first satires (edition of 1613) thus:

Readers; . . . doe not looke for Spencers or Daniels well-composed num-
bers; or the deepe conceits of now-flourishing Iohnson. Say, 'Tis honest
plaine matter, and there's as much as I expect. . . . Some no doubt will

---

[29] *Abuses Stript and Whipt,* Works, IX, 290.   [30] *Ibid.,* p. 287.

mistake my plaines, in that I haue so bluntly spoken what I haue ob-
serued, without any Poeticall additions or fained Allegories: I am sorry I
haue not pleased them therein, but should haue bin more sorry if I had dis-
pleased my selfe in doing otherwise; for I know if I had wrapt up my mean-
ing in darke riddles, I should haue been more applauded, and lesse vnder-
stood, which I nothing desire.

. . . This wants some fine Phrases, and such flourishes; as you find other
mens writings stuft withall; And if that be a fault . . . I could with ease
haue amended it, for it cost me more labour to obserue this plainenesse, than
if I had more Poetically trim'd it.[31]

He conceded, however, that his was the less "Poeticall" procedure,
and in that very work he spoke with the greatest reverence of those
who rightly merited the title of poet:

> And now thinke not you
> Oh Daniel, Drayton, Iohnson, Chapman, how
> I long to see you with your fellow Peeres,
> Sylvester matchlesse, glory of these yeeres;
>
> . . . . .
>
> . . . know you Muses Darlings, Ile not craue
> A fellowship amongst you for to haue,
> Oh no; for though my euer-willing hart
> Haue vow'd to loue and praise You and your Art,
> And though that I your stile doe now assume,
> I doe not, nor I will not so presume;
> I claime not that too-worthy name of Poet;
> It is not yet deseru'd by me, I know it;
> Grant me I may but on your Muses tend,
> And be enroul'd their Seruant, or their Friend;
> And if desert hereafter worthy make me,
> Then for a Fellow (if it please you) take me.[32]

Yet in *The Mistresse of Phil'arete*, printed in 1622 but probably
written about ten years earlier, his comments were more critical. He
already doubted the value of work that was pleasing, but not
profitable. His most admired contemporaries seemed to have obeyed
the shallow promptings of the traditional Muses and to have neg-
lected, with decided detriment to their works, the deeper inspiration
of Faire-Vertue:

---

[31] *Ibid.*, p. 17. [32] *Ibid.*, p. 292.

Which, if she had pleased to add,
To that Art sweet Drayton had,
Or that happy Swaine that shall
Sing Britanias Pastorall;
Or to thiers, whose Verse set forth
Rosalind, and Stella's worth;
They had doubled all their skill,
Gained on Apollos Hill

.   .   .   .

They, had vnto heights aspired,
Might haue iustly been admired. . . .[33]

Wither apparently associated the names of Apollo and the Muses
with the adventitious and artificial aspects of poetry, and with classi-
cally derived rules and types, against all of which he was gradually
turning:

Let those doters on Apollo
    That adore the Muses, so,
(And, like Geese, each other follow)
    See, what Love alone can doe.

Once againe, come lend an eare,
    And, a Rapture you shall heare,
(Though I tast no Thespian Spring)
    Will amaze you, whilst I sing.[34]

The divergence created by his emphasis on matter rather than on
manner, on the sensible rather than the sensuous, continued to in-
crease. He explained over and over to his own satisfaction why he
found it necessary to use dull and commonplace language and to
violate the most elementary rules of his art:

The language is but indifferent; for, I affected Matter more than Words.[35]

. . . that makes me oftentimes affect some things in regard of their use-
fulnesse: which being considered according to the Method of Art, and rules
of Scholler-ship, would seeme ridiculous.[36]

He deliberately rejected the sensuous element in poetry:

And whosoever takes delight in me,
For any quality that doth affect
His *Senses* better, than his *Intellect*:
I *care not* for his love.[37]

---

[33] Works, XI, 796.   [34] *The Mistresse of Phil'arete*, Works, XI, 714.
[35] *Wither's Motto*, Works, XI, 625.   [36] *Ibid.*, p. 627.   [37] *Ibid.*, p. 684.

In *Britain's Remembrancer* (1628), his whole effort was bent toward securing ready intelligibility and literal accuracy. He realized that this was an unusual procedure and carefully distinguished his poem from the products of other poets:

> It may be that to some it will appeare,
> My Muse hath onely poetized here;
> And that I fain'd expressions doe rehearse
> As most of those that use to write in verse:
> But, in this Poeme I pursue the story
> Of reale Truth, without an Allegory.[38]

By 1628 Wither had begun to scorn non-didactic poetry. Those who read it were frivolous,

> And more delight in Poems worded out,
> Then those that are Gods works employ'd about.[39]

His "Muse defends her lowly stile":

> We love not, in affected paths, to goe.
> For, to be understood, is language used.[40]

> Let no man thinke I'le racke my memory
> For pen and inkhorn terms to finify
> My blunt invention.[41]

He was in revolt against "lines over-dark or over trimm'd" and wished to write so

> That ev'ry one my meaning may discerne;
> And they be taught, that have most need to learne.
> It is the usefull matter of my Rimes
> Shall make them live.[42]

He would have nothing to do with romantic metaphor and titillating conceits, declaring "Greenes phrase" and "Lillies language" now out of fashion. A passage in a later work, commenting on contemporary poets, shows the full extent of his departure from their standards:

> The scoffs and jeers, cast on me by the Rimes,
> Of some reputed *Poets* in these times
> Have been my great advantage: for, th'esteem
> Which in my youthful dayes I had of them

---

[38] *Britain's Remembrancer*, Works, XXVIII, 255.   [39] *Ibid.*, p. 256.
[40] *Ibid.*, p. 85.   [41] *Ibid.*, p. 86.   [42] *Ibid.*, pp. 85, 86.

Had else perhaps, from my simplicity
Drawn me, by their familiarity
To those affected *Vanities,* with which
They have infected fools, and claw'd their itch.
Were I but as ambitious of that name
A POET, as they are, and think I am,
It might a little vex me when I hear
How often in their *Pamphlets* me they jear,
Because, Truth seasonably I convey
To such as need it, in a homely way.
Best pleasing unto those who do not care
To crack hard *shells* in which no *kernels* are;
Or for *strong Lines* in which is little found,
Save an affected phrase, and empty sound.[43]

Since Wither's expository aim did not particularly require poetry, and since he disapproved of so many of the practices of the acknowledged poets, the question arises as to why he did not use prose for his works. Sometimes he was forced to do so:

The Muses language suits with few of those
Who most need this; I therefore now in Prose
Express my mind.[44]

The reverse process is illustrated by an execrable transition in the hybrid *Epistolium-Vagum-Prosa-Metricum.* He feels a "rapture" coming on, "and therefore I will walk to the conclusion of what remains, upon my Feet in Verse." His main reason for preferring verse was that the poet was not so strictly bound by the laws of structure as the prose writer. Milton had turned to prose as the proper medium for logical argument, finding it more exact; Wither deliberately clung to the less rigorous medium of poetry:

I'll warn you . . .
That method not to look for, which by those
Is used, who express their Mindes in Prose:
For Things, not in premeditated Thought
I took in as they came; and what they were
Oft knew not, till in Words, they did appear.[45]

[I] plainly tell things as I find they are
And then concerning them, my thoughts declare;

---

[43] *A Triple Paradox,* Works, XIII, 38.   [44] *Paralellogrammaton,* Works, XXXIII, 6.
[45] *Salt upon Salt,* Works, XVIII, 5.

> Not limited by Method like to those
> Who make expressions of their minds in prose;
> But by digressions as the Muses do,
> When sudden Raptures them incline thereto.[46]

The final vindication for his rimed exposition was his strong belief that God had conferred on him the talent of verse, so that by using it he might secure a wider audience for his later-day revelations.

As he was indifferent to current practice in creation, so he was impervious to all criticism, because he felt that the critics were basing their comments on a theory of poetry that he had rejected:

> If my Methode they deride,
> Let them know, Loue is not tide
> In his free Discourse, to chuse
> Such strict rules as Arts-men use.
>
> Pedants shall not tye my straines,
> To our Antique Poets vaines;
> I will sing, as I shall please.[47]

If a man postulates self-gratification as the sole purpose of his poetry, he may very properly insist that the only critical test is that of self-approval:

> If the Verses heere vsed, be
> Their dislike; it liketh me.
>
> If this Prologue tedious seeme,
> Or the rest too long they deeme:
> Let them know my loue they win,
> Though they goe ere I begin,
>
> For, I will for no mans pleasure
> Change a Syllable or measure:
> No; let them know, who do their length condemn,
> I make to please my selfe, and not for them.[48]

In the same way, during his second period Wither insisted that it was his duty as a religious teacher to speak simply and return to his theme frequently, however much the critics might belabor him for dull language and repetition.

In his third period, feeling that he was a directly inspired agent of

---

[46] *Speculum Speculativum*, Works, XXII, 15.
[47] *Mistresse of Phil'arete*, Works, XI, 738.
[48] *Ibid*.

God, Wither again made no attempt to control or revise his poetic effusions; indeed he claimed that frequently he did not know what he was writing until he re-read his own work:

> For what I had to write when I begun
> I knew not; nor shall I know when 'tis done,
> What by my Prompter I was moved unto
> Until I read it over as you do,
> To see what is of God in ev'ry line
> As if those writings had been none of mine.[49]

He admitted that his poetry was inordinately long, but he did not understand how a pious work could ever be too long except to a wicked reader:

> If any thinks these *Odes* are over long,
> Let him not do his *credit* so much wrong
>
> There can arise no great *discommendation,*
> By lengthening out a *Pious Recreation.*[50]

Similarly, he failed to see how there could be any objection to repeating a helpful lesson:

> I hear my snarling Censurers Object,
> That, al I write, is to the same effect.[51]

But Wither did not think that the lesson had been learned and therefore he looked

> . . . to be excus'd if I shall thrice,
> Write that, which I have writ already twice.[52]

Wither's patriotic poetry was also a phase of his religious didacticism. Like the work of Browne and Drayton and Spenser, Wither's work has intensely patriotic passages, but his patriotism sprang not so much from the love of Britain's geography or history as from his sense that Britain was the country most highly favored by God, as witness the following speech of God concerning England:

> Is this the Land whom we have lov'd so long,
> And in our love, elected from among

---

49 *Tuba-Pacifica,* Works, XVI, 13.
50 *Three Grains of Spirituall Frankincense,* Works, XXII, title-page.
51 *Speculum Speculativum,* Works, XXII, 160, postscript.
52 *Tuba-Pacifica,* Works, XVI, 24.

> The Heathen Iles (and at the first was hurl'd
> Into the utmost corner of the world)
> That we might raise the glory of her name,
> To equall Kingdomes of the greatest fame?
> Is this that Iland, which our love did place
> (Within our bosome) in the safe embrace
> Of great Oceanus?
>
> Is this the Kingdome which our hand hath made
> The Schoole and Shop, of ev'ry Art, and Trade? [53]

He wanted to make England conscious of her glorious destiny, and in a most reverently patriotic passage he wrote an earnest panegyric of God's past goodness to England:

> Oh! looke about thee; yea, looke backe, and see
> What wondrous things thy God hath done for thee.
>
> God lookt upon thee, with the first of all
> Those Gentiles, whom in mercy he did call.
>
> God kept thee as the apple of an eye;
> And, as when Eglets are first taught to flye,
> Their Dam about them hovers; so, thy God,
> Doth over thee, display his wings abroad.
>
> Thou hadst a Deborah bestow'd upon thee,
> Who freed thee from thy Foes, and glory won thee.
> In spight of Sisera: For, God did please
> To make the Stars, the Clouds, the Winds, and Seas,
> To fight thy battels.
>
> The Jewish Commonwealth was never daigned
> More great Deliverances then thou hast gained.
> Moreover, that no meanes might passe untride,
> Which God did for the Jewes of old provide;
> To thee he also sends his onely Sonne:
> Not, as to them, a poore contemned one,
>
> But, in a glorious wise to thee he came. [54]

The patriotic strain did not appear in Wither's poetry until the religious strain had been well established. It did not lead to building up legends of Brut and Arthur nor to praising British hills and rivers

[53] *Britain's Remembrancer*, Works, XXVIII, 37.
[54] Works, XXIX, 325–29, *passim*.

in personified form, but concerned itself with the more awful task
of demonstrating from history and legend and geography the ex-
traordinary love of God for England.

In the matter of earthly immortality and fame, so much desired
by the children of the Renaissance, Wither was again peculiar. The
inherent immortality of poetry did not fascinate him, as it did his
contemporaries. His later writings were almost journalistic and he
believed that his work would live not for its artistic merit, but for
its value as a record:

> In sight of GOD, of Angels, and of Men,
> These things were done, and, this, compels my pen
> To leave it on Record, here to be read
> By future Ages, when that I am dead.[55]

After his earliest period, there was no attempt to immortalize his
friends or himself through his poetry. He looked to the future only
for appreciation of his faithfulness as a remembrancer and as a
prophet:

> For, I will tell thy Fortune; which, when they
> That are unborne shall read, another day;
> They will beleeve Gods mercy did infuse
> Thy Poets brest with a prophetick Muse.[56]

Equally atypical was his attitude toward the classics. His slight
education had been just about sufficient to reveal that the writers
of antiquity had said many of the things that everyone wished to
say. He childishly begrudged the fact that they had been born first
and had covered the ground well,[57] with the exception, of course, of
recent events and later religions:

> For many Bookes I care not; and my store
> Might now suffice me, though I had no more,
> Then Gods two Testaments, and therewithall
> That mighty Volume, which the World we call.
> For, these well lookt on, well in minde preseru'd
> The present Ages passages observ'd:
> My priuate Actions, seriously oreview'd,

---

55 *A Suddain Flash*, Works, XIII, 55. Cf. *Britain's Remembrancer*, Works, XXVIII,
32–33.
56 *Britain's Remembrancer*, Works, XXIX, 511.
57 *Wither's Motto*, Works, XI, 700.

My thougts recal'd, and what of them ensu'd:
Are Bookes, which better farre, instruct me can,
Then all the other Paper-workes of Man.[58]

He emphasized, whenever possible, how slight an influence earlier writers had had upon him and upheld his underived type of poetry:

Perhaps, the nicer Critickes of these times,
When they shall sleightly view my lowly Rimes
(Not to an end, these Poems fully reading
Nor their Occasion, nor my Aymes, well heeding)
May taxe my Muse that she at random flyes;
For want of Method, makes Tautologies.

They who in their Composures keep the fashion
Of older times, and write by imitation;
Whose quaint Inventions must be trimd and trickt
With curious dressings, from old Authors pickt;
And whose maine workes, are little else, but either
Old scattered Peeces, finely glewd together,
Or, some concealed Structures of the Braine.

Sometime, as well as they I play the Bee:
But, like the Silkeworme, it best pleaseth me
To spin out mine owne Bowells and prepare them
For those, who thinke it not a shame to weare them,
My matter, with my Method, is mine owne;
And I doe plucke my Flow'rs as they are blowne.[59]

Although Wither terminated his career as an iconoclast, his early work was planned to fall well within the recognizable categories of seventeenth-century theory. He departed slightly from the usual order by commencing as a satirist. His next work, as was proper for a youthful poet, was in the pastoral style. Wither used the sonnet form in *Prince Henries Obsequies,* but devoted no sonnet sequence to love, substituting instead the long semi-allegorical *Faire-Virtue,* written in heptasyllabic couplets, interspersed with some of his early experiments in the love lyric, notably "Shall I Wasting in Despair." He tried his hand at an epic fragment in *Fidelia* and he later essayed epic proportions and purpose in his long descriptive poem, *Britain's Remembrancer.* Well within seventeenth-century convention, too, are his translations of the Psalms and Old Testament songs into meter

[58] *Ibid.,* p. 669.   [59] *Britain's Remembrancer,* Works, XXVIII, 276.

and his original hymns of praise. The most complete break with
tradition was made when he started pamphleteering in verse. This
switch to undisguised didacticism was a bold departure, forced on
him by the exigencies of his situation, even as Milton's pamphleteer-
ing was, and no part of his original poetic intent. Particularly im-
portant is Wither's attitude toward the heroic couplet as used in
expository and argumentative poetry. He does not try to imitate the
vigor and restraint of Drayton, the neatness and artistry of Browne;
his whole claim is that his verses are easy, clear, and couched in the
language of normal prose.

He greatly advanced the tendency, already present in satire, to
deal in a more direct way with subjects of immediate interest. His
sound journalistic sense in a prejournalistic era foreshadows Dryden.
Thus, in *Britain's Remembrancer*, Wither reproaches his brother
poets for their neglect of so promising a subject as plague-stricken
London:

> What, none but me? me only leave they to it,
> To whom they shame to yeeld the Name of Poet?
> Well; if they ever had a minde to weare
> The Lawreat Wreath, they might have got it here:
> For though that my performance may be bad,
> A braver Subject, Muses never had.[60]

As he grew more extreme, Wither mistook the province of poetry
and applied the mechanics of verse to unpoetical, though worthy
subjects. He scorned the seemingly adventitious elements in poetry
and had no sympathy with the theory that led other poets to exercise
themselves thoroughly in preliminary types before attempting to
handle a great and doctrinal theme. He did not realize that though
the mysterious poetic principle is not dependent on figures or fiction,
neither is it assured by verse. Nor did he sufficiently differentiate
between moral and artistic excellence. He argued fallaciously that
the value of the subject would supply any stylistic deficiencies. Un-
like Milton, who supplemented his sense of divine ordination by in-
tensive reasearch into all that human knowledge could offer, Wither
attempted to use his gift in its simplest form, ignoring the fact that
poetry was a well-established art with many successful models from

60 Works, XXVIII, 260.

which significant principles had been abstracted. His weaknesses were incorporated into a new theory of poetry, in which truth was literally beauty and the most honest man the best poet. His insistence upon ready intelligibility as a cardinal point of style was in accordance with the temper of the century, but his utter disregard of all previous traditions was too extreme and too purely personal. The century was seeking the proper employment of esthetic forces, not the blunt rejection of most of them.

CHAPTER VI

GILES FLETCHER AND PHINEAS FLETCHER

THE BROTHERS Fletcher published their first poetry upon the occasion of Elizabeth's death and James' succession. In such commemorative verse the technique, especially of the younger poets, was likely to be imitative and stereotyped. The Fletchers selected an artificial and ornate Spenserian style, well suited to memorials and celebrations of state. With very little more experience behind him, Giles Fletcher in 1610 wrote his only other work, *Christ's Victory and Triumph,* a startling attempt to achieve a major objective immediately. Acting on his belief that the glorification of God is the true function of poetry, he rejected the contemporary theory that a poet must rise slowly through the practice of lower forms to competence on the heroic level, and proceeded directly to the composition of a long religious poem. In the preface to this work, which outlines his theory of poetry, Fletcher tried to conciliate two groups that would be hostile to a religious poem: those who thought poetry a profane art that should not be applied to "divine and heavenly matters"; and those who, not content with limiting poetry to the secular field, proposed to banish it entirely, in accordance with the suggestion of Plato. The arguments of Giles Fletcher, which are strongly reminiscent of Sidney's *Defense of Poesie,* discuss briefly the nature and purpose of poetry. Religious poetry is clearly vindicated, since there is example for it in the songs of the Bible and since the inspiration derived from God should most fittingly be returned to the Giver as a hymn of praise.

Faced with the harder problem of defending and justifying poetry as a whole, he acknowledged that it had occasionally been misused, but, like Sidney, called attention to the great accomplishments of poets. What group of men should be encouraged if not poets? Philosophers, musicians, soldiers? Philosophers have borrowed all the lights of example, used to illustrate their precepts, from poets;

"without Homer's examples, Aristotle would be as blind as Homer."
Poets such as Pindar and Horace have infused the "verie soule" into
the inarticulate sounds of music. As for soldiers, who but the poet
recalls the dead hero to life? He ends by commending himself "to
those that love such Poets, as Plato speakes of, that sing divine and
heroical matters."

The matter of poetry, according to Giles Fletcher, should ideally
be the highest; that is, the praise of God. But, in advocating the use
of poetry for so glorious a purpose, Fletcher was confronted by the
fact that it was now employed extensively in the service of pas-
sion. The blame for this, he pleaded, must be laid on the poet and
not on his art. He did not hold with those who "will needs shoulder
them [poets] out for the onely Firebrands to inflame lust (the fault
of earthly men not heavenly Poetrie)," but he deplored love poetry
as a worthless and wanton product, and urged his fellow poets
away from their favorite theme. The issue was not only moral but
artistic. Of what use was a beautiful style if it was wasted on an
unworthy subject? In disgust at the amorous preoccupation of his
contemporaries he exclaims:

> Goe giddy braines, whose witts are thought so fresh,
> Plucke all the flowers that Nature forth doth throwe
> Goe stick them on the cheekes of wanton flesh
> Poore idol, (forc't at once to fall and growe)
> Of fading roses and of melting snowe:
>> Your songs exceede your matter, this of mine
>> The matter which it sings shall make divine
> As starres dull puddles guild, in which their beauties shine.[1]

And yet Giles Fletcher did not rely entirely upon his subject matter
and repudiate style, as Wither did in his later poetry. Rather, he
thought that the height of poetic art would be realized only in
the application of a perfected technique to a great theme. Both
Fletchers were careful workmen, adhering to their own modifica-
tion of the conscious and elaborate Spenserian tradition. The cardinal
rule in their doctrine of style was smoothness. Christ's victory, says
Giles, is matter "worthie the sweetest Singer." The necessity for a
beautiful, flowing style is ever before him:

[1] Giles Fletcher and Phineas Fletcher, Poetical Works, ed. by Boas, I, 59.

> How may weake mortal ever hope to file
> His unsmooth tongue and his deprostrate stile? [2]

> One look would polish my afflicted verse. [3]

One of the blessings conferred by Mercy is the gift of "golden phrases." [4] That these "golden phrases" are synonymous with smooth phrases is made evident a few stanzas later when we are told that Satan possesses the

> golden foyle of eloquence and can lime
> And licke his rugged speech with phrases prime. [5]

When Giles wished to depreciate his own poetry, he called it "unsmooth." [6] Normal expression was to him "rough speech." [7] The other attribute of poetic style, far less frequently mentioned, was strength. The dual ideal of strength and sweetness becomes explicit at least once in the poetry of Giles:

> Had I a voice of steel to tune my song,
> Wear every verse as smoothly fil'd as glasse,
> And every member turned into a tongue,
> And every tongue wear made of sounding brasse,
>   Yet all that skill and all this strength, alas,
>   Should it presume to guild, wear misadvis'd. [8]

Phineas Fletcher, in a complimentary poem prefacing his brother's work, calls attention to the same combination:

> Or stol'n from Heav'n thou brought this verse to ground,
> Which frights the nummed soule with fearefull thunder,
> And soone with honied dewes melts it twixt joy, and wonder. [9]

A reciprocal fraternal tribute serves as the conclusion to the younger man's only important poem. Calling his own muse "too greene" to sing of Christ's love for the Church, Giles passes that task on to his more practiced brother, though the experience of Phineas lay mainly in the field of low poetry:

> But let the Kentish lad, that lately taught
> His oaten reed the trumpets silver sound

> Let his shrill trumpet with her silver blast
> Of faire Eclecta and her Spousall bed
> Be the sweet pipe and smooth Encomiast. [10]

---

[2] Poetical Works, I, 28.   [3] Ibid., p. 29.   [4] Ibid., p. 30.   [5] Ibid., p. 44.
[6] Ibid., p. 81.   [7] Ibid., p. 86.   [8] Ibid.   [9] Ibid., p. 14.
[10] Ibid., p. 87.

Apparently Giles realized that his early condemnation of light toys and love poetry eliminated too completely the usual practice material. He acknowledged this weakness in his theory and recognized the greater efficiency of the traditional approach to lofty poetry in this final tribute to his brother.

The course of Phineas Fletcher's development was more nearly normal. His piscatory drama and eclogues are but a mild variation of the usual pastoral type. He composed many verses to his friends in the prevailing tradition of personal, almost epistolary poems. Typical also are his classical love exercise, *Venus and Anchises* (*Brittains Ida*), the epic aspiration of *The Purple Island,* and the brief, bilingual epic realization in *The Locusts.*

He has left no serious discussion of the matter of poetic feigning, probably because he considered it axiomatic, but he evinces an awareness of the question in an amusing occasional poem based on the premise that "Poets to feign and make fine lies endeavour." [11]

Something of his theory of poetry is seen in his first eclogue, which sketches the poetical development of his father. Giles senior is pictured as stressing technique rather than purpose in his earliest attempts at verse:

> I learnt to sing
> Among my Peers, apt words to fitly binde
> In numerous verse.

Phineas inherited an elder brother's share of the paternal interest in style; he was even more concerned than Giles with the mere sweetness of his poetry:

> Who now with Thomalin shall sit, and sing?
>   .   .   .   .
> Or tune sweet ditties to as sweet a string? [12]

Fletcher loved to "frame sweet ditties to thy [Thomalin's] sweeter string." [13] In his farewell to piscatory poetry, it is still this quality which he stresses:

> Go little pipe; for ever I must leave thee,
> My little, little pipe, but sweetest ever.[14]

---

[11] *Ibid.,* II, 240.
[13] *Ibid.,* p. 234.

[12] *Ibid.,* I, 185.
[14] *Ibid.,* p. 235. Cf. Poetical Works, II, 222.

Vergil is praised for singing the Greek pastorals "with sweeter voice." [15] Along with all his emphasis on sweetness, Phineas had no objection to a "merry pipe" or "rugged rimes," since he urged Chromis to resume his "jocund rimes." [16]

Phineas Fletcher seems never to have questioned the existence of a hierarchy of poetical types. In Eclogue I, Telgon lists his works:

> I sang sad Telethusa's frustrate plaint,
> And rustick Daphnis wrong . . .
> And rais'd my rime to sing of Richard's climbing.

To Thenot, who had obviously written urging him to ascend Parnassus, i. e., to try a loftier type of poetry, he replies that he is but a lowly shepherd, a singer of humble love songs. An ardent admirer and disciple of Vergil and Spenser, he acknowledged the epic as the ultimate type. Here he and Giles were in accord. But although he endorsed the theories of Giles concerning the "lower" kinds of poetry, and praised the direct essay of the younger man into a more worthy field; nevertheless Phineas, in his own more careful preparation, chose to follow in the steps of Vergil and Spenser, and to practice the very forms that his brother had so rigidly eschewed. In theory, his pastoral efforts were only the means of reaching a much higher poetic level. One critic feels that the *Piscatory Eglogs* show the transition between the love poems and the religious poetry, show Fletcher passing from apprenticeship under Colin Clout to discipleship under the author of *The Faerie Queene*.[17] Actually, Phineas Fletcher, like William Browne, found the pastoral so congenial a genre that he preferred to expand it far beyond its original bounds rather than transcend it, with the result that *The Purple Island*, like *Britannia's Pastorals*, is a hybrid, combining pastoral and epic characteristics. Fisher and shepherd types had acquired special significance for him and his Cambridge audience as university colleagues and parish clergymen respectively.[18] He loved to assume various conventional names as a fisher boy or shepherd, to maintain the pretense, the beloved semi-incognito and allegorical rusticity.

[15] Poetical Works, II, 14.   [16] *Ibid.*, pp. 192, 193.

[17] Cory, "The Golden Age of the Spenserian Pastoral," PMLA, XXV (April, 1910), 260.

[18] Langdale, *Phineas Fletcher*, p. 161.

Nor did Phineas, like Giles, frown upon love poetry. Dorus urges the fishers to "carol lowd of love, and loves delight." [19] Thomalin, lamenting the loss of Thirsil (Fletcher himself), complains:

> Who now those wounds shall 'swage in covert glade,
> Sweet-bitter wounds, which cruel love hath made.[20]

Eclogue V deals with love. Finally, at the instance of his "fayre Eliza," he attempted a classical love story, *Venus and Anchises*, which he never acknowledged but which has been assigned to him on strong internal evidence. The nature of this poem is the best proof we have of his sympathy with the tradition of passionate and sensuous love poetry. Probably his desire to remain unconnected with it arose out of his hope for advancement in the ministry. Compared to the Caroline verse makers, Fletcher exercised some restraint in his *Venus and Anchises;* yet it should be noted that this modesty was imposed only by inadequate technique and fear of criticism, rather than by any such rigid morality as controlled his brother's theory of poetry. The poet, who has been describing categorically the beauties of Venus, calls a somewhat reluctant halt:

> But stay bold shepherd, here thy footing stay,
> Nor trust too much unto thy new-borne quill,
> As farther to those dainty limbs to stray;
>
> But were thy Verse and Song as finely fram'd
> As are those parts, yet should it soone be blam'd,
> For now the shameless world of best things is ashamed.[21]

Nowhere is the contrast between the brothers more striking than in the reaction of each to the hierarchy of types which both acknowledged. The idealistic fervor of Giles disdained intermediary steps and scaled the heights at a single bound. Phineas was no such ardent and impulsive spirit. There were values on the lower levels that were not to be overlooked. In addition to the training to be derived from the lower types, there was the opportunity for personal allusion, for light themes. And yet, despite their different procedures, the brothers so strongly felt themselves to be working under one theory that each held the other in the highest regard as a poet. The author of *Venus and Anchises* quite sincerely praised

[19] Poetical Works, II, 180.
[20] *Ibid.*, p. 185.   [21] *Ibid.*, p. 354.

his brother for proving "the Muses not to Venus bound." In un-
grudging terms he lauded his brother's epic essay as far beyond the
slight love rimes of most youthful poets:

> Fond ladds, that spend so fast your poasting time,
> To chaunt light toyes, or frame some wanton rime,
> Where idle boys may glut their lustfull tast,
> Or else with praise to cloath some fleshly slime
> With virgin roses and faire lillies chast:
> While itching bloods, and youthfull eares adore it,
> But wiser men, and once your selves will most abhorre it.[22]

In return, Giles acknowledged the practical value of the way Phineas
had trod; he realized the advantage of acquiring skill in the low
forms. Perhaps he even felt the analogy between human and divine
love that struck the lyric poets of the age so forcibly when, in with-
drawing from the stage to make room for his brother, he said:

> But my greene Muse, hiding her younger head
> Dares not those high amours, and love-sick songs assay.[23]

There is every reason to believe that the reciprocal understanding
and esteem, similar interests, and close proximity of the brothers
led them into a jointly planned coöperative effort. Apparently both
brothers regarded *The Purple Island* as the complementary sequel
to *Christ's Victory*. The concluding stanza of Giles and the frequent
references to *Christ's Victory* in *The Purple Island* [24] would indi-
cate some such arrangement. In fact, Giles appears as co-equal poet
in the poem of Phineas:

> Among the rout they take two gentle swains,
> Whose sprouting youth did now but greenly bud:
>
> .   .   .   .
>
> Their nearest bloud from self-same fountains flow,
> Their souls self-same in nearer love did grow:
> So seem'd two joyn'd in one, or one disjoyn'd in two.
>
> Yet since the shepherd-swains do all consent
> To make thee lord of them, and of their art;
> And that choice lad (to give a full content)
> Hath joyn'd with thee in office, as in heart.[25]

---

[22] Poetical Works, I, 14.

[24] Poetical Works, II, 25, 72, 73.

[23] *Ibid.*, p. 87.

[25] *Ibid.*, pp. 12, 13.

It was not collaboration by any means, but more in the nature of the later experiment of Coleridge and Wordsworth in the *Lyrical Ballads,* an undertaking in which each poet worked at a congenial task. The province of Giles was to sing the nature, struggle, and triumph of the Saviour in the highest epic vein; whereas the function of Phineas was to expound the nature, struggle, and rescue of the saved in deliberately lower fashion. How elated the younger brother must have felt when he found himself entrusted with the more ineffable and glorious task, while Phineas pursued his current enthusiasm for research into the wondrous mechanism of the human body and mind! Phineas was well aware that he had delegated the grander subject to Giles; he consistently referred to the younger man's poem as being in a higher strain:

> My callow wing, that newly left the nest,
> How can it make so high a touring flight?
>
> .   .   .   .
>
> But thou, my sister Muse, mayst well go higher,
> And end thy flight; ne're may thy pineons tire: *
> Then let me end my easier taken storie,
> And sing this Islands new recover'd seat.[26]

* A book called Christ's Victorie and Triumph

But Phineas Fletcher, like William Browne, had found so many advantages in the pastoral that he was delighted to have the lower theme, since it permitted him to work in a thoroughly congenial medium.

In *The Purple Island* he utilized the shepherd material to provide convenient openings and closings for his cantos, deliberately forfeiting the stature of his work. Throughout the poem he vacillated, aware of the opportunity to soar strongly, yet unwilling to abandon the familiar strain. Not even his brother's brilliant example, of which he was so fully conscious, could inspire him to burn his pastoral bridges behind him; and yet his work is full of tentative epic excursions prefaced by transitional verses in which he does not hesitate to ask the direct inspiration of the divine spirit:

> Who now (alas) shall teach my humble vein,
> That never yet durst peep from covert glade
>
> .   .   .   .

---

[26] Poetical Works, II, 25.

> Who now shall teach to change my oaten quill
> For trumpet 'larms, or humble verses fill
> With graceful majestie, and loftie rising skill?
>
> Ah thou dread Spirit . . .
> Teach thou my creeping measures to aspire
> And swell in bigger notes, and higher art;
>   Teach my low Muse thy fierce alarums ring
> And raise my soft strain to high thundering:
> Tune thou my loftie song; thy battels I must sing.[27]

Yet he is always careful to remind the reader of the technically pastoral nature of his poem. He is no longer feigning "soft sighs of love unto a looser strain"[28] or singing purely biographical and personal matters, but he is still playing a shepherd's pipe:

> Low is the shepherds state, my song as low[29]

He is conscious of the fact that the subject of his poem far outweighs his treatment of it:

> But to describe the people of this Isle
>   these reeds are all too vile
> Some higher verse may fit and some more loftie style.[30]

Yet when Thenot urges him to higher effort, the answer is

> How dare I then forsake my well-set bounds
> Whose new-cut pipe as yet but harshly sounds?
> A narrow compasse best my ungrown Muse impounds.[31]

Giles, too, recognized the difference in technique between *Christ's Victory* and *The Purple Island,* and he provided a smooth transition from the formal tone of his epic to the rather familiar style of Phineas. Nothing could more accurately characterize the pastoral-epic compromise of Phineas than the fraternal introduction of him as

> the Kentish lad, that lately taught
> His oaten reed the trumpets silver sound.

A second reason for the reluctance of Phineas Fletcher to assume full epic style was the increasing difficulty of solving the problem of heroic subject matter. Whereas Giles built his poem about the usual unifying core of a great central figure, Phineas deliberately

---

[27] Poetical Works, II, 140. Cf. *ibid.*, pp. 152, 74, 19.   [28] *Ibid.*, p. 13.
[29] *Ibid.*, p. 44. Cf. *ibid.*, pp. 53, 170.   [30] *Ibid.*, p. 68.   [31] *Ibid.*, p. 69.

forsook that theme as one that had been exhausted by previous poets:

> Tell me ye Muses, what our father-ages
> Have left succeeding times to play upon:
> What now remains unthought of by those Sages,
> Where a new Muse may trie her pineon?
>   What lightning Heroes, like great Peleus heir,
>   May stirre up gentle heat, and vertues wane repair? [32]

Certainly in *The Purple Island* he did not get far from material that had already been better handled by Spenser, but in the poem that he evidently considered his masterpiece, *The Locusts,* he did hit upon a fresh and better centralized topic, well calculated, from his point of view, to "stirre up gentle heat, and vertues wane repair." The three Latin versions and the English paraphrase of *The Locusts* were the highest bid that Fletcher made for a patron.[33] They represent his full emergence from the shelter of the pastoral tradition. He abstains from the personal allusion so dear to him. The change from oaten pipe to high-sounding trumpet is unmistakable in the opening epic statement of theme, the invocation, the didactic purpose and lofty tone of the whole work, the first English satire in epic style. When he does drop back into the pastoral metaphor, it is only to ask for more power in the heroic vein:

> Oh thou great Shepheard, Earths, Heavens Soveraigne,
>
>   .   .   .
>
> Teach me thy groome, here dull'd in fenny mire,
> In these sweet layes, oh teach me beare a part:
> Oh thou dread Spirit shed thy heavenly fire,
>
>   .   .   .
>
> Teach thou my creeping Muse to heaven aspire,
> Learne my rude brest, learne me that sacred art,
>   Which once thou taught'st thy Israels shepheard-King:
>   Oh raise my soft veine to high thundering;
> Tune thou my lofty song, thy glory would I sing.[34]

The dedication to Townshend dwells on the sin of permitting a great blessing to be forgotten for lack of commemoration; Fletcher will set forth the deliverance from the Gunpowder Plot, in order to arouse the spirit of his countrymen and to pay honor to God: "ad

---

[32] *Ibid.*, p. 13.   [33] Langdale, *Phineas Fletcher*, pp. 158, 159.
[34] Poetical Works, I, 179–80.

animos Britannorum excitandos, honorèmque Deo Servatori resto-
randum, in lucem emiserim." [35]

Many passages might be cited to show that Phineas, like Giles,
considered the highest poetical inspiration to be of God:

> Great Prince of shepherds,
>
> .   .   .   .
>
> Thou first and last, inspire thy sacred skill;
> Guide thou my hand, grace thou my artlesse quill:
> So shall I first begin, so last shall end thy will. [36]

The brothers did not, however, like Milton, consider the function
of the poet to be as lofty as the more direct divine calling of the
minister. Giles wrote no more poetry after his one brilliant effort.
Phineas, upon taking sacred orders, registered his intention of aban-
doning secular verse:

> Sing what thou list, be it of Cupid's spite
>
> .   .   .   .
>
> Or Gemma's grief, if sadder be thy sprite:
>
> Ah, (said the bashfull boy) such wanton toyes
> A better minde and sacred vow destroyes,
> Since in a higher love I settled all my joyes. [37]

Upon assuming his duties as minister, he gave over further poetic
endeavors almost entirely:

> Go little pipe; for ever must I leave thee,
> My little, little pipe, but sweetest ever:
> Go, go; for I have vow'd to see thee never,
>
> .   .   .   .
>
> Go little pipe, for I must have a new:
> Thirsil will play no more; for ever now adieu. [38]

Although Phineas reiterated the current belief that the purpose of
worthy poetry was to disseminate virtue, he made little effort to
reach an audience. Unlike Giles, who published immediately upon
completing his work, Phineas seemed indifferent to any benefit that
his poetry might confer upon the public. The bulk of his work

[35] Poetical Works, I, 100.
[36] Poetical Works, II, 19.
[37] Ibid., p. 13.
[38] Ibid., p. 235.

was written between 1607 and 1612; yet it was not until 1627 that the energy and enthusiasm of Benlowes aroused him to the point of publishing the poem that he considered his greatest work, the only one to which he was proud to sign his full name—*The Locusts*. Then, apparently under the stimulus of Benlowes, he completely changed his policy and began to publish all his work, even pieces that he did not deem fit to sign, such as *Venus and Anchises*. Evidently *The Purple Island* was considered unduly light for a minister of the gospel, for he published it under only his initials, "P. F., Hilgay." To be sure, it was lighter than his fully acknowledged prose works and technically it fell within the pastoral or "low" classification.

Why had not Fletcher seen fit to publish earlier? Perhaps the main clue to his willingness to let his work rest in manuscript lies in the real purpose that underlay his poetic career. Concerning this, Langdale, in his book *Phineas Fletcher,* makes an illuminating comment: "Both Giles Fletcher and his two sons placed a strange value upon their poetic talent; it was to be the avenue of academic advancement." [39] In proof of this statement Langdale adduces the frequency and bitterness of Phineas Fletcher's attacks on those who hampered the promotion he proposed to win by the aid of the muses. His hope that writing would further his career accounts for his concentrated poetic activity between 1607 and 1612 and his comparative silence afterward. It also explains his sudden, sporadic turning to low drama in *Sicelides,* one last attempt to advance by attracting royal attention. The last stanza of Giles's published poem almost presumed a simultaneous publication of *The Purple Island,* since it so strongly directed readers to that work. But apparently Giles profited so little by his venture that Phineas left the indicated sequel in manuscript.

The limited circulation that manuscript permitted was adequate for Fletcher's purposes. His pastoral poetry, inspired by Cambridge and closely associated with it, was written primarily for a small group of college friends who understood the local and personal allusions. He seems to have been unaffected by the usual incentive to publish, the desire for poetic fame. There are few allusions to the prevailing theory of the earthly immortality of the poet and his

[39] Page 30.

work. Sometimes Fletcher drops into the conventional manner of speaking, notably in his praise of preceding poets:

> Nor may, nor ever shall those honour'd flowers
> Be spoil'd by summers heat, or winters showers;
> But last when eating time shall gnaw the proudest towers.[40]

The strongest reference to poetic fame occurs in his diatribe against his and Spenser's common enemy. He is addressing Spenser:

> Yet shalt thou live, when thy great foe shall sink
> Beneath his mountain tombe, whose fame shall stink;
> And time his blacker name shall blurre with blackest ink.[41]

Fletcher foreshadows Milton in feeling that fame did not lie in the applause of the multitude. He admonished his Muse to pay no heed to the vulgar but to "build her nest" in heaven. The praise of kings might be acceptable and worthy tribute for such an art as poetry:

> (Farre be dull thoughts of winning dunghill praise)
> Enough, if Kings enthrone thee in their breast
> And crown their golden crowns with higher baies.[42]

But he needs no patron to protect his song from the vulgar rout:

> What care I, if they praise my slender song?
> A shepherds blisse nor stands nor falls to ev'ry tongue.[43]

Fletcher desired the applause of his Cambridge fellows and the favorable attention of those who had offices to bestow. Beyond this audience, he desired no approval but that of God:

> Breath gracious Spirit, breath gently on these layes,
> Be thou my Compasse, Needle to my wayes,
> Thy glorious work's my Fraught, my Haven is thy prayse.[44]

Perhaps because of his indifference to the vulgar audience, Phineas Fletcher never quite decided between the conflicting merits of Latin and English as the medium for his art. There is at least one Latin parallel for nearly every type of English poem that Fletcher wrote.[45] *The Purple Island* is an exception to this rule, probably because of its original function as a sequel to the English *Christ's Victory*. In the case of his favorite work *Locustae,* there were three Latin versions as against one English treatment of the theme.

---

[40] Poetical Works, II, 14. [41] *Ibid.*, p. 16. [42] *Ibid.*, p. 17.
[43] *Ibid.*, p. 19. [44] Poetical Works, I, 129.
[45] Langdale, *Phineas Fletcher,* pp. 158–59.

Concerning the advantages and disadvantages of poetry as a career, Fletcher had the usual complaints to make:

> Of all the gifts that fair Parnassus uses,
> Onely scorn'd povertie, and fortunes hate
> Common I finde to me, and to the Muses:
> But with the Muses welcome poorest fate.[46]

Speaking of the classical poets, he calls them fortunate in two respects: the subject matter of poetry had not been so completely covered in their time as to afford no new themes, and they could look forward to a fair reward. But the present audience was neither appreciative nor generous:

> But wretched we, to whom these iron daies
> (Hard daies) afford nor matter, nor reward!
> Sings Maro? men deride high Maro's layes;
> Their hearts with lead, with steel their sense is barr'd.[47]

This audience listened only to the low, vulgar songs of a Bavius or Mævius. No one that liked such work could like true poetry. Witness the treatment of Spenser, who could not obtain his suit, who was discouraged and humiliated, who would not even have had a fitting burial had not Essex acted. At times the attitude toward poets seemed to him so shameful that he did not want to write at all,

> Yet when new spring her gentle rayes infuse,
>
> .   .   .   .
>
> I 'gin to chirp and sing:
> At length soft fires disperst in every vein,
> Yeeld open passage to the thronging train,
> And swelling numbers tide rolls like the surging main.[48]

Once again in the theory of the Fletchers we hear the familiar terms divine inspiration, high and low types of poetry, and the poetic office; but this time the theory is modified by the fact that the Fletchers were not primarily poets but ministers. Their efforts were directed mainly toward securing advancement in their chosen careers and only secondarily toward developing their poetic gift for its essential beauty or for its value to society. With the thesis that poetry was of heavenly origin they had no quarrel; yet they reserved a

[46] Poetical Works, II, 234.   [47] Ibid., p. 15.   [48] Ibid., p. 17.

higher place for the minister than for the poet. Their attitude is a far cry from the stubborn faith of Jonson or Drayton in the supremacy of the poetic office, and perhaps the truly clerical spirit can never quite comprehend the dream of mankind ennobled to godliness through the poet's art. Giles, the more intense and original spirit, eschewed that part of the poetic hierarchy that had no direct bearing on his religious interests; but Phineas, following his master Spenser, and, of course, his own inclination, made pleasant holiday among the shepherds, dallied in the temple of Venus, digressed to scourge his enemies, and approached his higher works by gradual and prescribed degrees.

CHAPTER VII

WILLIAM DAVENANT

THE SECOND poet laureate of England was worthy to succeed the far more gifted Ben Jonson in at least one respect, in the high purpose and clear principles of his theory of poetry. No very deep research is needed to disclose the main points of that theory, for the preface to *Gondibert* supplies most of Davenant's poetic creed. It is interesting to see how this completely formulated belief compares with those theories that have been assembled from the scattered pronouncements of his contemporaries.

In considering the source of poetry, Davenant is not impressed by the mystical experience of inspiration; he does not speak of the wondrous poetic rapture that so fascinated his older contemporaries. He is proud of poetry as an art of man rather than as a special gift of God. He censures Homer because

He often interrogates his Muse, not as his rational Spirit but as a Familiar, separated from his body.[1]

Davenant resented the arrogation of special divine guidance insisted upon by Wither and held him up to ridicule in *The Cruel Brother*:

> You, you must be a satirist forsooth!
> Calumniate by instinct and inspiration;
> As if just heaven would borrow gall of you,
> Wherewith to write our faults.[2]

In reducing poetry to a purely rational basis he was the disciple of Hobbes, who ridiculed the practice of poetic invocation because he could not understand why a man "enabled to speak wisely from the principles of nature and his own meditations loves rather to be thought to speak by inspiration, like a Bagpipe." [3] To Hobbes and to Davenant, as to Jonson, the origin of poetry lies in human experience. There is no direct, intuitive link between poetry and God;

---

[1] *Gondibert,* preface, p. 2.
[2] The Dramatic Works of Sir William Davenant, ed. by Maidment and Logan, I, 121.
[3] Preface to *Gondibert,* Hobbes' reply, p. 77.

the poet knows God, just as other men do, through His earthly manifestation in nature. Nature is God's first law to man,[4] and the poet is supreme on earth because he is the best expositor of nature.[5] Davenant liked to refer to the poet as nature's secretary.[6] From nature, which is the course of life as we know it, we can by experience reason out the ideal state of life originally intended for man, from which he has lapsed and toward which he should strive, a state characterized by purity in love, active courage, justice on the part of superiors, and loyalty among subordinates. For the individual it would be a state of virtue; for the civic body, a state of peace. The object of Davenant's greatest poetic effort was to draw a picture of perfect virtue that should serve not as a dim, superhuman ideal, but as an efficient and immediate model. He intended "to strip nature naked, and clothe her again in the perfect shape of virtue."

Although he normally worked in the medium of drama, for his greatest artistic effort Davenant chose heroic poetry, which "if exact in it self, yeelds not to any other humane work." [7] As he reviewed the contributions of previous epic poets to their art, he measured their "exactness" by how careful they had been to confine themselves to their proper function of analyzing and elevating human life. And no matter where he looked, he found no work that had completely adhered to this purpose: ". . . remembering with what difficulty the world can shew any Heroick Poem, that in a perfect glass of Nature gives us a familiar and easie view of our selves." [8]

He begins his study of epic development with Homer and lauds him as a great pioneer to whom all honor should be paid for having blazed a trail that is of the utmost help to succeeding poets. But the very merit of Homer has caused his followers to be content with "a perfection of imitating him." His achievement is a barrier to those who wish to try a new method, who are not satisfied "to stay and depend upon the authority of example." [9] The particular fault that Davenant has to find with Homer and the later writers who guided themselves closely by his procedure is a tendency to write of the supernatural. This is a double violation of Davenant's own

[4] Preface to *Gondibert*, p. 67.   [5] *Ibid.*, p. 64.
[6] *The Temple of Love*, Dramatic Works, II, 286. *Entertainment at Rutland House,* Dramatic Works, III, 212.
[7] Preface to *Gondibert*, p. 6.   [8] *Ibid.*, p. 1.   [9] *Ibid.*, p. 2.

theory, for he held a possible story to be both more pleasant and more instructive than an impossible one: "and story, where ever it seems most likely, growes most pleasant." [10] "He sometimes deprives us of those natural probabilities in a Story, which are instructive in humane life." [11] For the sake of probability a poet who is trying to reform society ought to avoid representing heaven and hell. He will reach his readers better through more familiar material. Certainly a Christian poet like Tasso, "whose Religion little needs the aids of Invention," had no reason to draw an imaginative picture of paradise and hell. Spenser, too, did not confine himself to the natural and therefore lost in usefulness. His allegorical story is too dreamlike. The moral visions and abstractions have not the force that human examples would carry.

The opposite error in poetry is illustrated by the work of Lucan, who followed contemporaneous truth with too close and too historical accuracy. The business of the poet is not to record a particular set of facts, but to generalize from his observation of mankind. He is an expert in character and passions, rather than a recorder of events:

for wise Poets think it more worthy to seek out truth in the Passions, then to record the truth of Actions; and practise to describe Mankinde just as we are perswaded or guided by instinct, not particular persons, as they are lifted, or levell'd by the force of Fate, it being nobler to contemplate the general history of Nature, then a selected Diary of Fortune. [12]

Lucan's fault is, however, relatively rare. Most of the epic poets, in their eagerness to follow Homer, have repeated his undesirable practice of using supernatural material. If the principle of imitation is adhered to overstrongly, it is impossible for anyone to progress beyond the original model. The examples of the ancients are not intended as goals but as guides: "Learning is not Knowledge but a continued progress toward it." [13] Fredoline, in "The Platonic Lovers," has the practical man's contempt for the accomplishments of scholarship; his comment on the achievements of science parallels Davenant's attitude toward art:

> Since your great Master Aristotle died,
> . . . what have you done?

---

[10] Preface to *Gondibert*, p. 2.   [11] *Ibid.*, p. 3.

[12] *Ibid.*, p. 4.   [13] *Ibid.*, p. 9.

Wrote comments on his works, 'light! I could beat
You all. Have you so many ages toil'd
T'interpret what he writ in a few years?
Is there yet nothing new, to render benefit
For human life? [14]

In his own epic, Davenant proposed to depart from the accepted heroic model wherever necessary in order to satisfy his own theory of usefulness and pleasure. The characters were to be Christian persons, since their example would be most effective with an audience of similar doctrine. Davenant found, furthermore, that early Christianity provided the very code of justice and honor that he wanted; it was designed to further the general welfare of men as individuals and in states. To avoid being bound by factual truth, he set his action in the dim past:

Truth narrative, and past, is the Idol of Historians, . . . and truth operative, and by effects continually alive, is the Mistris of Poets, who hath not her existence in matter, but in reason. [15]

He was shrewd enough to realize that men prefer hearing the virtues of predecessors rather than of contemporaries. Audiences are incredulous or envious in their attitude toward modern virtue, and he wanted their complete sympathy for the characters and their easy acceptance of the action. Because men tend to underestimate that which is native and to value more highly that which is foreign, he set his scene in Italy. Only comic poets teach through the use of local and contemporary representation.

Davenant's heroes have learned their morality in the court and in the camp. At this point in his discussion, Davenant explains that armies, though they would not be needed in a perfect world, are highly important in the world as it is constituted today, in order to control that monster, the multitude. The problem of controlling the multitude is variously approached by four groups: divines, leaders of armies, statesmen, and judges. Each of these groups would be more successful if it used the aid of poetry. [16] The churchmen are foolish to refuse the help of moralists, and poets are the most useful moralists, since they sweeten the lesson, thereby counterbalancing the repellent austerity of religion.[17] Generals ought to remember that poetic praise is a valuable reward of victory. The poet can also supply models of judgment and courage that strongly stimulate the imitative instinct in man. Statesmen and judges have foolishly frowned on poetry, forgetting that to work on the people's mind by persuasion there are none better than poets, for they educate the people and appeal to them by reason, they provide much-needed diversion and mirth: "Poets (who with wise diligence study the People, and have in all ages by an insensible influence governed their manners) may justly smile if Divines, Generals, Statesmen, Judges think to have good government without the muses." [18]

Davenant makes a sharp distinction between the heroic and other kinds of poetry. For the education of the general run of the people there are several kinds of poetry, of which the dramatic has been the most successful. When plays were banned, Davenant still insisted on the value of "Moral presentations as public entertainment," [19] even if they did not take the pleasant dramatic form.[20] As he gives no details concerning the other types suitable for the public, it is probable that he had in mind the analysis of Hobbes, which divided poetry into epic, tragedy, satire, comedy, bucolics, and pastoral comedy. Davenant did not consider the general populace sufficiently prepared to profit by heroic poetry,

which hath a force that overmatches the infancy of such minds as are not enabled by degrees of Education; but there are lesser forces in other kinds of Poesy, by which they may train and prepare their understandings.[21]

Thus the pattern taken from court and camp in *Gondibert* is not intended to teach virtue directly to all. It is a model fit to be imitated by "the most necessary men," the leaders by birth, education, and magnanimity. The multitude is to be governed by law and force, not directed by heroic example except as they imitate the example set by their princes and nobles who have been reformed by heroic poetry: [22]

The common Crowd (of whom we are hopelesse) we desert, being rather to be corrected by laws (where precept is accompanied with punishment)

---

[17] *Ibid.*, p. 64. [18] *Ibid.*, p. 47.
[19] *Entertainment at Rutland House*, Dramatic Works, III, 199.
[20] *Ibid.*, p. 229. [21] Preface to *Gondibert*, p. 60. [22] *Ibid.*

then to be taught by Poetry. . . . Nor is it needful that Heroick Poesy should be levell'd to the reach of Common men.[23]

Gondibert is designed to portray the noble passions of love and ambition and the undesirable results arising from a distemper of either. The intention of Davenant is to supply a lofty yet practical code of ethics. He has no use for the passive spiritual detachment and "melancholy precept of the Cloister." [24] The good should be ambitiously active; [25] they should be encouraged in the vigorous use of their God-given reason. They should strive to enjoy the best things in nature and help others to do so. God is no tyrant who resents the honest happiness of men. Poets should not be censured for praising beauty and encouraging love, for beauty is a work of God and love is nature's necessary prelude to the making of new life. The poet quite rightly tries to elevate and ennoble the relationship between man and woman. Love, moreover, is a necessary palliative of courage; honor that has known no touch of its softening influence is harsh, untempered, crude. This rough honor is represented in *The Platonic Lovers* by the comic character Gridonell, who has had no knowledge of women either in life or books. More seriously the theme of the perfect blending of gentleness and strength, and the function of poetry in promoting this ideal combination, is given in *Love and Honour:*

> O thou hast lost thy heart! hence doth proceed
> This recreant act, that to thy savage courage
> I could never join the temperature
> Of sweet philosophy. Had'st thou been learn'd,
> And read the noble deeds of gentle knights,
> Reason had checked thy rage, thy valour would
> Have been more pitiful than to have led
> A virgin into harsh captivity.[26]

In *Britannia Triumphans* Davenant had early indicated the role of poetry in stimulating heroic virtue. The name Bellerophon is given to the character representing heroic virtue, to suggest that it is the function of poetry to bring this heavenly quality to earth. Imposture recognizes Bellerophon in the following speech:

---

[23] Preface to *Gondibert*, p. 18.   [24] *Ibid.*, p. 19.
[25] Compare *Britannia Triumphans*, Dramatic Works, II, 277.
[26] Dramatic Works, III, 109. Cf. also p. 110.

> Cry mercy, Sir!
> You are heroic virtue, who pretend
> An embassy from heaven, and that y'are sent
> To make new lovers here on earth; you will
> Refine the ways of wooing, and prescribe
> To valour nobler exercise than what
> The ancient knights' adventurers taught.[27]

The distempers of love and ambition will not be shown in low and contemptible persons nor in horrifying extremes, since either of these presentations would weaken the applicability of the lesson.

In modifying the form of his epic, Davenant was influenced by his observation that the most pleasant and instructive representations of great actions had been achieved by the English playwrights. He desired to combine the effectiveness of drama with the acknowledged beauty and highest excellence of the heroic poem; therefore he followed dramatic form by planning his epic in five books that should be similar in function to the five acts of a play.[28] The cantos were to be equivalent to scenes.

His choice of stanza was determined by several considerations. In discussing Spenser, Davenant expressed his belief that it was Spenser's unlucky choice of a stanza requiring much rime that forced him to use obsolete language. Certainly Davenant burdened himself with no such difficulty when he chose an alternately riming four-lined stanza. He liked the plainness and brevity that the quatrain tended to produce and he did not feel that the alternate rime made the sound less heroic. He particularly desired a form in which there would be a pause after a brief period, since that rendered the poem better fit for being sung in *stilo recitativo*, a fate that Davenant hoped would befall it. The music of poetry itself did not greatly interest Davenant; he was far more concerned with the fascinating possibilities of employing music as an auxiliary, rather than improving it as a component of verse. He expounds his theory of *stilo recitativo* in *The Playhouse To Be Let*. The musician has a novelty to offer:

> I would have introduced heroique story
> In *Stilo Recitativo*.

---

[27] *Britannia Triumphans*, Dramatic Works, II, 276.   [28] Preface to *Gondibert*, p. 23.

The player argues that it is silly to sing what would naturally be spoken, but the musician informs him more fully:

> Recitative music is not compos'd
> Of matter so familiar, as may serve
> For every low occasion of discourse.
> In tragedy, the language of the stage
> Is rais'd above the common dialect;
> Our passions rising with the height of verse;
> And vocal music adds new wings to all
> The flights of poetry.[29]

Davenant's simple statement that the substance out of which he had woven the poem was "wit" may cause the student difficulty unless he remembers that the term wit, although frequently used as opposed to judgment, sometimes, as in this case, included judgment and was used to express the combined fanciful and limiting elements in composition. The wit of *Gondibert* covers both "the laborious and lucky resultances of thought." [30] Davenant is groping toward a clear distinction of the effects of each component which he does not fully realize:

All things proceed from chance or care; those proceeding from chance are accomplishments of an instant and have a dissimilitude; those from care are the works of time, and have their contextures alike.[31]

This is not so sharp and certain as Hobbes's theory, which clearly divides the creative source of memory into its products, judgment and fancy—judgment, which provides the strength and structure of a work, and fancy, which yields the ornaments.

Although Davenant is brief and perfunctory in his attempt to distinguish the swift from the slow element in poetic composition, he expands with assurance the statement that poetic wit is an epitome of the attributes required in all other professions:

It [Wit] is in Divines, Humility, Exemplarinesse and Moderation; in Statesmen, Gravity, Vigilance, Benigne Complacency, Secrecy, Patience and Dispatch: in Leaders of Armies, Valor, Painfulness, Temperance, Bounty, Dexterity in punishing and rewarding, and a sacred Certitude of Promise. It is in Poets, a full comprehension of all recited in all these; and an ability to bring those comprehensions into action, when they shall so far forget the true

---

[29] *The Playhouse To Be Let*, Dramatic Works, IV, 23.
[30] Preface to *Gondibert*, p. 26.   [31] *Ibid.*

measure of what is of greatest consequence to humanity (which are things righteous pleasant and usefull) as to think the delights of greatness equal to that of Poesy; or the Chiefs of any Profession more necessary to the world, then excellent Poets.[32]

This declaration of poetic scope and responsibility has the right Jonsonian flavor.

In a final effort to clarify the concept of poetic wit he turns, as Cowley has done, to the question of what is not wit. It is not mere dexterity with words, a musical fall of sound, conceits or epigrams written with no clear view of the subject. It is not partiality toward the past, nor the kind of gravity that automatically condemns youth and beauty.[33] Although wit provides a delightful leavening of philosophy, it is not unseemly levity and is a perfectly proper ornament of the heroic muse.[34]

Nowhere does Davenant sound more strikingly like Jonson than in his discussion of the composition of poetry and the discipline of the poet. The true poet must be a mature artist. The Davenant of *Gondibert* pronounces worthless all his early "hasty digestions of thought."[35] "You must not entertain a Nation (who are a Poets standing Guest and require Monarchicall respect) with hasty provisions."[36] The poet must be willing to take pains and perfect his work. Davenant is like Jonson in his belief that the poet should be well-informed and should use clear, intelligible language to convey the information to an audience. It might almost be Jonson who writes that his endeavor is "in bringing Truth (too often absent) home to mens bosoms, to lead her through unfrequented and new ways, and from the most remote Shades, by representing Nature, though not in an affected, yet in an unusual dress."[37]

Like Cowley, Davenant entered the field of poetry chiefly for the love of fame. Nor did he consider love of fame a vain longing. Good reputation is a commodity much desired by the living; it is a first taste of eternity. To the dead, it is "a musical glory" in which God shares, for they are praised for their godly works. Some poets write from conscience. In their unfortunate zeal they are likely to depict God as a terrible foe. Davenant had the deepest respect for

---

[32] Preface to *Gondibert*, p. 27. [33] *Ibid.*, p. 28.
[34] *Ibid.*, p. 3. Cf. *The Platonic Lovers*, Dramatic Works, II, 64.
[35] *Ibid.*, p. 31. [36] *Ibid.* [37] *Ibid.*, p. 30.

religious poetry, but he believed in restricting it to the sure ground of praise:

Poesy is the clearest light by which they find the soul who seek it . . . for divine Praise (when in the high perfection, as in Poets, and only in them) is so much the uttermost and whole of Religious worship, that all other parts of Devotion serve but to make it up.[38]

The only part of his work that he quotes reinforces this point:

Praise, is Devotion fit for mighty Mindes;
The diff'ring World's agreeing Sacrifice
Where Heaven divided Faiths united findes;
But Pray'r in various discord upward flyes.[39]

The religious impulse and experience of the Christian world finds its highest, most universally valid utterance in the poetic offering of praise.

Davenant's theory concerning poetic types other than the heroic is notable for its indifference toward the lyric. His volume of occasional verse contains few lyrics, and the songs in his plays have small merit as poetry and were confessedly interpolated to pander to the public taste [40] in much the same spirit as the amazing acrobatics of the priest's attendant in the *Cruelty of the Spaniards in Peru*. The theory of Hobbes gave the lyric short shrift, and Davenant saw no reason to go counter to the philosopher on this point. The love poem, with its lavish embroidering of emotion, had no appeal for this exponent of high and heroic passion. He refers to poets who specialize in such lyrics as "silly Priests" of lovers.[41]

Satire had his endorsement as a type, although his own effort in that direction was light. In his castigation of Wither, he takes care to make it clear that it was Wither's special manner of satire that he was ridiculing:

Satires are more useful now than ever.
Nor grieves it me to see the humour us'd,
But thus abus'd.[42]

---

[38] Preface to *Gondibert*, p. 42.
[39] *Ibid.*, p. 43, quoted from *Gondibert*, Bk. II, Canto 6.
[40] *The Wits*, Dramatic Works, I, 226.
[41] The Works of Sr William D'avenant K^t, p. 232.
[42] *The Cruel Brother*, Dramatic Works, I, 141.

He praises a Mr. Ogilby for satirical writing that fits Jonson's borrowed and well-loved formula of assailing the fault and not the person:

> Or as thy Muse in her Satyrick strain
> Doth spare the person, whilst the Vice is slain.[43]

Davenant's attitude toward romances may readily be deduced from his belief that poetry ought to eschew supernatural subject matter. He used the giants, squires, ladies, knights, and dwarfs as the basis for farce in *The Playhouse To Be Let*:

> What think you
> Of romances travestie?
>
> .   .   .   .
>
> The garments of our fathers you must wear
> The wrong side outward
>   the mock-heroique must be it
> Which draws the pleasant hither i'th' vacation.[44]

His attempt to parody the heroic vein in *Jeffereidos,* though not completed or especially successful, is significant as an unexalted use of the heroic couplet.

Davenant's theory of drama has been well treated by Alfred Harbage in his book *Sir William Davenant*. Little, therefore, is required, except to emphasize a few significant details. As in his epic, the "turns, counter-turns, double walks, and interweavings of design" in Davenant's serious plays were utilized to illustrate various aspects of love and honor.[45] He felt that he had furthered the reform of the stage:

for as others have purg'd the stage from corruptions of the art of the drama, so I have endeavour'd to cleanse it from the corruption of manners: nor have I wanted care to render the ideas of greatness and virtue pleasing and familiar.[46]

He had contracted to provide "not only harmless delights, but useful and instructive representations of human life." [47] More specifically, he hoped through the theater to achieve his general aim for worthy

---

[43] Works, p. 309.
[44] Dramatic Works, IV, 28.
[45] *Siege of Rhodes*, Dramatic Works, III, 234.
[46] *Ibid.*, p. 258.
[47] Nicoll, *A History of Restoration Drama: 1660–1700*, p. 286.

poetry and to heighten "the characters of valour, temperance, natural justice, and complacency to government." [48]

In comedy, Davenant followed the general theory of Jonson to the extent of believing that comedy should aim to correct humors. Like Jonson, he set little value on purely farcical writing, although occasionally he was forced back on it by the hard theatrical conditions of his day. The very Frenchman who produces the farce in *The Playhouse To Be Let* comments:

> De vise nation bi for tings heroique,
> And de fantastique, vor de farce. [49]

And Davenant admits that farce is a commercial necessity for him:

> But, till the nation be more civiliz'd,
> Your Fool and Devil may be entertain'd;
> They'll get the money; none now but very choice
> Spectators will vouchsafe to see a play
> Without'm. [50]

He was well aware that he had compromised repeatedly in an effort to retain his audience; yet he never gave in completely. To the end he insisted on some moral value:

> The Muse, disdain'd, does as fond women do;
> Instead of being courted she courts you:
>
> .   .   .   .
>
> Well, our old poet hopes this comedie
> Will some what in the fine new fashion be;
> But if all gay, 'twould not with age agree.
>
> A little he was fain to moralize
> That he might serve your mind as well as eyes:
> The proverb says, "Be merry and be wise." [51]

In the attitude he assumed toward an audience, Davenant was strongly influenced by Jonson. The first act of *The Playhouse To Be Let*, with its tirewoman, charwoman, actor, and various applicants, has the quality of Jonson's familiar explanatory dialogues. Davenant's prologue, like those of the older playwright, comments on unfriendly factions, the audience's habit of overexpectation, the

[48] *Siege of Rhodes*, Dramatic Works, III, 235.   [49] Dramatic Works, IV, 18.
[50] *The Playhouse To Be Let*, Dramatic Works, IV, 24.
[51] *The Man's the Master*, Dramatic Works, V, 7.

desire of some spectators to demonstrate their wit by criticizing adversely:

> And still the reputation of their wit grows strong
> As they can first contemn be't right or wrong.[52]

He exhibits a good degree of contempt for the audience,[53] combined with the rueful realization that they hold the whip hand.[54] He was, above all, a practical man and he rather easily resigned himself to including whatever dross he deemed necessary to make his plays popular:

> Th' allay's coarse metal makes the finer last
> Which else would in the people's handling waste.
> So country jigs and farces mixt among
> Heroic scenes make plays continue long.[55]

Restoration literature is all too frequently associated with licentiousness and immorality. While these qualities unquestionably characterize the last quarter of the century, they were not rampant earlier. In fact, a quite opposite atmosphere prevailed in which the emphasis was heavily on heroic virtue and the hope that through poetry it might be made increasingly a part of life. As Harbage reminds us in speaking of Davenant's efforts in the heroic vein, "These works too, in their mistaken way, have wrought in the cause of sweetness and light." [56] Although Davenant did not, like Jonson, publish a complete edition of his works during his own lifetime, we know from Herringman's statement that he longed to see a one-volume collection of all the pieces he had designed for the press. If, on Davenant's own authority, we dismiss as worthless all his hasty youthful efforts, the remaining portion of his work, though mediocre as poetry, is devoted to the lofty aim of improving the human race by pleasant persuasion. Perhaps for that alone Davenant deserves the modest reward he aspired to:

> And I deserve a little sprig of Bay
> To weare in Greece on Homers Holy-day.[57]

---

[52] *The Unfortunate Lovers*, Dramatic Works, III, 84.
[53] *The Man's the Master*, Dramatic Works, V, 107.
[54] *The Wits*, Dramatic Works, I, 243.   [55] *Ibid.*, p. 226.
[56] Harbage, *Sir William Davenant*, p. 250.   [57] Davenant, Works (1673), p. 213.

CHAPTER VIII

ABRAHAM COWLEY

IN A DOCTORAL DISSERTATION on *Abraham Cowley: sa vie, son œuvre*, Loiseau concludes that Cowley, whose contemporaries hailed him almost unanimously as "the prince of poets," was highly esteemed in his own age because both in personality and writing he was thoroughly representative of that age.[1] A supplementary publication, *Abraham Cowley's Reputation in England*,[2] affords ample proof that however diverse critical opinions on Cowley may be, they are all in agreement as to one point: that in him all the literary tendencies of his age found brilliant and conscious expression. For the purpose of this study, then, Cowley is an ideal subject. The poetry of this many-sided gentleman, who was scholar, writer, royal secretary, scientist, and Sabine farmer, covers almost the whole seventeenth-century range of subject matter and style, and in the explanatory prefaces and notes which he affixed to many of his works, there is a mine of direct information on his literary theories.

In the preface to his collected works (1656), Cowley, explaining his intended withdrawal from the practice of poetry, gives as one reason that his mind is not now fit for the "exercise or divertisement" of poetry:

There is nothing that requires so much serenity and chearfulness of Spirit. The Soul must be filled with bright and delightful Idoeas when it undertakes to communicate delight to others; which is the main end of Poesie.[3]

The desirability of instructive subject matter is set forth in *A Proposition for the Advancement of Experimental Philosophy:*

the truth is we want good Poets (I mean we have but few) who have purposely treated of solid and learned, that is, Natural Matters (the most part indulging to the weakness of the world and feeding it either with the follies of Love, or with the Fables of gods and Heroes).[4]

---

[1] Loiseau, *Abraham Cowley*, Introduction, p. ix.
[2] Loiseau, *Abraham Cowley's Reputation in England*.
[3] Poems of Abraham Cowley, ed. by Waller, p. 7.
[4] Essays, Plays and Sundry Verses of Abraham Cowley, ed. by Waller, p. 256.

Here, separately stated, are the pleasure and instruction of Horatian doctrine, and Cowley subscribes himself a full disciple by combining them so as to provide for the double aim:

> If Life should a well-order'd Poem be
> (In which he only hits the white
> Who joyns true Profit with the best Delight).[5]

He clearly places the emphasis where Horace implied it, on the purpose of delight. The choice of poetry as a medium of expression is *ipso facto* evidence of an attempt to present the informative element pleasingly. Furthermore, as Cowley noted, the practice of the great poets has leaned more to delight than to instruction.

Cowley's works exemplified all the purposes indicated by Horace. *The Mistress* had no other aim than pure delight. His Latin poem on plants combined a maximum of instruction with a minimum of pleasure. The ideal combination of the purposive and pleasurable aims seemed to him to lie in the field of religious poetry, and the introduction to the *Davideis* presents a powerful argument for the religious epic as the ultimate and loftiest type. Scripture, said Cowley, affords many magnificent subjects, "in the wise managing and illustrating whereof, the Glory of God Almighty might be joined with the singular utility and noblest delight of Mankind."[6] In stressing the communication of delight as the main purpose of poetry, Cowley is more akin to Browne, Herrick, and Carew than to poets like Drayton, Wither, Milton, and the Fletchers, who considered this "delight" a characteristic of poetry which enabled it to fulfill other more important functions.

Consistent with his purpose is Cowley's comment on the conditions desirable for the writing of poetry:

a warlike, various, and a tragical age is best to write of but worst to write in.[7]

The Truth is, for a man to write well, it is necessary to be in good humor; neither is Wit less eclipsed with the unquietness of Mind, then Beauty with the Indisposition of Body. So that 'tis almost as hard a thing to be a Poet in despight of Fortune, as it is in despight of Nature.[8]

---

[5] *Ibid.*, p. 391.
[7] *Ibid.*, p. 7.
[6] Poems of Abraham Cowley, p. 12.
[8] *Ibid.*, p. 7.

Indeed, he goes so far as to insist that the only place to write poetry
of any value is the country:

The truth is, no other place is proper for their work; one might as well
undertake to Dance in a Crowd, as to make good Verses in the midst of
Noise and Tumult.[9]

Cowley's view of the relationship of the poet to his art, as ex-
pressed in the Preface to the 1656 edition of his *Works*, is singularly
cool, detached, judicial, and scientific. He felt that he had "married
poetry too young before I realized those more profitable matches
which I might have made among the richer Sciences." Consequently
"the decay of his affection to Poesie" was not to be wondered at.
This edition was the "fruit of his resolve never to practise poetry
more." The very choice of words in these remarks on poetry is
cold. One thinks of a practicing physician, but hardly of a prac-
ticing poet. His inclusion of poetry among the sciences, even though
he later distinguishes it as the "Divine science," is striking. He ac-
knowledges the singularity of his attitude toward poetry in words
that sound most unlike the Muse-worshiping Elizabethans, "when
once we fall in love with that bewitching Art, we do not use to
court it as a Mistress, but Marry it as a wife." [10] It is not hard to
account for this peculiar tone. As certain "rules" of poetry began
to emerge, it seemed for a while as if art, like Bacon's vision of
science, could be reduced to formulae by analysis of the works of
acknowledged poets. This possibility tended to remove the mys-
terious, ineffable concept of poetry. The worship of the muses gave
place to the gallant or prosaic wooing of poetry, in which the author
felt complacently sure of success. Just as the Elizabethan delighted
in poetic "raptures," so the typical Caroline poet distrusted them as
defying analysis and logical criticism and, consequently, imitation.
Notice Cowley's tribute to the poet he admired most, Vergil:

> Whose verse walks highest but not flies
> Who brought green Poesie to her perfect Age;
> And made that Art which was a Rage.[11]

In the same way, although Cowley recognized the exalted nature
of the office of the poet, he was also well aware of certain serious

9 Essays, Plays and Sundry Verses, p. 405.
10 Poems of Abraham Cowley, p. 6.   11 *Ibid.*, p. 15.

drawbacks attaching to the poetic career. One of these he attempted to obviate by his 1656 edition, namely, that the works of poets, if posthumously printed, were very largely at the mercy of their editors.[12] Cowley considered that by deliberately terminating his poetical career, he could have the great advantage of being his own editor.

Cowley's second complaint against poetry is that it is an unprofitable career:

> Though other Arts poor and neglected grow
> . . . Po'esie . . . was always so.[13]

Alupis, a somewhat autobiographical character in *The Guardian*, speaks of that prime madman, the poet, who depends for a precarious living on the noble deaths or marriages to be commemorated.[14] Further on, this same merry shepherd, Alupis, observes in a song

> 'Tis better to dance than sing
> The cause is if you will know it,
> That I to my selfe shall bring
> A Poverty
> Voluntary
> If once I grow but a Poet.[15]

That this is not merely the mood of his play is shown in the "Ode on Lord Broghill's Verses," and in the preface to *The Guardian* [16] in both of which Cowley complains that he has given up much to serve the muse, but has never been repaid.[17] He remarks, too, that at the Restoration the dews of Charles's bounty were not quite universal:

> Enriching moisture drop'd on everything
> And nothing but the Muses Fleece was dry.[18]

Except at the very beginning of his career as a poet, Cowley derived relatively slight satisfaction from the prospect of posthumous fame. He started with the Elizabethan coveting of immortality, of leaving a deathless name. The conventional attitude toward fame is reflected everywhere in his early works. We get the lisping echoes of his models in "Pyramus and Thisbe," who "have left their loves to Fame." The theme is unmistakable in "Constantia and Philetus":

[12] Poems of Abraham Cowley, p. 5.   [13] *Ibid.*, p. 31.
[14] Essays, Plays and Sundry Verses, p. 72.   [15] *Ibid.*, p. 82.
[16] *Ibid.*, pp. 265–66.
[17] Poems of Abraham Cowley, pp. 406–7.   [18] *Ibid.*, p. 437.

> Heere stay my Muse, for if I should recite
>   Her mournefull Language, I should make you weep
> . . . and so not see to write,
>   Such lines as I and th' age requires to keepe
>   Mee from sterne death, or with victorious rime,
>   Revenge their Masters death, and conquer time.[19]

At nineteen, he wrote, in the introduction to his *Poetical Blossoms*, "he is the worst homicide who strives to Murther anothers fame." [20] In the poem to his godfather, Cowley stresses the hope of immortalizing his name.[21] He has the best of grounds for this expectation in the authority as well as the example of his beloved Horace, whom he broadly paraphrases:

> 'Tis not a Tombe cut out in Brasse, which can
>   Give life to th' ashes of a man,
> But Verses onely; they shall fresh appeare,
>   Whil'st there are men to reade, or heare.
>
> .   .   .   .
>
> Poets by death are conquered, but the wit
>   Of Poets triumphs over it.[22]

As further evidence, he cites Vergil's deathless fame.[23] In his early poem "The Motto" it is for the sake of fame that he turns to poetry:

> What shall I do to be for ever known
>   And make the Age to come my own? [24]

He is not great by birth or wealth; therefore he will be "the Muse's Hannibal" and under her banner will conquer all obstacles and win renown. In the "Praise of Pindar" he expresses the usual corollary of the main theory: namely, that the poet could confer fame on others and save their names from death by his power. The favored subject shall

> . . . Live and Grow in fame
> Among the Stars he sticks his Name:
> The Grave can but the Dross of him devour,
> So small is Deaths, so great the Poets power.[25]

This power extends to inanimate things too, and becomes the basis of the excellent conceit in the poem on Drake's chair:

---

[19] Poems of Abraham Cowley, p. 13.   [20] Essays, Plays and Sundry Verses, p. 3.
[21] *Ibid.*, p. 53.   [22] *Ibid.*, p. 59.   [23] *Ibid.*, p. 41.
[24] Poems of Abraham Cowley, p. 15.   [25] *Ibid.*, p. 178.

Great Relique . . .
Hast still one way of Making Voyages
The breath of fame, like an auspicious Gale
Shall drive thee round the World . . .
. . . steer the endless course of vast Eternitie,
Take for thy Sail this Verse, and for thy Pilot Mee.[26]

As with their frequent references to the gods and the muses, seventeenth-century poets paid lip service to the idol of poetic fame long after they had come to distrust its godhead. Admirer of Horace though he was, Cowley could not rest content in contemplation of *monumentum aere perennius*. For one reason, he was also a disciple of Anacreon:

After death I nothing crave.
Let me Alive my pleasures have.[27]

The ever-present good sense of Cowley, the instinct that made him cultivate above all things the fine art of living, made him realize that such fame was a "Posthumous and imaginary happiness." [28] The Muse

. . . rewardest but with popular breath
And that too, after death.[29]

One of his essays summarizes the case for fame with shrewd practicality:

I love and commend a true good Fame, because it is the shadow of Virtue, not that it doth any good to the Body which it accompanies, but 'tis an efficacious shadow, and . . . cures the Diseases of others. The best kind of Glory . . . is that which is reflected from Honesty . . . but it . . . is seldom beneficial to any man whilst he lives, what it is to him after his death, I cannot say, because I love not Philosophy merely notional and conjectural, and no man who has made the Experiment has been so kind as to come back and inform us.[30]

The furthest departure from the worship of poetic immortality occurs in his poem on "Life and Fame":

We poets madder yet than all
Think we not only Have, but Give Eternitie,
Fain would I see that Prodigal,

[26] Poems of Abraham Cowley, p. 413.   [27] *Ibid.*, p. 56.   [28] *Ibid.*, p. 6.
[29] *Ibid.*, p. 440.   [30] Essays, Plays and Sundry Verses, p. 399.

> Who his To-morrow would bestow,
> For all old Homers Life e're since he dy'ed till now.[31]

Finally, in commenting on the abuses of poetry, Cowley touches on the practice of using it to build "vain Pyramids to mortal pride." [32]

But posthumous fame, whatever its worth, was the only reward that the poet might expect from his art. In his "Complaint," the Muse reproaches Cowley for having sought the world

> . . . when I meant t'adopt thee for my Son,
>
> .   .   .   .
>
> When I resolv'd t'exalt thy anointed Name,
> Among the Spiritual Lords of peaceful Fame.[33]

Again, in his praise of Orinda, Cowley by pointing out her superior chances for fame, inasmuch as poetesses were rarer than poets, stresses the desirability of such "Glory managed by the Pen." [34]

Among the other differences that distinguish a poet from ordinary men is his willingness to gamble on the future and his ability to derive a present satisfaction from the contemplation of the fair promised land of fame. But even this slight happiness is partly destroyed by the vicious attacks of ignorant critics:

> the Muse reply'd
> That she had given me Fame
> Bounty Immense! And that too must be try'd,
> When I my self am nothing but a name.
> Who now, what Reader does not strive
> T' invalidate the gift whilst w'are alive?
> For when a Poet now himself doth show,
> As if he were a common Foe,
> All draw upon him, all around,
> And every part of him they wound,
> Happy the Man that gives the deepest blow:
> And this is all, kind Muse, to thee we owe.[35]

Criticism was beginning to be a popular rage. In both the preface and the prologue to *The Guardian*, Cowley alludes to this new plague of the poet, the amateur critic.

A final disadvantage that attaches to poetry is the trick that the

---

[31] Poems of Abraham Cowley, pp. 202, 203.   [32] *Ibid.*, p. 48.
[33] *Ibid.*, p. 436.   [34] *Ibid.*, p. 442.
[35] *Ibid.*, p. 407. Cf. Essays, Plays and Sundry Verses, p. 265.

ignorant have of judging a poet's life by his writings. Cowley banters his audience:

It is not in this sense that Poesie is said to be a kind of Painting; it is not the Picture of the Poet, but of things and persons imagined by him. . . . He professes too much the use of Fables (though without the malice of deceiving) to have his testimony taken even against himself.[36]

To recapitulate, Cowley considered that the career of a poet had decided disadvantages: it was poorly compensated; it was the object of vicious attacks by critics; the reward of fame was posthumous and enjoyed only in imagination; it led to unwarranted deductions as to the poet's character. And yet Cowley cultivated his poetical gift, in spite of the many other interests and talents that he possessed. In the "Complaint" he pictures himself delightfully as an unwilling victim of the muse, stolen in infancy, rebelling in verse against the tyranny of verse, lost to more gainful pursuits because of her spell. But again, in a stronger mood, he accepts his birthright proudly:

> Me from the womb the Midwife Muse did take:
> She cut my Navel, washt me, and mine Head
> With her own Hands she Fashioned,
>
> .   .   .   .
>
> Thou of my Church shalt be,
> Hate and renounce (said she)
> Wealth, Honor, Pleasures, all the World for Me.
> Thou neither great at Court, nor in the War,
> Nor at th'Exchange shalt be, nor at the wrangling Bar.
> Content thy self with the small Barren Praise,
> That neglected Verse does raise
>
> .   .   .   .
>
> Do thou nor grieve nor blush to be
> As all th'inspired tuneful Men,
> And all thy great Forefathers were from Homer down to Ben.[37]

Rarely, however, does Cowley exalt the poetic office as in his passionate eulogy on Crashaw:

> Poet and Saint! to thee alone are given
> The two most sacred Names of Earth and Heaven.[38]

---

[36] Poems of Abraham Cowley, p. 10.   [37] Ibid., p. 193.
[38] Ibid., p. 48.

It is tempting to guess at the reason for Cowley's disillusioned estimate of the genus *poet*. He was a very precocious and observant boy, as witness his satire on the law courts. His first introduction to poets had been to the classical and revered figures of Vergil, Horace, and Ovid, magnified by the long perspective of centuries. At fifteen he was an acknowledged poet, probably seeking out his own kind and welcome among them. Sharp indeed must have been the contrast between his schoolboy models and some of the less fortunate specimens of his brethren in art. Alupis is surely a mouthpiece for Cowley and he claims to have learnt all his wit and knowledge of the world by a three years' residence in the city (Cowley had been at Westminster just three years) during which he wasted all his money on pseudo captains and poets.[39] It is noteworthy that when, a few years later, Cowley had to turn out a play in mad haste for Prince Charles's visit to Cambridge, the two comedy butts were a pseudo captain, Worm, and a poet, Dogrel. Cowley had two concepts of a poet: the traditional one and the conflicting picture arising from his own experience with poetasters. Both are indicated in the following passage, but, as it occurs in a comedy, the higher concept is interrupted as soon as it has been hinted at.

> You have a vice call'd Poesie which much
> Displeaseth me, but no matter for that neither.
> *Alupis:* Alas! Hee'le leave that straight
> When he has got but money;
> Besides, when he hath married Hylace
> Whom should he wooe, to praise her comely feature?
>
> .   .   .   .
>
> oh! those vanities,
> Things quite as light, and foolish as a Mistris,
> Are by a Mistris first begot, and left
> When they leave her.
> *Pol:* Why doe you thinke that Poesie
> An art which even the gods. . . .[40]

We have seen that the purpose of Cowley's poetry was primarily the giving of delight to his audience, that he regarded the poet as a man who contrived to give the world delight in spite of its churlish

[39] Essays, Plays and Sundry Verses, p. 98.
[40] *Ibid.*, p. 123.

acceptance of his present. What theories did Cowley hold as to the nature of this art? Wherein did the delight lie? Was there a general formula for its production or a different one for each different genre? Strangely enough, the same fundamental principles underlie all of his varied works. Invariably there is an appeal to the intellect of the reader through ideas expressed with vigor, ease, and clarity amounting occasionally to brilliance, and neatly articulated within a shell of perfect unity; all of this tempered by excellent taste and a saving sense of humor. In the terminology of the day, his formula was the union of wit and judgment in proper proportions. The requisites for the composition of all poetry include "fertility of Invention, wisdom of Disposition, Judgment in the observance of decencies, lustre and vigor of Elocution, modestie and majestie of number." [41] The same idea is expressed with even more detail in describing the equipage of the Muse:

> Unruly Phansie with strong Judgment trace,
>   Put in nimble-footed Wit,
>   Smooth-pac'd Eloquence joyn with it,
> Sound Memory with young Invention place. [42]

Nature is to be the postilion and Art the coachman; the attending footmen are figures, conceits, raptures, sentences, innocent loves, pleasant truths, and useful lies.

The most interesting and difficult of these elements to define and handle, the one that is most essentially poetical, is wit. Cowley's definition of wit and his thorough destruction of any false ideas concerning it is very important:

> 'Tis not to force some lifeless Verses meet
>   With their five gouty feet
> All ev'ry where, like Mans, must be the Soul
> And Reason the Inferior Powers controul.
>
> Yet 'tis not to adorn, and gild each part;
>   That shows more Cost, then Art.
> Jewels at the Nose and Lips but ill appear;
> Rather then all things Wit, let none be there. [43]

---

[41] Poems of Abraham Cowley, p. 14.   [42] Ibid., p. 184.
[43] Ibid., p. 17.

Neither, Cowley continues, is wit punning or anagrammatic writing or obscenity or indecency. It is not strong, "mighty" lines, nor bombastic metaphors, nor pithy wisdom, nor strained similes. It is a highly complex ingredient, for it comprises all sorts of creative ingenuity: wit dictates the clever conceit; wit evolves the thought progressively through the most intricate stanzas; wit knits and welds to the central idea whatever may support and adorn it; wit furnishes the suave and subtle exhibition of mental skill that gives a scintillating finish to the whole work. It is fancy, invention, memory, and intellect, combining under the discipline of judgment and the restriction of form to effect brilliant poetry:

> In a true piece of Wit all things must be,
> Yet all things there agree.

Cowley reminds us of Drayton in his attempts to reconcile the conflict between the two opposing elements in any art, the free energy of the creative urge and the restrictive power that is just as necessary to the complete artist. The ideal combination of the two results in "wit," for you have wit when the inspiration is brilliant and powerful but nowhere out of control, where the restraint is complete but not deadening. Fancy controlled by judgment, nature controlled by art, Pegasus obedient to Bellerophon—such compromises are the basis of all poetry. Since it is impossible to maintain a perfect balance between these basic elements, there will be two possible styles: i. e., a style in which control is uppermost and a style in which the free element predominates. In the obviously controlled style, Cowley's great master was Vergil,[44] the epitome of the correct school of writing, Vergil, who "made that Art which was a Rage." Cowley thought he had found in Pindar the authority he needed for experiments in "Numbers loose and free." Pindar's odes had the one element that he missed in Vergil, the *poeticus furor*, the soaring, inspired, lyric note, free to digress, to turn and wind at will.

His convictions about the subject matter of poetry were just as broad and sure as his theories concerning style. Certainly no one ever defined the scope of poetry more liberally than Cowley:

44 Essays, Plays and Sundry Verses, pp. 265, 400.

Poetry treats not only of all things that are, or can be, but makes Creatures of her own as Centaurs, Satyrs, Fairies &c. makes persons and actions of her own as in Fables and Romances, makes Beasts, Trees, Waters . . . to understand and speak, nay makes what Gods it pleases too without idolatry.

That is, The Subject of Poetry is all Past, Future, and Present Times, and for the Past, it makes what choice it pleases out of the wrack of Time of things that it will save from Oblivion.[45]

Like the other poets of his day, Cowley had a definite hierarchy of subject matter in mind and held certain styles to be peculiarly appropriate for certain kinds of work. If we can believe Sprat, it would seem that a discussion of this point was to form a major division of his proposed discourse concerning style:

We had persuaded him to look back into his former studies, and to publish a discourse concerning style. In this he had designed to give an account of the proper sorts of writings, that were fit for all manner of arguments, to compare the perfections and imperfections of the authors of antiquity with those of this present age, and to deduce all down to the particular use of the English genius and language.[46]

It is possible to piece together more of Cowley's discourse than Nethercot has assembled in his short article.[47] Low in the scale of poetic types stand satire and comedy, romantic or fantastic tales, and love poetry. Of a loftier order are poems dealing with the three verities: man, nature, and God. For these Cowley reserved the highest types of form, the ode and the epic.

His conscious progress through the hierarchy had an unusual prelude in which a gifted little boy exhibited his precocious skill. The essay "Of Myself" tells in Cowley's own quietly charming fashion how he came to be a poet:

I believe I can tell the particular little chance that filled my head first with such Chimes of Verse, as have never since left ringing there. . . . In my Mother's parlour . . . was wont to lie Spencer's Works; this I happened to fall upon, and was infinitely delighted with the Stories of the Knights, and Giants and Monsters, and brave Houses, which I found everywhere there:

---

[45] Poems of Abraham Cowley, p. 187.
[46] Nethercot, "Abraham Cowley's Discourse Concerning Style," *Review of English Studies*, II (Oct., 1926), 385.
[47] *Ibid.*, pp. 385–404.

(Though my understanding had little to do with all this), and by degrees
with the tinckling of the Rhyme and Dance of the Numbers . . . read him
all over before I was twelve . . . and was thus made a Poet as immediately
as a Child is made an Eunuch.[48]

While Cowley acknowledged a debt to Spenser for his sense of rime
and rhythm, the subject matter of *The Faerie Queene* left no impres-
sion on him but that of vague, wondering, childish delight. He had
no sense of his entertainer as "sage and serious," "a better teacher
than Scotus or Aquinas." Nor did he long admire Spenser's style,
which he burlesqued through the medium of Dogrel:

> Or hither in triumph 'twixt two panniers ride,
> And sell the bouls of wheat and butter in Cheapside.
> The last is a little too long: but I imitate Spencer.[49]

As he grew older, he relegated Spenser to the same category as his
other early favorite, Ovid, whose tales had evidently delighted him in
youth but seemed puerile and unworthy of imitation as he matured.
His two earliest poems, "Pyramus and Thisbe" and "Constantia and
Philetus," are Ovidian in subject and Spenserian in tone, exhibiting
the two influences which he tended most strongly to reject as he
reached years of discrimination. What might be considered the start-
ing point of his more mature poetic theory is the pastoral comedy,
Love's Riddle, in which is exhibited decided critical acumen as well as
creative ability. In the preface the Ovidians are scored:

> 'tis not stuff'd with names of Gods, hard words,
> Such as the Metamorphosis affords.[50]

He has already a keen sense of the artificiality of certain poetic
practices and ridicules them pleasantly by means of his merry shep-
herd, Alupis. Especially does he omit no opportunity to attack the
sonnet, as for instance his mocking description of lovers who "cry
my Cœlia" and wring their brains for sonnets: [51]

> I have seen all your beautyes of the Court,
> And yet was never ravisht, never made
> A dolefull Sonnet unto angry Cupid,
> Either to warme her heart, or else coole mine.[52]

---

[48] Essays, Plays and Sundry Verses, p. 457.
[49] *Ibid.*, p. 205.
[50] *Ibid.*, p. 69.   [51] *Ibid.*, p. 73.   [52] *Ibid.*, p. 75. Cf. p. 97.

The bombast of the stage has not impressed him either. After listen-
ing to the high-sounding speeches of the mad Aphron, Alupis says,

> 'Tis pitty that these huge Gigantick speeches
> Are not upon the stage. They would doe rarely
> For none would understand them, I could wish
> Some Poet here now, with his table-booke.[53]

Later he was to designate bombast and strong lines along with
clinches (*clichés*) as the two crying sins of the English muse.[54] His
next play, the hastily contrived *Guardian*, continued to exhibit, in
his comments on Dogrel and Puny, a penetrating criticism of cheap
wits and poets.

The theater evidently had a great attraction for the young Cowley.
Frequent allusions to drama and dramatist in his early work testify
to this.[55] He makes reference to almost all of Marlowe's plays [56] and
to many of Jonson's and Shakespeare's.[57]

In view of his deep interest in plays, it is not strange that Cowley
served his real apprenticeship as a writer to the drama. The fact
that he wrote pastoral comedy for his early practice brought him
much nearer to reality and humor than the more usual *Shepheards
Calendar* type of pastoral poetry. In fact, there were times when he
introduced the satiric element to an extent unusual in the eclogue:

> What so Satyricke Shepheards? I beleeve
> You did not learne these flashes in the Woods.[58]

Alupis confesses to a three years' residence in the city, thus account-
ing for the ultra-pastoral train of satire. Cowley had a lovely faith
that the country could not bring forth evil or give birth to its
remedy, satire:

> God the first Garden made, and the first City, Cain.[59]

Conversely, the city "will bear nothing but the Nettles or Thornes
of Satyre, which grow most naturally in the worst Earth." [60]
As in the case of his pastoral poetry, Cowley's most important work
in satire was dramatic. The exceptions are his boyish poems: "The
Vote," in which he mildly satirizes various professions before ex-

[53] Essays, Plays and Sundry Verses, p. 108.
[54] *Ibid.*, p. 44.
[55] *Ibid.*, pp. 51, 217, 296.
[56] *Ibid.*, pp. 195, 284, 367.
[57] *Ibid.*, pp. 206, 208, 228, 306, 335.
[58] *Ibid.*, p. 73.
[59] *Ibid.*, p. 423.
[60] *Ibid.*, p. 405.

pressing his own moderate, Horatian ambitions; and a schoolboy re-taliation for not being admitted to witness the proceedings in a law court. His one attempt at serious satire, "The Puritan and the Papist," is poor because Cowley could not be deliberately immoderate.[61] Cowley's sane and salutary theory of satire is set forth in his defense of *The Cutter of Coleman Street*:

> It is hard for any Party to be so Ill as that no Good, Impossible to be so Good as that no Ill should be found among them. And it has been the perpetual privilege of Satyre and Comedy to pluck their vices and follies though not their Persons out of the Sanctuary of an Title. A cowardly ranting Souldier, an Ignorant Charlatanical Doctor, a foolish Cheating Lawyer, a silly Pedantical Scholar, have always been and still are the Principal Subjects of all Comedy.[62]

Cowley's comedy combined the types of Horace and the humors of Ben Jonson. He was well aware that it was a "low" kind of writing:

> If you be to choose parts for a Comedy out of any noble or elevated rank, the most proper for that work are the worst of that kind. . . . Comedy is humble of her Nature, and has always been bred low, so that she knows not how to behave her self with the great or the accomplisht. . . . If I had designed here the celebration of the Virtues of our friends. . . . They should have stood in Odes, and Tragedies, and Epique poems . . .[63]

But satire performs a necessary function for which the smoother forms are unsuited by their very nature, as Dogrel comically demonstrates:

> Scorn'd by a mistress? with a friend to fight?
> Hence, lighter Odes; I'll biting Satyres write.[64]

(Dogrel uses the word *ode* incorrectly to mean an irregular love poem.) [65] That satire should be governed by certain artistic laws appears in the discourse on Cromwell. After remarking that, unlike every other great man, Cromwell left behind him not one memory of a "wise or witty Apothegm," Cowley adds:

> That little in print which remains upon a sad record for him, is such, as a Satyre against him would not have made him say, for fear of transgressing too much the rules of Probability.[66]

[61] Essays, Plays and Sundry Verses, p. 265. [62] *Ibid.*, p. 261.
[63] *Ibid.*, p. 263.   [64] *Ibid.*, p. 172.   [65] *Ibid.*, p. 170.
[66] *Ibid.*, p. 363.

The first lengthy essay into nondramatic poetry is the group of lyrics in imitation of the pseudo Anacreon. These show Cowley as still willing to work over well-worn topics and as an easy master of the short line and simple style. He was, moreover, still interested in being purely amusing.

The next logical phase for the young poet was love poetry, and Cowley pays tribute to the importance of this genre in the preface to his collected works:

The Second is called, The Mistress (or) Love-Verses for so it is that Poets are scarce thought Free-men of their Company without paying some duties, and obliging themselves to be true to Love. . . . But we must not always make a judgment of their manners from their writings of this kind. . . . He may be in his own practice . . . a Stoick, and yet speak with the softness of an amorous Sappho. He professes too much the use of Fables . . . to have his testimony taken even against himself. . . . I speak to excuse some expressions (if such there be) which may happen to offend the severity of supercilious Readers; for much excess is to be allowed in Love, and even more in Poetry; so we avoid the two unpardonable vices in both, which are Obscenity and Prophaneness.[67]

How these poems could be considered as the fruit of any passion other than the passion to write is hard to tell. Their very lightness, brilliance, polish, ease, and wit argue against depth. Throughout the poems, moreover, are passages that give away his real reason for writing in this fashion. Consider the beginning with its unmistakable keynote:

> I Have often wisht to love; what shall I do?
> Me still the cruel Boy does spare
> And I a double task must bear,
> First to woo him and then a Mistress too.[68]

That this type of poetry may have been prompted by the success of Waller is suggested in the lines

> I'll fix thy title next in fame
> To Sacharissas well sung name.[69]

But the object of his poetry is so shadowy that she remains unnamed! In a poem written expressly to cover this point, he evades the issue neatly. He has given the lady no name, not even such a substitute

[67] Poems of Abraham Cowley, p. 10. [68] Ibid., p. 65. [69] Ibid., p. 70.

as Astrœa or Cœlia, and he will not reveal her name until she is wedded to him.

About two-thirds of the way through *The Mistress* stands a poem with the title "The Dissembler," which again warns the reader of the shallowness of the waters that are making such a display of upheaval:

> Unhurt, untoucht did I complain;
>
> .   .   .   .
>
> I thought, I'll swear, an handsome ly
> Had been no sin at all in Poetry:
>
> .   .   .   .
>
> Dart, and Wounds, and Flame and Heat,
> I nam'd but for the Rhime, or the Conceit.
>
> .   .   .   .
>
> Truth gives a dull propriety to my stile,
> And all the Metaphors does spoil.[70]

The central idea of this poem is that he has at last "become Lame with counterfeiting Lame," but this is no more to be believed than his previous protestations.

Cowley's next experiment was in the "translation" and imitation of Pindar's odes. His theory of translation was perhaps the most liberal ever devised. Word-for-word translation he dismissed absolutely, declaring, with good reason, that such a method applied to the flights of Pindar would make it seem as though "one Mad man had translated another." [71] He was not even content to make a free translation that should strive merely to preserve the beauties of the original. He went a step further and argued that as these beauties had of necessity faded with time, the object of the translator should be to restore the lost loveliness, to give the poem a significance for its modern audience such as the original had had for its contemporaries. Because of their failure to do this, he censured the translations of the Psalms made by Sandys and Buchanan. He did not insist on being called a "Translator"; he repeats that he has "taken, left out, and added" what he pleased, "nor make it so much my aim to let the Reader know precisely what he spoke, as what was his way and man-

[70] Poems of Abraham Cowley, p. 132.   [71] Ibid., p. 155.

ner of speaking . . . the noblest and highest kind of writing in verse." [72] As Shafer points out, there is no reason to believe that Cowley attempted an exact imitation of the Pindaric structure and failed through lack of understanding of the principles governing the ode.[73] In the section devoted to the *Pindariques* in the preface of 1656, Cowley mentions specifically those characteristics of Pindar's style which he aimed to reproduce: free digressions, unusually bold figures, and irregular numbers. The *Pindariques* were to have more "weight and height" than the love poems, which he designated as "light."

Cowley had not always had so lofty a concept of the ode. The term ode, before Cowley and Marvell established models for the Pindaric and Horatian types respectively, meant little more than a lyric, usually a lyric with irregular lines. Thus Dogrel, who has a fondness for impromptu verse, finds odes the easiest type to invent. "I'm onely for Odes, by the Muses, and the quickest for them, I think, in the Christian world." [74] He explains that he plans to win the lady by his love-odes and a little further on another character tells us "if one line forget it self, and run out beyond his elbow, while the next keeps at home . . . and dares not shew his head; he calls that an Ode." [75] But later Cowley, like Milton, came to realize that irregularity might be a sign of complete control over one's medium, rather than an indication of weakness:

> Stop, stop, my Muse, allay thy vig'orous heat,
>
> .   .   .   .   .
>
> Hold thy Pindarique Pegasus closely in,
> Which does to rage begin.
>
> .   .   .   .   .
>
> Disdains the servile Law of any settled pace
> Conscious and proud of his own natural force.
> 'Twill no unskilful Touch endure
> But flings Writer and Reader too that sits not sure.[76]

He was trying, not to imitate Pindar, but to catch the apparent fire and freedom of his strain:

[72] Poems of Abraham Cowley, p. 155.
[73] Shafer, *The English Ode to 1660*.
[74] Essays, Plays and Sundry Verses, p. 162.   [75] *Ibid.*, p. 170.
[76] Poems of Abraham Cowley, p. 183.

> The more Heroique strain let others take,
> Mine the Pindarique way I'le make.
> The Matter shall be Grave, the Numbers loose and free.
> It shall not keep one settled pace of Time,
> In the same Tune it shall not always Chime,
> Nor shall each day just to his Neighbour Rime,
> A thousand Liberties it shall dispense,
> And yet shall manage all without offence;
> Or to the sweetness of the Sound, or greatness of the Sence,
> Nor shall it never from one Subject start,
> Nor seek Transitions to depart,
> Nor its set way o're Stiles and Bridges make,
> Nor thorough Lanes a Compass take
> As if it fear'd some trespass to commit,
> When the wide Air's a Road for it.[77]

The ode retained seriousness and musical value, while permitting escape from an inflexible scheme of rime and rhythm and allowing for lyric soarings and digressions. The desire to write in a freer vein led Cowley, as it had led Drayton, to the ode. Cowley was evidently unfamiliar with Drayton, as he makes no allusion to the *Pindarics* and considers himself an innovator in that field. He may have been indifferent to Drayton's work because of its insularity, for Cowley's writings, in sharp contrast to those of Drayton, Wither, and Browne, are not strongly British in sentiment or allusion.

The last division of Cowley's collected works is devoted to four books of his unfinished religious epic, the *Davideis*. Cowley's purpose in writing a religious epic must be carefully distinguished from the strong attraction to a holy subject that led Giles Fletcher to write of Christ's victories, or the sense of dedication that inspired Milton, or the kindred impulse that led Herbert, Vaughan, and Crashaw to pour out their spirituality in verse. As early as 1638 Cowley had had ideas of a scriptural epic. He chose a biblical subject not because of his intense preoccupation with religion, but because it was artistically an ideal topic. He was not trying primarily to redeem or convert or pour forth praise or justify the ways of God to men, but to show a fresher and fairer field for the exercise of the poetic gift. Although he recognized the fact that poetry could create its own gods without idolatry, he felt that in failing to use the Scriptures

[77] Essays, Plays and Sundry Verses, p. 391.

poets had been neglecting the richest source of subject matter. It seemed a pity that most of his fellow poets should occupy themselves with the "lower" types, to the exclusion of nobler possibilities:

It is not without grief and indignation that I behold that Divine Science employing all her inexhaustible riches of Wit and Eloquence, either in the wicked and beggarly Flattery of great persons, or the unmanly Idolizing of Foolish Women, or the wretched affectation of scurril Laughter, or at best on confused antiquated Dreams of senseless Fables and Metamorphoses.

These continued "feasts of Love and Fables," even if wholesome, have been so oft repeated as to be nauseating; "they ought to appear no better arguments for Verse, then those of their worthy Successors, the Knights Errant." [78] Cowley, to be sure, mentions as one advantage of a religious poem the desirability of converting poetry from the uses of the devil to the uses of God, but he is far more detailed and convincing when he lists the artistic advantages. Poetry, he argued, would not be contracted but expanded in its scope by being "confined to Heaven," and accordingly he praised Crashaw for bringing the Muses "nobly home back to their Holy Land." Truth was just as good a subject for poetry as lies. "Feasts of Love and Fables" had been but parrot-like imitations of the classics. Truly to imitate the ancients, a modern poet should follow their spirit and sing of Christian God and heroes as they had sung of ancient gods and heroes. Nothing of value would be lost by this change, as all the classical stories had biblical parallels. His concluding argument on the suitability of religion for poetry (not the suitability of poetry for religion!) is:

All the Books of the Bible are either already most admirable and exalted pieces of Poesie, or are the best Materials in the world for it. [79]

A first glance at the enthusiastic preface to the *Davideis* might make the reader think that Cowley was advocating the use of religious topics only, throughout the whole range of poetry. That this was not the case is evident in many ways: first, the *Davideis* is almost his only religious poem; second, it was deliberately abandoned after the fourth book for a return to secular poetry adorned with heathen tales; third, it was published together with *The Mistress*, concerning

[78] Poems of Abraham Cowley, pp. 12, 13. Cf. Essays, Plays and Sundry Verses, p. 48.
[79] Ibid., p. 13.

which he said that poets were scarcely thought full-fledged until they had paid their respects to love. Cowley's feeling was, I believe, that divine poetry was a very lofty type, and that divine subject matter was particularly well suited to the epic. He nowhere praises and seldom practices the divine lyric; in the lyric his preference is for the noble abstract theme, as in the odes. He wrote no original religious lyrics and makes no mention of those of Donne or Herbert. The admiration he expressed for the poetry of his dear friend Crashaw was probably largely for the *Sospetto d'Herode,* which he imitated to some degree in the *Davideis.* It was the epic possibilities of Scripture that thrilled Cowley. His ambition was to compose an epic in accordance with the ancient rules, and with true instinct he turned to a record of primitive times for his material, recognizing in the Bible a comparatively unworked vein of "great, heroical and supernatural action." Such action, he explains in parentheses, verse will either find or make; and he adds the significant comment "there is not so great a Lye to be found in any Poet, as the vulgar conceit of men, that Lying is Essential to good Poetry." [80] Cowley is not, like Sidney, arguing the old point that invention is not the same as lying, but he is defending the right of the poet to use truth as well as fiction for subject matter, a right that becomes increasingly important during the next century.

In the copious notes to the *Davideis,* Cowley expounds many "rules" which he undoubtedly would have incorporated in his projected discourse under the heading of "epic style." Some of these are peculiar to the epic, while others characterize all forms of higher poetry, as we learn by reading the similar notes on the *Pindariques.*

The models for the epic are Vergil and Homer, and the greater of these is Vergil: "in . . . almost everything . . . I prefer the judgment of the Latins." [81] He planned his epic to have the classical twelve books, initial "Proposition of the whole work," and invocation of God for assistance. It was to end after the manner of Vergil and Homer.[82] He liked the use of unfinished lines and considered that he had sufficient authority for this practice in Vergil.[83] The principle of decorum is used to explain why he makes an angel repeat a message

[80] Poems of Abraham Cowley, p. 13.   [81] *Ibid.,* p. 266.   [82] *Ibid.,* p. 11.
[83] *Ibid.,* p. 269.

from God exactly as it was given: "to have made him [the angel] say a long, eloquent, or figurative speech . . . would have pleased perhaps some Readers, but would have been a crime against . . . Decency." [84] He rejected certain words because they were not suitable for verse, i. e., lad, spouse; [85] and he noted the strength to be gained by saying Light Divine instead of Divine Light.[86] He permitted himself a digression and an innovation, the insertion of an ode.[87]

In treating of the rules governing all lofty poetry, Cowley stressed the ideal of pleasure with profit. The ancient poet—and he was the model for the modern poet who essayed the higher types—was a delightful instructor. Pleasure was still fundamental and must be preserved, even at the sacrifice of accuracy. For instance, poetry should never stoop to exact statistics; the nearest round number should be substituted. Poetry, moreover, was not bound to take account of the latest scientific truths. It might properly utilize such doctrines as the music of the spheres or the transmigration of souls:

To speak according to common opinion, though it be false, is . . . far from being a fault in Poetry . . . Vergil did not look upon what might be spoken most truly, but what most gracefully; and aimed more at Delighting his Readers, than at instructing Husbandmen.[88]

In fine, whatever the truth may be, this opinion makes a better sound in Poetry.[89]

What he cannot handle well, the poet may omit.[90] He may write irregular lines to give a rough or tumbling effect.[91] In sum, Cowley enunciated a complete and detailed theory of the style befitting "noble numbers."

He soon had cause to regret some of the statements in the preface to the *Davideis*. In his enthusiasm over the religious epic, he had made biblical topics alone seem worthy of sustained lofty verse. When a year later he published two books of Latin verse on plants, his position was awkward. To read the first part of the introduction to this work, one would think there was no such thing as religious subject matter. He speaks of

[84] *Ibid.*, p. 274. [85] *Ibid.*, p. 311. [86] *Ibid.*, p. 307. [87] *Ibid.*, pp. 275, 277.

[88] *Ibid.*, p. 272. [89] *Ibid.*, p. 314.

[90] *Ibid.*, p. 312. [91] *Ibid.*, p. 217.

the incredible Veneration which the best poets always had for Gardens, Fields, and Woods, insomuch that in all other Subjects they seem to be banished from the Muses Territories. (But no one has celebrated *Plants*) . . . certainly a copious Field of Matter and what would yield them a plentiful return of Fruit.[92]

Plants have not been hitherto neglected as improper subjects for poetry, but because they were too vast an undertaking and poets despaired of completing such a work. Cowley is again feeling the lure of "fresh fields and pastures new" for poetic exploitation. But finally he comes to the rub. Why had he left the *Davideis* unfinished? Why this change of front? His first answers are very lame: he did not wish to weary the reader; he was not to be blamed for stopping but for starting; he has pioneered and now some better poet may continue. At length he confesses the truth about his religious epic:

I thus employed my self not so much out of Counsel, as the Fury of my Mind; for I am not able to do nothing, and had no other diversion of my Troubles; therefore through a wearisomeness of humane Affairs to these more pleasing Solaces of Literature (made agreeable to me by Custom and Nature) my sick Mind betakes it self, and not long after from an irksomeness of the selfsame things, it changes its course and turns off to some other Theme.[93]

But what of his use of "exolete and interpolated repetitions of old Fables in poetry," which he had "declaimed so vehemently against . . . when Truth . . . in the sacred books of God . . . Has laid open a new more rich and ample World of Poetry for the Wits of Men to be exercised upon"? Cowley now finds them legitimate embellishment, just as he now finds a work on nature to be closely allied to a work on nature's God:

I esteem that which celebrates the wonderful Works of Providence, not to be far distant from a sacred Poem. . . . Those Fictions are not to be accounted for Lies, which cannot be believed nor desire to be so. But that the Names of Heathen Deities and fabulous Transformations are sometimes Intermixt, the Matter it self compell'd me against my Will being no other way capable of embellishment, and it is well if by that means they are so.[94]

He added notes in sober prose, lest anyone think he had overworked a poet's privilege and "feigned those Qualities which would afford

[92] The Works of Mr. Abraham Cowley, Part III, b.   [93] *Ibid.*
[94] *Ibid.*

the greatest Matter for Pomp and empty Pleasure." For poets, who deal largely in fiction, are not always believed when they tell plain truth. Here once again is displayed the Horatian principle that underlies his whole work; the primary function of poetry is pleasure and to that the poet may join as much of profit as he will. Too little serious purpose leaves his poetry light and less lastingly pleasurable; too much thought content will overweight it hopelessly.

As the preface to the Latin poems clearly indicates, Cowley's attitude was experimental; he was the poet who came nearest to viewing his art objectively. As T. S. Eliot points out, "There was, in Cowley's world, no object of belief capable of eliciting from him a response of the highest poetic intensity." [95] He was one of the first English poets to be greatly affected by poetic theories advanced by men whose contact with poetry was preëminently critical and scientific, i. e., Hobbes, and through him Bacon. The proper blending of law and inspiration to form wit was to him the Divine Science. Even as his fellows of the Royal Society explored other fields in the hope of demonstrating valuable laws, so Cowley used his great knowledge of and control over his art to deduce and illustrate poetic theory, to establish "the proper sorts of writing that were fit for all manner of arguments." His research led him to substitute the love song for the sonnet, the dramatic for the narrative pastoral, to return to the classical epic, to develop the ode; in short, to vary, as every individual artist must, from the practice of his contemporaries. But he is at one with them in affirming a hierarchy of poetry, based on the extent to which each type permits the poet to fulfill his obligations as a delightful teacher of mankind.

[95] Eliot, "A Note on Two Odes of Cowley," *Seventeenth Century Studies Presented to Sir Herbert Grierson,* p. 238.

CHAPTER IX

JOHN MILTON

REVIEWING poetic inspiration as manifested by the greatest of his predecessors, Milton came to the following conclusion:

These abilities, wheresoever they be found, are the inspired guift of God rarely bestow'd, but yet to some (though most abuse) in every Nation.[1]

The consciousness that he was one of the chosen few who had received this gift and was destined to use it rightly runs through all his work. In all his serious poetry, it is directly to God, in one of his manifestations, that Milton appeals for inspiration:

> Thou Spirit who ledst this glorious Eremite
> Into the Desert . . .
> > inspire,
> As thou art wont, my prompted Song else mute.[2]

Characteristic of his more expanded style are the appeal for an irradiation of celestial light [3] and his prayer to the Spirit that "from the first was present." [4] Even when Milton uses a seemingly more traditional invocation and personifies divine inspiration as a muse, he is most careful to distinguish his Urania from the Olympian figure. His muse inhabits Sinai or Sion, and though she bears the same name as the most celestial of the classical muses, Milton leaves the reader in no doubt that he is using the familiar name to convey a more transcendent concept:

> Descend from Heav'n Urania, by that name
> If rightly thou art call'd, whose Voice divine
> Following, above th'Olympian Hill I soare,
> Above the flight of Pegasean wing.
> The meaning, not the Name I call: for thou
> Nor of the Muses nine, nor on the top

---

[1] *The Reason of Church-government*, The Works of John Milton, Frank A. Patterson, general ed., 18 vols., New York, Columbia University Press, III, 238. Hereafter referred to as Works, Columbia ed.

[2] *Paradise Regain'd*, Works, Columbia ed., II, 405.

[3] *Paradise Lost*, Works, Columbia ed., II, 79.   [4] *Ibid.*, p. 9.

Of old Olympus dwell'st, but Heav'nlie borne,
Before the Hills appeerd, or Fountain flow'd,
Thou with Eternal wisdom didst converse,
Wisdom thy Sister . . .
                                        Up led by thee
Into the Heav'n of Heav'ns I have presum'd
An Earthlie Guest and drawn Empyreal Aire,
Thy tempring.[5]

In the philosophy of Milton, a special gift such as the gift of
poetry was not merely a pleasing personal endowment to be em-
ployed at the discretion of the possessor, but a grant of extraordinary
power to be used in furthering some divine purpose. The possession
of such a power carried with it the great responsibility not only of
using it, but of using it correctly.[6] Thus in his *Apology for Smec-
tymnuus* he explains his attitude toward these "guifts of Gods im-
parting, which I boast not, but thankfully acknowledge, and feare
also lest at my certaine account they be reckon'd to me many rather
than few."[7] It was spiritual death to hide such a talent. The great
task-master could be satisfied in only one way, by the attempt, suc-
cessful or unsuccessful, to realize his purpose. Despite his argument
in the sonnet on his blindness that those who are unable to serve
actively may show their obedience by patient acceptance of God's
will, the sense of special obligation because of special power enabled
Milton to overcome even the great obstacle of blindness.

To a man with such belief, the question of the true function of
poetry is more than a merely academic or artistic problem. As soon
as Milton recognized his special ability, he began to speculate upon
its proper use and decided that it was to further the glory of God by
instructing his countrymen in truth and virtue. The duty of the
Christian poet was to bring his nation nearer to the Christian ideal
by means of an art which had in every century been rightly used by
its great exponents to teach the current concept of perfection. Like
most of his poetical principles, this is enunciated in versions varying
from a simple statement to a richly detailed and magnificently writ-
ten passage:

[5] *Paradise Lost*, Works, Columbia ed., II, 211.
[6] *Reason of Church-government*, Works, Columbia ed., III, 232 ff.
[7] *Apology for Smectymnuus*, Works, Columbia ed., III, 282.

. . . if I were certain to write as men buy Leases, for three lives and down-ward, there ought no regard to be sooner had than to Gods glory, by the honour and instruction of my country. . . . That, what the greatest and choicest wits of Athens, Rome, or modern Italy, and those Hebrews of old did for their country, I, in my proportion, with this over and above, of being a Christian, might do for mine.[8]

. . . what religious, what glorious and magnificent use might be made of poetry, both in divine and human things.[9]

These abilities . . . are of power, beside the office of a pulpit, to imbreed and cherish in a great people the seeds of vertu and publick civility, to allay the perturbations of the mind, and set the affections in right tune; to cele-brate in glorious and lofty Hymns the throne and equipage of Gods Al-mightinesse. . . . Teaching over the whole book of sanctity and vertu, through all the instances of example with such delight to those especially of soft and delicious temper, who will not so much as look upon Truth herselfe, unlesse they see her elegantly drest, that the paths of honesty and good life . . . will then appear to all men both easy and pleasant.[10]

. . . to sing and celebrate thy divine Mercies and marvellous Judgements in this Land throughout all Ages; (whereby this great and Warlike Nation, instructed and inur'd to the fervent and continuall practice of Truth and Righteousnesse . . . may presse on hard to that high and happy emulation to be found the soberest, wisest, and most Christian People. . . .[11]

To summarize Milton's belief in Horatian terms, the right end of poetry was spiritual profit through delightfully gained knowledge.

Exactly the same conclusion may be reached from an entirely dif-ferent starting point. In *Of Education,* Milton defines the purpose of all learning and explains the special way in which poetry con-tributes to that purpose:

The end then, of Learning is to repair the ruines of our first Parents by re-gaining to know God aright, and out of that knowledge to love him, to imitate him, to be like him, as we may the neerest, by possessing our souls of true vertue, which, being united to the heavenly grace of faith, makes up the highest perfection.[12]

Under the general heading of learning he lists poetry as one of the "organic" arts, that is, an art instrumental in the conveyance of

[8] *Reason of Church-government*, Works, Columbia ed., III, 236.
[9] *Of Education*, Works, Columbia ed., IV, 286.
[10] *Reason of Church-government*, Works, Columbia ed., III, 238.
[11] *Of Reformation in England*, Works, Columbia, ed., III, 78.
[12] *Of Education*, Works, Columbia ed., IV, 277.

thought. He groups it with logic and rhetoric, with this difference: that logic is the art of writing perspicuously; rhetoric, the art of writing elegantly; poetry, the art of writing "according to the fitted stile of lofty, mean, or lowly." Having discussed logic and rhetoric briefly, he adds, "to which Poetry would be made subsequent, or, indeed, rather precedent, as being less suttle and fine, but more simple, sensuous and passionate." [13] This ambiguous statement deserves careful attention because of the light that one interpretation of it sheds on an otherwise apparently derogatory comment on the poetry of the Psalms made in the *Pro populo anglicano defensio,* namely: "but however this may be, the words and thoughts of the psalmist, rhapsodical and passionate, are nowise fitted to expound law, nor should be dragged into that use." [14] That is, poetry is not an art of exact statement; it is far more powerful because it is suggestive, more eloquent because it has freer license. It is subsequent, i. e., last, in Milton's scheme of study, because it is precedent in its power to affect mankind:

For Eloquence the Soul, Song charms the Sense.[15]

From the evidence of these statements, too, the purpose of poetry, according to Milton's theory, is to enlist the force of sensuous appeal to aid in the increasing of human virtue and divine glory through the dissemination of knowledge.

That Milton considered intensive preparation necessary to the accomplishment of such an aim is obvious from his frequent reference to the thoroughness of his training. He proudly relates that as a young boy he rarely left his studies before midnight.[16] As a college student, he rose early and read good books until his mind was wearied.[17] The Horton period was devoted to intensive study by a man whose disciplined mind could absorb material rapidly and retain it well, because Milton considered a vast fund of knowledge indispensable for a great poet. This, of course, followed logically from his purpose; the poet could not lead his reader to the truth unless he

[13] *Of Education,* Works, Columbia ed., IV, 286.
[14] *Pro populo anglicano defensio,* Works, Columbia ed., VII, 121. Cf. *Tenure of Kings and Magistrates, ibid.,* V, 13.
[15] *Paradise Lost,* Works, Columbia ed., II, 57.
[16] *Defensio secunda,* Works, Columbia ed., VIII, 119.
[17] *Apology for Smectymnuus,* Works, Columbia ed., III, 299. Cf. *ibid.,* p. 282.

himself had acquired as much of that truth as possible. He thoroughly scorned "the mercenary crew of false pretenders to learning" [18] and proudly included himself among "those who had prepared their minds and studies above the vulgar pitch to advance truth in others, and from others to entertain it." [19] Again he writes with gusto of the host of those who, like himself, stand ready to defend the truth:

there be pens and heads there, sitting by their studious lamps, musing, searching, revolving new notions and ideas . . . others as fast reading, trying all things, assenting to the force of reason and convincement. [20]

He speaks of "labouring the hardest labour in the deep mines of knowledge" [21] and explains that divine and human learning have in many cases to be "rak't out of the embers of forgotten Tongues." [22] The principles of amassing knowledge are outlined clearly in *Of Education*. One is to study the world he lives in and the world beyond his horizon in space and time:

our understanding cannot in this body found itself but on sensible things, nor arrive so clearly to the knowledge of God and things invisible, as by orderly conning over the visible and inferior creature. . . .
And seeing every Nation affords not experience and tradition enough for all kind of Learning, therefore we are chiefly taught the Languages of those people who have at any time been most industrious after Wisdom. [23]

The ability to sing was given; the truth to be sung was not to be acquired passively, but by strenuous endeavor. Once sure of his genius, and that assurance possessed him very early, the only limit to his scope was his effort:

I thought with my self by every instinct and presage of nature . . . that what imbold'd them [the elegiac poets] to this task might with such diligence as they us'd imbolden me. [24]

. . . by labour and intent study, (which I take to be my portion in this life,) joyn'd with the strong propensity of nature, I might perhaps leave something so written to aftertimes, as they should not willingly let it die. [25]

[18] *Areopagitica*, Works, Columbia ed., IV, 323.   [19] *Ibid.*, p. 330.
[20] *Ibid.*, p. 341.   [21] *Areopagitica*, Works, Columbia ed., IV, 347.
[22] *Of Reformation*, Works, Columbia ed., III, 5.
[23] *Of Education*, Works, Columbia ed., IV, 277, 278.
[24] *Apology for Smectymnuus*, Works, Columbia ed., III, 302.
[25] *Reason of Church-government*, Works, Columbia ed., III, 236. Cf. *Familiar Letters*, Works, Columbia ed., XII, 19.

A letter to Diodati tells how his studies and literary meditations were being disrupted by the turbulent times. But though he would have liked an even longer period of preparation, Milton acknowledged gratefully that God had given him not only talent but also ample opportunity to develop it:

> ease and leasure was given thee for thy retired thoughts out of the sweat of other men.[26]

To summarize, it was incumbent upon the true poet to remember that his inspiration was divine and to prepare himself for its proper use as far as worldly knowledge permitted. Milton's formula for preparation was both mystical and specific:

> by devout prayer to that eternall Spirit, who can enrich with all utterance and knowledge, and sends out his Seraphim, with the hallow'd fire of his Altar, to touch and purify the lips of whom he pleases: to this must be added industrious and select reading, steddy observation, insight into all seemly and generous arts and affaires.[27]

To prayer for inspiration and to study Milton added actual practice, and yet the poetic output of the early period was very slight for a man with Milton's capacity for sustained literary labor. Unlike the diffuse initial experiments of Drayton, Browne, Wither, Phineas Fletcher, and Cowley, Milton's early English poems were restricted almost to the minimum essential to establish the fact of his control over each type. They were proofs of his progress rather than publishable exercises. He exercised himself more fully in Latin verse, and later attributed his ear for good cadence and scansion to an early acquaintance "with the best and elegantest authors of the learned tongues." [28] He enjoyed "the smooth elegiac poets for the pleasing sound of their numerous writing, which in imitation I found most easy and most agreeable to nature's part in me." [29] He also practiced that favorite imitation from the classics, the epistle in verse, thereby improving his power to express himself "in that cramped mode of speech, straitened by fixed feet and syllables." [30]

But while Milton was developing his high natural power in prosody by practice, there were also other aspects of poetic composition

---

[26] *Reason of Church-government*, Works, Columbia ed., III, 232.
[27] *Ibid.*, p. 241.   [28] *Apology for Smectymnuus*, Works, Columbia ed., III, 328.
[29] *Ibid.*, p. 302.   [30] *Familiar Letters*, Works, Columbia ed., XII, 5.

on which he lavished his attention. Much of his research was devoted
to the study of various types of poetry. We have already noted that
in his pamphlet *Of Education* he made the statement that poetry
was the art of expression "according to the fitted style of lofty,
mean, or lowly," thus readily acknowledging a hierarchy of poetry.
Like most of the major poets, he had only a passing interest in the
lower types. He did not condemn that class of verse; he merely
found little to hold him long where the emphasis lay admittedly on
technique rather than on subject matter. Even during his enjoyable
apprenticeship to low poetry he was careful to distinguish between
such poetry used as a means and as an end. There was no point of
comparison between the light poet and the serious poet. Their in-
spiration was as utterly different as their discipline or purpose. Thus
Milton assured Diodati that "light" poets ought to eat and drink and
be merry, that the light elegy is inspired by many gods, Bacchus,
Erato, Ceres, Venus, Cupid. It was far different in his own case:

But if a poet sings of wars, of Heaven controlled by a Jove full grown, of
duty-doing heroes, of captains that are half gods, if he sings now the holy
counsels of the gods above, now the realms deep below wherein howls a
savage hound, let him live a simple frugal life . . . On such a poet is im-
posed, too, a youth free of crime, pure and chaste, and a character unyield-
ing, and a name without taint; such an one must he be as *you* are, augur, as,
resplendent with holy vestments and with lustral waters, you rise, minded to
go forth to face the angry gods.[31]

The major poet was dedicated to disciplined living:

He who would not be frustrate of his hope to write well hereafter in laudable
things, ought him selfe to bee a true Poem; that is, a composition and pat-
terne of the best and honourablest things; not presuming to sing high praises
of heroick men, or famous Cities, unlesse he have in himselfe the experience
and practice of all that which is praise-worthy.[32]

Work such as Milton contemplated was, unlike the lesser verse, "not
to be rays'd from the heat of youth, or the vapours of wine, like that
which flows at wast from the pen of some vulgar Amorist, or the
trencher fury of a riming parasite; nor to be obtain'd by the invoca-
tion of Dame Memory and her Siren daughters." [33] He early sat in

[31] *Elegia sexta,* Works, Columbia ed., I, 211, 213.
[32] *Apology for Smectymnuus,* Works, Columbia ed., III, 303.
[33] *Reason of Church-government,* Works, Columbia ed., III, 241.

judgment on his favorite elegiac poets and felt the greater potentiality within himself because he had a greater love and comprehension than they of those "high perfections" which they had prided themselves on understanding and celebrating:

what judgement, wit or elegance was my share, would herein best appeare, and best value it selfe, by how much more wisely, and with more love of vertue I should choose . . . the object of not unlike praises.[34]

A recent article, "Milton as a Satirist," has shown that "Milton was capable of humor, that he was acquainted with the classics of satire, and that a very considerable tinge of satire pervades his prose works." [35] In view of these facts and of his strong desire to lash certain abuses, it is remarkable that he did not write much poetry which, according to the theory of the period, would have been classed as satire. The youthful "In Quintum Novembris" is the nearest approach to it. The two sonnets on the reception of his divorce tracts, while they illustrate interestingly the extent to which he used the sonnet as a mirror for his own emotions, certainly do not adequately indicate Milton's concept of satiric form and function. For the mildly derisive satire he had complete aversion. It seemed to him to be laughing at the flaws in God's world, instead of undertaking the Christian duty of scoring the wrong or teaching the right.[36] He was particularly vitriolic on the subject of Hall's works. Although his criticism in this case was prompted by personal antipathy, he musters sound theoretical objections against the "toothless satires." That designation represented a contradiction in terms. The meter of the poems was halting, their subject matter common; the author had failed to take advantage of good models, had failed to understand the true purpose of satire:

the ordinary subject of freshmens tales, and in a straine as pittifull. Which for him who would be counted the first English Satyr, to abase himselfe to, who might have learned better among the Latin, and Italian Satyrists, and in our own tongue from the vision and Creed of Pierce plowman, besides others before him. . . . For a Satyr as it was born out of a Tragedy, so ought to resemble his parentage, to strike high, and adventure dangerously at the most eminent vices among the greatest persons, and not to creepe into

---

[34] *Apology for Smectymnuus*, Works, Columbia ed., III, 303.
[35] French, "Milton as a Satirist," PMLA, LI, 414–29.
[36] *Apology for Smectymnuus*, Works, Columbia ed., III, 294, 295.

every blinde Taphouse. . . . But that such a Poem should be toothlesse, I
still affirm it to be a bull, taking away the essence of that which it calls it
selfe. For if it bite neither the persons nor the vices, how is it a Satyr? [37]

Milton evidently derived satire from the satyr play that concluded
the Greek tragic trilogies, and did not, like Jonson, consider that it
sprang from *vetus comoedia*. Yet he had no prejudice against strong
or humorous writing; he fully justified necessary vehemence when
it served the purpose of virtue: "even this veine of laughing (as I
could produce out of grave Authors) hath ofttimes a strong and
sinewy force in teaching and confuting." [38] At least once he con-
sidered using his power as a poet to pillory an unworthy adversary;
the critic of the divorce tracts might have been poetically enthroned
along with Theobald and Cibber had not Renaissance convention
outlawed personal detraction in verse:

what defence can properly be used in such a despicable encounter as this,
but either the slap or the spurn? . . . Since my fate extorts from mee a
talent of sport, which I had thought to hide in a napkin, he shall be my
Batrachumuomachia, my Bavius, my Calendrino, the common adage of
ignorance and overweening. Nay, perhaps, as the provocation may bee, I
may bee driv'n to curl up this gliding prose into a rough Sotadic, that shall
rime him.[39]

Milton had no desire to execute the threat. He preferred to teach in
the high, grave, and dignified spirit of the tragic muse rather than
to expose "clowns and vices" by the rough and boisterous aid of
comedy. The problems with which he desired to cope in poetry were
too lofty to be disposed of by subjecting them to a stream of ridicule.
He favored the more academic method of destroying the false argu-
ments of the opposition by superior reasoning, after having first pre-
sented them through such an *advocatus diaboli* as Comus or through
Satan himself. On the other hand, he did not hesitate to apply scath-
ing satire when he thought it was deserved by interpolating such
passages as the diatribe against the bishops in *Lycidas* or the Paradise
of Fools in *Paradise Lost*.

His early poems frequently strain toward the higher type, in an-

[37] *Apology for Smectymnuus*, Works, Columbia ed., III, 329.
[38] *Animadversions*, Works, Columbia ed., III, 107. Cf. *Apology for Smectymnuus, ibid.*,
pp. 317 ff.
[39] *Colasterion*, Works, Columbia ed., IV, 272.

ticipation of his poetic coming of age. And Milton let them go in that direction as far as decorum would permit. The lofty goal toward which he was moving overshadowed his work from the very beginning. Most incongruously his great purpose makes itself felt in the midst of academic merrymaking:

> Yet I had rather, if I were to chuse,
> Thy [Poetry's] service in some graver subject use,
> Such as may make thee search thy coffers round,
> Before thou cloath my fancy in fit sound.

> Then sing of secret things that came to pass
> When Beldam Nature in her cradle was;
> And last of Kings and Queens and Hero's old

> But fie my wandring Muse how thou dost stray! [40]

He dismisses the early products of his pen with a conventional formula of depreciation, designed to enhance the serious purpose of his subsequent efforts. He characterizes the youthful works as "idle trophies of my worthlessness" written "once on a time, with warped and twisted mind, and with all true zeal laid prostrate." [41]

His early religious poetry resolved temporarily the struggle between his subject matter and his purpose. But Milton soon decided that he was not sufficiently equipped to attempt the higher reaches of his art. During his period of further preparation he again practiced the lower types occasionally, and again the consciousness of his ultimate purpose left its impress. Thus his masque *Comus* charmingly cloaks morality; his parallel pastorals lack Arcadian scenes and situations, but treat instead of the idyllic rustication of a young man whose life was, as he best knew, "a true poem." His sonnets soon changed from imitative love poems to a crystallization of brief and intimate self-expression. Following Tasso and following, too, his own inclination toward the heroic, he introduced into English the sonnet in praise of a public figure. In *Lycidas* the pressure toward a higher type of poetry is reflected in his consideration of fame and in the St. Peter passage. Milton emphasized the elevated tone of these digressions:

[40] *Sixth Academic Exercise,* Works, Columbia ed., I, 20. Cf. Elegy V, Works, Columbia ed., I, 197.
[41] *Elegies,* Works, Columbia ed., I, 223.

         O Fountaine Arethuse
   That strain I heard was of a higher mood;
   But now my Oate proceeds.[42]

   Return Alpheus, the dread voice is past,
   That shrunk thy streams; Return Sicilian Muse.[43]

Even the pastoral elegy for his best friend digresses to give a detailed account of Milton's epic project:

I myself shall sing of Dardan ships [making their way] through Rutupian [Kentish] waters, and of the realm, in days of old, of Imogene, daughter of Pandrasus; I shall sing of Brennus and Arviragus, captains [both] and of ancient Belinus, too, and of the settlers from Amorica subject at last to Briton's laws. Next I shall sing of Igraine, mother-to-be, through fateful trickery, of Arthur, I shall sing of lying features, of the taking of the arms of Gorlois, guile, all, of Merlin. O, if only life shall endure for me, you, my Pan's pipe, will hang, far away [from me] on an aged pine, utterly forgot by me, or else, transmuted, you will with the aid of native Muses, sound forth a truly British strain.[44]

Thus Milton, after a youth spent in long and arduous preparation, arrived at last on the heroic plane and, looking back, regarded the output of his early period kindly but criticially:

Twin books, rejoicing in a single robe [i. e., binding], bright, it may be, with double leaves of laurel [i. e., with two title-pages], and with neatness [of contents] not overlabored, neatness that a boyish hand bestowed on you, an earnest, zealous hand, but as yet no sure poet's hand.[45]

The collected *Poems* of 1645 was a thoroughly satisfactory volume of "low" poetry, a brilliant example of the apprentice's and journeyman's skill, but not until now had Milton felt himself master of his art, rich in subject matter and learned in the basic laws which previous masters had deduced. Indeed, it was in terms of these laws that Milton most concretely defined "lofty" poetry as "that sublime Art which in Aristotles Poetics, in Horace, and the Italian Commentaries of Castlevetro, Tasso, Mazzoni, and others, teaches what the laws are of a true Epic Poem, what of a Dramatic, what of a Lyric, what Decorum is, which is the grand masterpiece to observe." [46]

[42] *Lycidas*, Works, Columbia ed., I, 79.   [43] *Ibid.*, p. 81.
[44] *Epitaphium Damonis*, Works, Columbia ed., I, 311, 313.
[45] *Ad Joannem Rousium*, Works, Columbia ed., I, 317, 319.
[46] *Of Education*, Works, Columbia ed., IV, 286.

From the above quotation it is evident that Milton had studied classical and Renaissance critical authorities, in his effort to gather the full tradition concerning the three great divisions of "lofty" poetry: the epic, the drama, and the lyric. He was vitally concerned with the different functions, rules of composition, and the best examples of each. A detailed discussion of his researches and speculations is given in *The Reason of Church-government*. In the case of the epic, there were four different yet excellent models from which to choose: Homer, Vergil, Tasso, and the Book of Job. Were the rules of Aristotle strictly to be kept? What Christian hero should he sing? Or should he follow the example of Sophocles and Euripides—an example confirmed by the direct dialogue of the Song of Solomon and the Apocalypse—and dramatize his material? Perhaps that would prove "more doctrinal and exemplary to a nation." There was the third possibility of developing a lyric technique which should follow the classic examples of Pindar and Callimachus and, far more important, would have the strong authority and numerous incomparable models afforded by the Bible. The choice among the three genres really rested on a differentiation in purpose, for when Milton explains that poetic ability has the power "to inbreed and cherish in a great people the seeds of vertu and publick civility, to allay the perturbations of the mind, and set the affections in right tune, to celebrate in glorious and lofty Hymns the throne and equipage of Gods Almightinesse," [47] he is referring successively to the special properties of the epic, the drama, and the lyric.

The bias of his early days was decidedly toward the epic. The bulk of the evidence up to the year 1641 points to the fact that he had decided on an Arthurian heroic poem, written in English, as his first and perhaps supreme piece of lofty poetry. In his tribute to Mansus, Milton longs for a like patron

if ever I shall bring back to my songs the kings of my native land, and Arthur, who set wars in train even 'neath the earth [i. e., in Fairyland], or shall tell of the high-hearted heroes bound together as comrades at that peerless table, and—O, may the spirit come to my aid—I shall break to pieces Saxon phalanxes under the might of Briton's warring. [48]

---

[47] *Reason of Church-government*, Works, Columbia ed., III, 238.
[48] *Mansus, Works*, Columbia ed., I, 293.

Epitaphium Damonis, quoted before, is even more specific as to the
scope of his projected poem, and most emphatic that it is to be in
English. The patriotic spirit of the times was reflected in his choice.
Milton, who was soon to suspend his cherished career as a poet in
order to serve his state as a pamphleteer and later as Secretary for
Foreign Tongues, at first thought himself destined to be the singer
of his nation's history. Everything seemed to indicate that. Save for
Spenser, the matter of Britain had never received adequate treat-
ment:

these British Ilands . . . whose fortune hath hitherto bin, that if the
Athenians, as some say, made their small deeds great and renowned by their
eloquent writers, England hath had her noble atchievments made small by
the unskilful handling of monks and mechanicks.[49]

As soon as the current difficulties were straightened out, he would
play a poet's part; he indicated that his contribution would take
the form of a historical epic:

Then amidst the Hymns, and Halleluiahs of Saints, some one may perhaps
bee heard offering at high strains in new and lofty Measures to sing and cele-
brate thy divine Mercies, and marvellous Judgements in this Land through-
out all Ages.[50]

But as Milton became more and more involved in contemporary
national events, his interest in recording remote and fabulous British
exploits waned. Charles was not Gloriana, and to sing of Arthur
was to strengthen Charles.[51] He now saw his destiny in another
light as the narrator of the Parliamentary victories:

I thought, therefore, that if it were the will of God those men should per-
form such gallant exploits, it must be likewise his will, that when per-
formed, there should be others to set them forth with becoming dignity and
ornament.[52]

He was already fulfilling his function as an English chronicler. At
the end of the *Second Defence* the blind Milton, recalling his early
ambitions and promises, seems to feel that his great prose defense is
a substitute in heroic prose for the national epic by which he had
originally planned to celebrate his country. The Horatian formula

[49] *Reason of Church-government*, Works, Columbia ed., III, 237.
[50] *Of Reformation*, Works, Columbia ed., III, 78.
[51] Brinkley, *Arthurian Legend in the Seventeenth Century*.
[52] *Defensio secunda*, Works, Columbia ed., VIII, 11.

for poetic fame and the reference to a familiar rule of epic theory reminds his audience of former hints and promises that were not otherwise to be fulfilled:

I have celebrated, as a testimony to them, I had almost said, a monument, which will not speedily perish, actions which were glorious, lofty, which were almost above all praise; and if I have done nothing else, I have assuredly discharged my trust. But as the poet, who is styled epic, if he adhere strictly to established rules, undertakes to embellish not the whole life of the hero whom he proposes to celebrate in song, but, usually, one particular action of his life, as for example, that of Achilles at Troy, or the return of Ulysses, or the arrival of Aeneas in Italy, and leaves alone the rest; so likewise will it suffice for my duty and excuse, that I have at least embellished one of the heroic actions of my countrymen.[53]

Even after he had abandoned British material as the subject of his epic, Milton never forgot the need which he felt existed for a worthy recounting of his country's story. He supplied it in part with his *History of Britain,* which covers the time from the beginning to the Norman Conquest. Hanford feels that the late publication (1670) of this work indicates that Milton hoped to bring it down to his own day,[54] but a sentence from a letter written in 1659 seems to contradict that:

Of any such work as compiling the history of our political troubles . . . I have no thought whatever: they are worthier of silence than of commemoration.[55]

There was the alternative possibility, which Milton had recognized in his early poems, of choosing a religious rather than a national hero. The Cambridge manuscript shows that he considered both types in his experiments in drama, with the emphasis decidedly on the biblical figures. When, after the exigencies of civil war, he again resumed his literary career, he had settled upon epic treatment of a religious theme.[56] In his earlier selection of a national

---

[53] *Defensio secunda,* Works, Columbia ed., VIII, 253.

[54] Hanford, *A Milton Handbook,* p. 104.

[55] *Familiar Letters,* Works, Columbia ed., XII, 109.

[56] Masson feels Milton chose the theme of *Paradise Lost* because he felt the subject would enable him to throw into epic form the largest possible amount of his own philosophy of "man and history," from *Life of Milton Narrated in Connexion with the History of His Time,* VI, 522. Cf. Tillyard, "Milton and the English Epic Tradition," *Seventeenth Century Studies,* p. 230: "'Paradise Lost' offered the chance to combine all the literary themes and epic types known and esteemed by Milton except the heroic poem."

hero, Milton had followed closely the example of the classics. The shift to a biblical figure meant the thrilling possibility of "higher argument" than either Homer or Vergil had treated: not the wrath of Achilles, but the wrath of God; not the founding of a nation, but the founding of the world. Aristotle had taught that the vital element of a heroic poem is the action which it represents. There could be no greater action than the revolt of the angels and the fall and the indicated redemption of man. Thus instead of carefully imitating the external components of the classical epic, as Cowley did, Milton consciously transcended the established heights:

> yet argument
> Not less but more Heroic than the wrauth
> Of stern Achilles on his Foe pursu'd
> Thrice Fugitive about Troy Wall; or rage
> Of Turnus for Lavinia disespous'd,
> Or Neptun's ire or Juno's that so long
> Perplex'd the Greek and Cytherea's Son;

> this Subject for Heroic Song
> Pleas'd me long Choosing, and beginning late
> Not sedulous by Nature to indite
> Warrs, hitherto the onely Argument
> Heroic deem'd, chief maistrie to dissect
> With long and tedious havoc fabl'd Knights
> In Battels feign'd; the better fortitude
> Of Patience and Heroic Martyrdom
> Unsung; or to describe Races and Games,
> Or tilting Furniture, emblazon'd Shields,
> Impreses quaint, Caparison and Steeds;
> Bases and tinsel Trappings, gorgious Knights
> At Joust and Tournament; then marshal'd Feast
> Serv'd up in Hall with Sewers, and Seneshals;
> The skill of Artifice or Office mean,
> Not that which justly gives Heroic name
> To Person or to Poem. Mee of these
> Nor skilld nor studious, higher Argument
> Remaines, sufficient of itself to raise
> That name.[57]

Clearly it had not been the adventitious and colorful details that had attracted Milton to heroic narrative. Even in his youth, when he

[57] *Paradise Lost*, Works, Columbia ed., II, 260.

had delighted in the fabulous and the wonderful, he had praised
Spenser's tale of knights because it had used the chivalric mech-
anism to teach and had not treated it as matter in itself worthy:

> And if ought els, great Bards beside,
> In sage and solemn tunes have sung,
> Of Turneys and of Trophies hung;
> Of Forests, and inchantments drear,
> Where more is meant then meets the ear.[58]

Now, abandoning the romantic tradition, Milton boldly extended
the term "heroic" upward to include his greater argument, and
emphasized the fact that it was not necessarily synonymous with
knightly, martial, or spectacular. The significant phrase

> the better fortitude
> Of Patience and Heroic Martyrdom
> Unsung [59]

foreshadows his ultimate return in *Paradise Regain'd* to a concept
which had lain dormant since his early religious poetry, the concept
of Jesus as the perfect hero:

> Most perfect Heroe, try'd in heaviest plight
> Of labours huge and hard, too hard for human wight.[60]

In *Paradise Regain'd* he summons his epic power once again to treat
of a theme beyond the conventional bounds of the term heroic:

> to tell of deeds
> Above Heroic, though in secret done
> And unrecorded left through many an Age,
> Worthy t'have not remain'd so long unsung.[61]

Perhaps, too, Milton's own experiences with the discrepancies be-
tween the fortunes of war and merit, between might and right, af-
fected his later definition of heroic poetry:

> For in those dayes Might onely shall be admir'd,
> And Valour and Heroic Vertu call'd;
> Thus fame shall be achiev'd, renown on Earth,
> And what most merits fame in silence hid.[62]

---

[58] *Il Penseroso*, Works, Columbia ed., I, 44.
[59] *Paradise Lost*, Works, Columbia ed., II, 261.
[60] *The Passion*, Works, Columbia ed., I, 23.
[61] *Paradise Regain'd*, Works, Columbia ed., II, 405.
[62] *Paradise Lost*, Works, Columbia ed., II, 370.

To recapitulate, Milton, who had originally planned a national Arthurian epic, developed instead the ultimate type of heroic poetry by applying the epic technique to a grander theme.

What of Milton's theories concerning the second of the subdivisions of lofty poetry, the drama? His first excursions into this field were made, apparently, as a recreation from his studies in nondramatic poetry. In the first elegy he tells Diodati that he is now giving his time to the Muses, adding, "when I am weary grown, the splendor of the rounded theatre welcomes me." [63] The references following are all to classical drama. In "Il Penseroso" tragedy seems to have been elevated to the rank of a study, for it is mentioned between his readings in philosophy and poetry:

> Som time let Gorgeous Tragedy
> In Scepter'd Pall com sweeping by,
> Presenting Thebs, or Pelops line
> Or the tale of Troy divine,
> Or what (though rare) of later age
> Ennobled hath the Buskind stage.[64]

From the beginning the favored dramatic type was Greek tragedy. True, in "L'Allegro" he refers to contemporary English comedies, but the whole tone of "L'Allegro" demands a reference to comedy. In alluding to Ben Jonson, Milton cites the most classical of English comedy writers. His admiration for Shakespeare's comedies was apparently based on the attraction of opposites. The highly trained classical genius of Milton accorded frank admiration to a less cultured romantic genius, unaided as well as unhampered by too thorough a grounding in the "rules":

> Then to the well-trod stage anon,
> If Jonson's learned Sock be on,
> Or sweetest Shakespear fancies childe,
> Warble his native Wood-notes wilde,[65]

Milton's general attitude toward comedies was that they were to be handled with care, since they were not completely salutary. He had certainly been most unfavorably impressed by the comedies pre-

---

[63] *Elegia prima*, Works, Columbia ed., I, 171.
[64] *Il Penseroso*, Works, Columbia ed., I, 43.
[65] *L'Allegro*, Works, Columbia ed., I, 39.

sented at Cambridge during his residence there.[66] In *Of Education* he advises that the reading of comedies be introduced into the course of study, but with "good antidote." [67] In regard to contemporary English tragedy, he felt that it had produced little of value and that it had lost heavily by violating the old Greek concept. Yet in the Elizabethan drama only could Milton have found that which his classical studies had taught him to seek, a pattern for unrimed English heroic verse.[68]

In addition to an academic pageant, Milton's other early dramatic compositions were two masks, *Arcades,* and *Comus,* written to be presented at family celebrations. In the latter he had already begun to use his art for what he considered its proper purpose, to set forth virtue attractively. The Cambridge manuscript is devoted principally to plans for drama. This does not mean that by 1642 he had abandoned all idea of an epic.[69] It is, however, very likely that Milton was unusually interested in the possibilities of dramatic presentation of his ideas at this time. In *The Reason of Church-government* Milton seems to be advising the magistrates to adopt the old Greek policy, so effective in securing virtue in Athens, of combining religion with recreation through drama, just as he also advised reviving the Greek practice of martial sports. The Cambridge manuscript indicates that he had considered using the material of Britain, which he had already been pondering in connection with his epic, but that he had passed on to an even fuller consideration of biblical subjects. The closing of the theater rather than its utilization was, however, the Puritan answer to its corruption. By the time Milton again turned to literary composition, he was no longer interested in adapting his forms to instruct the vulgar. He had gone back to considering art forms as they suited his material: the epic for the fall of man and the pure Greek tragedy for *Samson Agonistes.* He deliberately chose to write a closet drama. What attracted him to the form was its unrivaled power as an artistic instrument of moral instruction, a power inherent in dia-

[66] *Apology for Smectymnuus,* Works, Columbia ed., III, 300.
[67] *Of Education,* Works, Columbia ed., IV, 285.
[68] *Paradise Lost,* Works, Columbia ed., II, 6.
[69] Gilbert, "The Cambridge Manuscript and Milton's Plans for an Epic," *Studies in Philology,* XVI (1919), 172–76.

logue, as Plato and the writer of *Job* had also realized. That Milton
considered the Greek tragedy a form peculiarly fit for the teaching
of exalted thought is evident from *Paradise Regain'd*. Satan, in
offering Jesus all worldly knowledge, offers the culture of Greece
including

> what the lofty grave Tragœdians taught
> In Chorus or Iambic, teachers best
> Of moral prudence with delight receiv'd
> In brief sententious precepts, while they treat
> Of fate, and chance, and change in human life;
> High actions and high passions best describing.[70]

So far this is only Satan's evaluation and as such open to suspicion.
But the answer of Jesus gives it unexpected confirmation. Jesus dis-
misses the Greek epic and lyric as inferior to the Scriptures, par-
ticularly in subject matter:

> Ill imitated, while they loudest sing
> The vices of their deities and their own
> In fable, hymn, or song, so personating
> Their gods ridiculous, and themselves past shame.
> Remove their swelling Epithets, thick laid
> As varnish on a harlot's cheek, the rest
> Thin sown with aught of profit or delight,
> Will far be found unworthy to compare
> With Sion's songs, to all true tastes excelling,
> Where God is praised aright and Godlike men.[71]

Exempt from this scathing criticism, however, are the tragedians,
who, guided by the light of nature (which was the nearest ap-
proach of the pagan world to the revealed light of the Christian
world), had expressed moral teachings that were still valid:

> Unless where moral virtue is expressed
> By light of nature, not in all quite lost.[72]

In drama, as in the epic, Milton desired to combine an already noble
type with still nobler matter, to graft the scriptural subject on the
stock of Greek tragedy. The result of that experiment was *Samson
Agonistes*. In the preface Milton summarizes and briefly expounds

---

[70] *Paradise Regain'd*, Works, Columbia ed., II, 468.   [71] *Ibid.*, p. 471.
[72] *Ibid.*

the Greek theory of tragedy, which he had chosen to follow in composing his dramatic poem:

Tragedy, as it was antiently compos'd, hath been ever held the gravest, moralest, and most profitable of all other Poems . . . This is mention'd to vindicate Tragedy from the small esteem, or rather infamy, which in the account of many it undergoes at this day with other common Interludes; hap'ning through the Poets error of intermixing Comic stuff with Tragic sadness and gravity; or introducing trivial and vulgar persons, which by all judicious hath been counted absurd; and brought in without discretion, corruptly to gratifie the people.

Milton suggests that those familiar with the three great Greek tragedians will be the best judges of his success in observing the unities and working within a limit that would correspond to five acts, although the divisions were not marked since the poem was intended to be read and not staged. He also comments on the complete freedom of the verse used in the choruses, a freedom possible because the choruses were to be read and not sung.

Thus Milton exceeded his models in the epic and dramatic fields theoretically by matching their form and surpassing their subject matter. There remained a third subdivision of lofty poetry, the lyric; but in this type he made no further experiments, probably because the lyric form throws the emphasis on manner of expression rather than on subject, whereas Milton tended to slough off the restricting bondage of rime and complex verse patterns so as to obtain the maximum freedom in his expression of thought. Through his other works Milton had both in general and in particular justified the ways of God to men. He had thus in part fulfilled what he deemed the purpose of the lyric—"to celebrate the throne and equipage of God's almightiness," even though he had not done it specifically in "glorious and lofty hymns." [73]

In addition to teaching him the laws of epic, dramatic, and lyric poetry and indicating models in each type, the study of classical and Renaissance critics had taught Milton "what decorum is (which is the grand master-piece to observe)." [74] The concept of decorum in Milton's theory of poetry is very broad, embracing all

[73] *Reason of Church-government*, Works, Columbia ed., III, 238.
[74] The punctuation of the quotation follows J. H. Hanford and Ida Langdon.

questions of suitable procedure. The most important point is to see that the great force of poetic art is applied only to worthy persons and actions. Milton flays the violators of this rule, the talented men who misapply their gift:

libidinous and ignorant Poetasters, who, having scars ever heard of that which is the main consistence of a true poem, the choys of such persons as they ought to introduce, and what is morall and decent to each one, doe for the most part lap up vitious principles in sweet pils.[75]

Having guided the choice to the right persons, the principle of decorum would also insure their speaking appropriately. Evil characters will advance plausible but specious arguments; virtuous figures will maintain the truth; nor will an excerpt arbitrarily chosen from the speeches of his characters necessarily represent the poet's own thoughts:

know then, I say, that we must not regard the poet's words as his own, but consider who it is that speaks in the play, and what that person says; for different persons are introduced, sometimes good, sometimes bad, sometimes wise men, sometimes fools, and they speak not always the poet's own opinion, but what is most fitting to each character.[76]

The poet's own thoughts are usually given to the most worthy characters.[77] But the whole matter is not as simple as that. Sometimes unrighteous characters speak most piously; the sanctimonious speech is frequently found in the mouth of the tyrant:

From Stories of this nature both Ancient and Modern which abound, the Poets also, and som English, have bin in this point so mindfull of Decorum, as to put never more pious words in the mouth of any person, than of a Tyrant.[78]

There is still another type of decorum which Milton frequently commented on. The suiting of style to subject involves a question of propriety. Elevated topics require an elevated tone; mean topics should be accorded a lower tone: "Proceeding on to speak of mysterious things in nature, I had occasion to fit the language thereafter." [79] Milton twits an opponent with violating decorum through insufficient ability: "(for I suppose he cannot even name

[75] *Reason of Church-government*, Works, Columbia ed., III, 238.
[76] *Pro populo anglicano defensio*, Works, Columbia ed., VII, 307.
[77] *Ibid.*, p. 327.   [78] *Eikonklastes*, Works, Columbia ed., V, 84.
[79] *Colasterion*, Works, Columbia ed., IV, 266.

the brave and courageous without nauseous affectation)." [80] A nice problem arises when a lofty subject is introduced where stylistic considerations require simple treatment:

I confess it is with difficulty I restrain myself from soaring to a more daring height than is suitable to the purpose of an exordium, . . . for I . . . surpass . . . the orators of all ages in the nobleness and in the instructiveness of my subject.[81]

This conflict gave rise to the device of consciously transcending a type for additional emphasis. Brilliant examples previously quoted are the artful digressions in *Lycidas*. The principal rule when breaking the bounds of strict type decorum was, with Milton as with Drayton, to indicate and explain your digression, as in the following case:

This story, though seeming otherwise too light in the midst of a sad narration, yet for the strangeness thereof, I thought worthy enough the placeing, as I found it plac't in my Authour. But to digress no farder.[82]

Decorum emerges as a term of wide application. It might concern the proper employment of poetry for worthy subjects. In its more common use, it included differentiation of character through appropriate speech, and suiting the type of poetry or prose to the topic treated. This last was a rule more honored in the breach than the observance, as a brilliant digression was always in order.

Closely related to the principle of decorum is the question of the proper use of fiction. A distinguishing quality of poetry, according to Milton, was that it employed fiction to teach truth. It was not required to be literally accurate; the function of poetry was to present truth figuratively and allegorically:

Certainly, in this he imitated . . . the poets . . . , by whom no secret and hidden mystery is exhibited in public, unless clad in some covering or garment.[83]

Inasmuch as poetry makes no pretense of being an exact art, the reader must not attempt to analyze the fable too minutely, but he should strive to get the general impression that the poet intended

[80] *Pro populo anglicano defensio*, Works, Columbia ed., VII, 21.
[81] *Defensio secunda*, Works, Columbia ed., VIII, 13.
[82] *History of Britain*, Works, Columbia ed., X, 308.
[83] *Prolusiones*, No. 2, Works, Columbia ed., XII, 151.

to leave. Milton has no patience with the kind of person who reasons from the details of a poem or story "as if a parable were to be straind through every word or phrase, and not expounded by the general scope thereof." [84] Yet nothing could be more ignorant than to reject poetry because it does not deal in demonstrable fact. That function is fulfilled by other kinds of writing. In its own fashion poetry treats of more profound truths than may well be directly stated:

> Ile tell ye, 'tis not vain or fabulous,
> (Though so esteem'd by shallow ignorance)
> What the sage Poets taught by the heav'nly Muse,
> Storied of old in high immortal vers. [85]

Milton takes advantage of the fact that the free use of fiction is typical of poetry and extraordinary in prose to cast a slur on *Eikon Basilikon*:

I begun to think that the whole Book might be perhaps intended a piece of Poetrie. The words are good, the fiction smooth and cleanly. [86]

In his own prose writings Milton was always careful to distinguish fictional interpolations as such:

as they fable happened of old to Tmolus, the popular god of the Lydian mountain. [87]

Not with so much labour, as the fables have it, is Ceres said to have sought her daughter Proserpina, as it is my habit day and night to seek for this idea of the beautiful. [88]

Madness, says the tale, turned Hecuba into a dog. [89]

His ideas on the correct use of unauthenticated material are most clearly shown at the beginning of the *History of Britain*. Milton was emphatic on the point that history should deal in truth; [90] he

[84] "Civil Power in Ecclesiastical Causes," Works, Columbia ed., VI, 27. Cf. *Prolusiones*, No. I, Works, Columbia ed., XII, 129; *Defensio secunda*, Works, Columbia ed., VIII, 219; *Pro populo anglicano defensio*, Works, Columbia ed., VIII, 111.

[85] *Comus*, Works, Columbia ed., I, 104.

[86] *Eikonoklastes*, Works, Columbia ed., V, 125.

[87] *Familiar Letters*, Works, Columbia ed., XII, 9.

[88] *Ibid.*, p. 27.

[89] *Pro populo anglicano defensio*, Works, Columbia ed., VII, 343.

[90] I think J. Milton French goes too far in his article "Milton as a Historian" (PMLA, L, 469–79), when he argues from this that Milton's interests were primarily prosaic, that he was a "reluctant poet."

would not even assign probable speeches to kings and generals in order to enliven the chronicle; but there were no facts for the earliest period and so, after a long explanation, he began with material that was merely fabulous. The stories were not utterly unbelievable; there was the possibility of some truth in them. He included them, however, chiefly for the sake of poets:

I have therefore determin'd to bestow the telling over ev'n of these reputed Tales; be it for nothing else but in favour of our English Poets, and Rhetoricians, who by thir Art will know, how to use them judiciously.[91]

In view of these considerations, it is hard to agree with Mr. P. F. Jones, who, in an article on "Milton and the Epic Subject" suggests that Milton abandoned his proposed British epic because he "would be unwilling to employ his Muse on a tale of questionable authenticity, which, . . . he thought had been besmirched in the handling." [92] Certainly the details of the conclave in hell are as purely fictional as the sessions of the Round Table. Milton did not, like Cowley, choose a completely historical part of the Scriptures as his subject, for the ability to use fiction properly was one of the prime characteristics of the true poet.

Like most of the major poets of the era, Milton exhibited a strong feeling of nationalism. He saw in England "a Nation not slow and dull, but of a quick, ingenious and piercing spirit, acute to invent, suttle and sinewy to discours, not beneath the reach of any point, the highest that human capacity can soar to." [93] He felt, as Wither did, that England had been specially marked out for favor by God. His trip to Italy had made him conscious of the large freedom he had enjoyed at home.[94] His faith in the future of England was far too great to make him seek in the past for proofs of her nobility. Thus he exposes the childish effort to link Britain with Rome by means of the Brut legend.[95] But he was deeply interested in doing his part to shape a glorious and god-like nation. The Englishman was excellent raw material and, properly in-

[91] *History of Britain,* Works, Columbia ed., X, 3.

[92] Jones, "Milton and the Epic Subject from British History," PMLA, XLII (Dec., 1927), 901-9.

[93] *Areopagitica,* Works, Columbia ed., IV, 339.   [94] *Ibid.,* p. 329.

[95] *History of Britain,* Works, Columbia ed., X, 6.

structed, would take first rank.[96] He saw himself cast in the role of instructor:

Then, . . . some one may perhaps bee heard offering at high strains in new and lofty Measures to sing and celebrate thy divine Mercies, and marvellous Judgements in this Land throughout all Ages; (whereby this great and godlike nation, instructed and inured to the fervent and continual practise of truth and righteousness, and casting far from her the rags of her whole vices, may press on to that high and happy emulation to be found the soberest, wisest, and most Christian people.[97]

It was partly a result of his patriotism that, although he had prepared to write both Latin and English poetry,[98] he abandoned all idea of writing in Latin in order to instruct his countrymen in their own tongue:

For which cause, [the honor and instruction of his country] and not only for that I knew it would be hard to arrive at the second rank among the Latines, I apply'd myself . . . to fix all the industry and art I could unite to the adorning of my native tongue; not to make verbal curiousities the end (that were a toylsom vanity,) but to be an interpreter and relator of the best and sagest things, among mine own Citizens throughout this Iland in the mother dialect. That what the greatest and choycest wits of Athens, Rome, or modern Italy, and those Hebrews of old did for their country, I, in my proportion, with this over and above, of being a Christian, might do for mine.[99]

His very desire to conform to classical procedure became a reason for writing in his own language. He realized that the greatest of his forerunners had written in tongues native to them. Nor did he pretend to be equally at ease in both tongues. In his university address, against custom he broke over from Latin prose into English verse.[100] By 1640 he had already determined on the use of English for his epic.[101] The same choice is evident in his prose. He nowhere uses Latin unless the occasion demands it. He gives patriotism and a kind of loyal preference for his native tongue as his reasons for writing *The Doctrine and Discipline of Divorce* in English.[102]

[96] *Reason of Church-government*, Works, Columbia ed., III, 225.
[97] *Of Reformation*, Columbia ed., III, 78.
[98] *Familiar Letters*, Works, Columbia ed., XII, 17.
[99] *Reason of Church-government*, Works, Columbia ed., III, 236.
[100] *Sixth Academic Exercise*, Works, Columbia ed., I, 19.
[101] *Epitaphium Damonis*, Works, Columbia ed., I, 313.
[102] *Doctrine and Discipline of Divorce*, Works, Columbia ed., III, 378.

Furthermore, Milton held the theory that it was a mark of unsoundness in a country if its great men employed a foreign language.[103] Conversely, he considered the correct use of the native tongue an index of a healthy state. In a letter to the Florentine grammarian, Bonmattai, he accounts it as next in importance to good government "to establish in maxims and rules the methods and habits of speaking and writing received from a good age of the nation." [104]

If Milton had expected the British public to be grateful for his patriotic endeavors to enlighten it, he was soon bitterly disillusioned. From his student days, he had had little feeling for an audience. He realized that he attracted a very limited group of listeners and was content to accept that situation and dismiss the inattentive ones as not worth holding:

By these indeed, however few, for my part, I would prefer to be approved, than by innumerable companies of the ignorant.[105]

He paid no attention to current trends of public taste, but wrote acknowledgedly for a chosen few and continually thrust away the vulgar. Even in the pamphlets which by their very nature were addressed to the general reading public, he frequently inserts passages designed for a more limited group. He appeals to the "intelligent and equal auditor" and wishes to "be heard only, if it might be, by the elegant and learned reader, to whom principally for a while, I shal beg leav I may addresse my selfe." [106] Again he discriminates among his hearers: "All persons of gentle breeding . . . I know will apprehend and bee satisfy'd in what I spake." [107]

The vulgar he belabors for their many failings, especially for their love of words rather than ideas, their foolish admiration of a florid style. "Pomp and ostentation of reading is admir'd among the vulgar." [108] He criticizes the writings of Salmasius as having no practical value and as being "stuffed with scraps of citation from eminent authors; than which nothing sooner excites the wonder-

---

103 *History of Britain*, Works, Columbia ed., X, 292.
104 *Familiar Letters*, Works, Columbia ed., XII, 31.
105 *Prolusiones*, Works, Columbia ed., XII, 121.
106 *Reason of Church-government*, Works, Columbia ed., III, 234.
107 *Colasterion*, Works, Columbia ed., IV, 261.
108 *Civil Power in Ecclesiastical Causes*, Works, Columbia, ed., VI, 41.

ment of the literary vulgar." [109] Milton soon regretted having written on divorce in English and having thereby laid himself open to the reaction of the "vernacular readers." [110] In proportion as he mistrusted the majority, he pinned his faith to the chosen few.[111] In *Eikonoklastes* there is the sharpest contrast between such expressions as "the blockish vulgar" and "what a miserable, credulous, deluded thing that creature is, which is call'd the Vulgar," and the audience he desires,[112]

Few perhaps, but those few, such of value and substantial worth, as truth and wisdom, not respecting numbers and bigg names, have bin wont in all ages to be contented with.[113]

This attitude concerning an audience was equally characteristic of Milton the poet. He rejoices that his book of early poems is lodged in the Bodleian "into which the wanton tongue of the rabble will not make its way, from which the throngs of worthless readers will speed afar." [114] *Paradise Lost* continues to stress "How few sometimes may know, when thousands err." [115] It reiterates his desire for "fit audience . . . though few." [116]

Milton's requirement for a desirable critic was a thorough grounding in the theory of the art he was judging:

none can judge of a painter, or statuary, but he who is an artist, that is either in the practice or theory, which is often separated from the practice and judges learnedly without it.[117]

In *Of Education* he proposed a careful course in the theory of poetry, using Aristotle, Horace, and the Renaissance Italian critics as texts and the great masterpieces as illustrations. He asked Bonmattai, a Florentine grammarian, to add a critical section to his work, evaluating the lesser-known Italian works so that foreigners might have guidance similar to that offered by Cicero and Fabius in Latin.[118] Altogether his ideal reader-critic would have exactly that basis for judgment which the vulgar lacked, a background of

[109] *Defensio secunda*, Works, Columbia ed., VIII, 101.
[110] *Ibid.*, p. 115. Cf. *Familiar Letters*, Works, Columbia ed., XII, 73.
[111] *Defensio secunda*, Works, Columbia ed., VIII, 155.
[112] *Eikonoklastes*, Works, Columbia ed., V, 64, 143. [113] *Ibid.*, p. 65.
[114] *Ad Joannem Rousium*, Works, Columbia ed., I, 325.
[115] *Paradise Lost*, Works, Columbia ed., II, 183. [116] *Ibid.*, II, 212.
[117] *Apology for Smectymnuus*, Works, Columbia ed., III, 346.
[118] *Familiar Epistles*, Works, Columbia ed., XII, 37.

selected reading and some conversance with the theory of poetry.

Just as Milton's theories of poetic procedure show a consecrated employment of the rich store of traditional patterns, so his theory of poetic fame represents a Christian adaptation of the pagan concept of *fama*. That the whole question was never far from his mind is attested by his frequent references to various aspects of it. The immortality of poetry was primarily important to Milton as a means of preserving that knowledge which should add to human virtue and divine glory, but there was also the secondary question of personal fame to be considered. A new responsibility rests on the poet from the very fact that

> he knows the charms
> That call Fame . . .
> And he can spred thy Name o're Lands and Seas.[119]

Like Drayton, Milton was most eager to fulfill the purpose of heaven in his use of this power. That its function was to perpetuate glorious deeds and to immortalize their doers he deduced from historical evidence. First, epic talent was rare:

> Yea, since in so many ages as are gone over the world, there has been but here and there a man found, able to recount worthily the actions of great heroes and potent states.[120]

Second, it seemed to appear when it was needed to celebrate worthy acts; it seemed designed to serve as a reward for the actor:

> For worthy deeds are not often destitute of worthy relators: as by a certain fate, great acts and great eloquence have most commonly gone hand in hand, equalling and honoring each other in the same ages. But he whose just and true valour uses the necessity of war . . . to bring in liberty . . . knowing that when he conquers all things else, he cannot conquer Time or Detraction, wisely conscious of this his want, as well as of his worth not to be forgotten or concealed, honours and hath recourse to the aid of eloquence . . . by whose immortal record his noble deeds, which else were transitory, become fixed and durable against the force of years and generations.[121]

Conversely, "eloquence . . . with the decrease and fall of virtue, corrupts also and fades." [122] Milton's deduction from this was that the two were related in the divine scheme of things:

119 "Sonnet VIII," Works, Columbia ed., I, 60.
120 *Pro populo anglicano defensio*, Works, Columbia ed., VII, 7.
121 *History of Britain*, Works, Columbia ed., X, 32.   122 *Ibid.*

I thought, therefore, that if it were the will of God those men should per-
form such gallant exploits, it must be likewise his will, that when performed,
there should be others to set them forth with becoming dignity and orna-
ment.[123]

By force of circumstances, most of Milton's recording of the
worthy deeds of his contemporaries was in prose, but in the earlier
writings he looked forward to immortalizing the victories of his
side in poetry, when time should permit. He apologizes to God,
the victory-giver, for his lesser offering, by proposing a better one:

And he that now for haste snatches up a plain ungarnish't present as a
thanke-offering to thee, which could not bee deferr'd in regard of thy so
many late deliverances . . . may then perhaps take up a Harp and sing thee
an elaborate Song to Generations.[124]

In line with his belief that individual merit should have the reward
of fame, he carefully introduces the name of Lord Brook into
Areopagitica: "Ye know him, I am sure; yet I for honours sake,
and may it be eternall to him shall name him, the Lord Brook." [125]
Similarly, he devotes a paragraph in the *Defensio secunda* to com-
memorating the names of some of the outstanding Commonwealth
men.[126]

In his poetry, it is the idea of preserving rather than mourning
the memory of the dead that animates his elegies. "Is merit such as
yours to pass thus, nameless, and to be joined with a host of ob-
scure shades?" [127] Not, answers Milton, if it means anything for a
man to have been good and to have had a poet for a friend. He
invokes the Muses for Edward King, in the hope that someone will
perform the same office for him when he dies. That hope brings us
to the question of the poet's own prospect of fame. Did Milton,
like many of his forerunners, consider personal fame one of the
chief rewards of his art?

His early tribute to Shakespeare, enlarging upon Ben Jonson's
theme of Shakespeare's immortality, exhibits a purely Horatian at-
titude:

[123] *Defensio secunda*, Works, Columbia ed., VIII, 11.
[124] *Animadversions*, Works, Columbia ed., III, 148.
[125] *Areopagitica*, Works, Columbia ed., IV, 346.
[126] *Defensio secunda*, Works, Columbia ed., VIII, 235.
[127] *Epitaphium Damonis*, Works, Columbia ed., I, 299.

Dear son of memory, great heir of Fame,

. . . . .

Thou . . .
Hast built thyself a life-long Monument.

In 1632 he touches on the distinction that he will enjoy through his gift:

Therefore, since I am already a part, albeit the lowliest, of the learned [poetic] throng, I shall sit amid the victors' crowns of ivy and of laurel; no more now shall I mingle, a figure obscure, with the witless populace.[128]

But a disquieting thought had obtruded itself, the thought that earthly fame is not awarded in proportion to merit. This he considers in a Cambridge exercise which presents a debate between Ignorance and Learning. Ignorance declares that glory is mankind's most powerful incentive and points out that later-day writers will have a shorter span of glory because there will be fewer generations to succeed them. The answer is twofold: first; "But, in truth, not to value fame when you have done well, that is beyond all glory," and second;

May we hope for an eternal life, which will never wipe out the memory at least of our good deeds on earth: in which, if we have nobly deserved anything here, we ourselves, being present, shall hear it.[129]

His reply carries him far beyond the old Renaissance concept of *fama,* in that he extends the discussion to the heavenly enjoyment of merited glory. Milton's immortality of fame is no longer purely Horatian, but one that the worthy person begins to receive on earth and continues to know in heaven. It is this that Milton so ardently longs for in the letter to Diodati (1637): "You ask what I am thinking of? So may the good Deity help me, of immortality!" [130] His altered concept of fame is evident again when, speaking of learning (and learning, it must be remembered, was Milton's preparation for poetry), he includes fame, in the same bracket as the service of God and the love of truth, as a valid end of study:

such as evidently were born to study, and love learning for it self, not for lucre or any other end but the service of God and of truth, and perhaps that

---

128 *Ad patrem,* Works, Columbia ed., I, 277.

129 *Prolusiones,* No. 7, Works, Columbia ed., XII, 279, 281.

130 *Familiar Epistles,* Works, Columbia ed., XII, 27.

lasting fame and perpetuity of praise which God and good men have con-
sented shall be the reward of those whose publisht labours advance the good
of mankind.[131]

Having revised the Renaissance concept by the addition of a
heavenly element, Milton gradually began to emphasize his own
amendment and to withdraw further from the original idea. In the
last analysis, the longing for an earthly immortality was a human
weakness. It was, to be sure, the noblest of human weaknesses, in
that the effort to satisfy it, when properly directed, led to glorious
results. It was in no sense reprehensible, since God approved of hu-
man desires when they led to virtue. "Wherefore did he create pas-
sions within us, pleasures round about us, but that these, rightly
temper'd are the very ingredients of vertu?"[132] But fame was no
fair or certain reward. What of the man who devoted his life to
arduous preparation, yet did not live to achieve a work that should
merit glory? In order to resolve this difficulty, Milton had to aban-
don almost entirely the classical and Renaissance position and give
a purely Reformation answer: such a man loses, of course, the
earthly renown which it was natural and noble to have desired;
glory of another kind awaits him, not the praise of men, but the
approbation of God, a truly immortal reward:

> Fame is no plant that grows on mortal soil,
> Nor in the glistering foil
> Set off to th' world, nor in broad rumour lies,
> But lives and spreds aloft by those pure eyes,
> And perfet witnes of all judging Jove;
> As he pronounces lastly on each deed,
> Of so much fame in Heav'n expect thy meed.

Thus *Lycidas* develops the theory of two kinds of fame, earthly
and heavenly, with the latter far more important. Renaissance
fama had value mainly as an immediate, self-evident reward that
would stimulate the writer to work; it was important as an activat-
ing force rather than as a result.

A second consideration that caused Milton to distrust earthly
fame was that it depended so frequently on arousing the admira-
tion of the vulgar. Nothing could have been more directly opposite

---

[131] *Areopagitica*, Works, Columbia ed., IV, 323, 324.   [132] *Ibid.*, p. 319.

to his tastes and aims.[133] Those who wrote only to secure the praise of the vulgar Milton assigned contemptuously to the Paradise of Fools:

> . . . and all who in vain things
> Built their fond hopes of Glorie or lasting fame,
>
> .   .   .   .
>
> Naught seeking but the praise of men, here find
> Fit retribution, emptie as thir deeds.[134]

The fullest exposition of the whole question occurs in *Paradise Regain'd,* where Satan presents the old point of view in offering earthly fame to Jesus:

> wherefore deprive
>   . . . thy self
> The fame and glory, glory the reward
> That sole excites to high attempts the flame
> Of most erected Spirits, most temper'd pure
> Aetherial, who all pleasures else despise.

The answer of Jesus shows that the older Milton, thoroughly disillusioned as to his audience, had lost almost all interest in earthly fame and had centered his faith on a just and merited heavenly renown:

> For what is glory but the blaze of fame,
> The peoples praise, if always praise unmixt?
> And what the people but a herd confus'd,
> A miscellaneous rabble, who extol
> Things vulgar, and well weigh'd, scarce worth the praise
>
> .   .   .   .
>
> And what delight to be by such extoll'd
> To live upon thir tongues and be thir talk,
> Of whom to be disprais'd were no small praise?
>
> .   .   .   .
>
> Th'intelligent among them and the wise
> Are few, and glory scarce of few is rais'd.
> This is true glory and renown, when God
> Looking on the Earth, with approbation marks
> The just man, and divulges him through Heaven.[135]

---

[133] *Familiar Letters*, Works, Columbia ed., XII, 105.
[134] *Paradise Lost*, Works, Columbia ed., II, 93.
[135] *Paradise Regain'd*, Works, Columbia ed., II, 443, 444.

The reward of heavenly fame is sufficient not only for men but for angels, and the terrible doom of heavenly oblivion is not the least punishment of the fallen angels:

> I might relate of thousands, and thir names
> Eternize here on Earth; but those elect
> Angels contented with thir fame in Heav'n
> Seek not the praise of men, the other sort
> In might though wondrous and in Acts of Warr,
> Nor of Renown less eager, yet by doome
> Canceld from Heav'n and sacred memorie,
> Nameless in dark oblvion let them dwell.
>
> .   .   .   .   .
>
> Therefore Eternal silence be thir doome.[136]

Although Milton's ultimate ideas were a far cry from the starting point of Renaissance fame, his theory represented not a rejection but an intensification of the original. He never questioned the validity of the basic concept, the public recognition of exceptional individual merit. But because that principle was not equitable in its action on earth, Milton translated the whole phenomenon into heavenly terms, a procedure to which his religious background strongly predisposed him.

Even when he was still vitally interested in his earthly fame, Milton abandoned the project by which he had the best hope of securing renown to do what he considered his duty. In a passage in the *Reason of Church-government,* he was very careful to point out that his discussion of spectacular political issues was not a mere bid for immediate fame; his bid was to be a poetic one.[137] In *Eikonoklastes* he again denies the charge that he sought fame through his pamphleteering:

Neither was it fond ambition, nor the vanity to get a Name, present, or with Posterity, by writing against a King: I never was so thirsty after Fame, nor so destitute of other hopes and means, better and more certaine to attaine it.[138]

It was to be his poetry that the world would not willingly let die. But even in his poetry he was willing to forego the prospect of in-

---

136 *Paradise Lost,* Works, Columbia ed., II, 191.
137 *Reason of Church-government,* Works, Columbia ed., III, 235.
138 *Eikonklastes,* Works, Columbia ed., V, 63.

ternational fame in order to achieve a higher end, and accordingly greater heavenly glory, by instructing his own people:

I apply'd my selfe to that resolution . . . to fix all the industry and art I could unite to the adorning of my native tongue; not to make verbal curiousities the end (that were a toylsom vanity,) but to be an interpreter and relator of the best and sagest things, among mine own Citizens throughout this Iland in the mother dialect . . . not caring to be once nam'd abroad, though perhaps I could attaine to that, but content with these British Ilands as my world.[139]

The degree of the subjective element in Milton's poetry is closely related to his general theory. Almost every reference to himself involves some aspect of his poetic career. The two parallel pastorals are composite sketches of the days and nights of a youthful poet. *Lycidas* gives his answer to the problem of fame. The *Epitaphium Damonis* outlines his epic plans. The personal passages are a constant reminder that Milton considered his early poetry as part of his preparation for heroic measures. His "low" poetry should therefore mark the milestones of progress, give assurance of what was to come. The poet, when exalted by inspiration, is permitted to speak of himself as the instrument of his gift, without accusation of vanity:

For although a Poet, soaring in the high region of his fancies with his garland and singing robes about him might without apology speak more of himself than I mean to do, yet for me sitting here below in the cool element of prose, a mortall thing among many readers of no Empyreall conceit, to venture and divulge unusual things of my selfe, I shall petition to the gentler sort, it may not be envy to me.[140]

This privilege Milton carried over into prose when he considered it necessary to vindicate his motives or his character. Accusations against his character could not be ignored as irrelevant personalities since, in his theory, only the good man could write good works: "So that how he should be truly eloquent who is not withall a good man, I see not." [141] Thus in the *Defensio secunda* he goes into the greatest biographical detail to save his good reputation. In *Paradise Lost* he stretches beyond classical bounds Aristotle's permission for

[139] *Reason of Church-government*, Works, Columbia ed., II., 236.
[140] *Ibid.*, p. 235.
[141] *Apology for Smectymnuus*, Works, Columbia ed., III, 287. Cf. *ibid.*, III, 303.

a very slight subjective element, so that he may include two personal points: first, the fact of his blindness, which he accepted with greater faith than Job; second, the fluent and easy quality of his divine inspiration. Strongly he sings that he is still himself, still, by virtue of his predestination and preparation, a great poet only now engaged in his long-delayed task. He sings with voice

> unchang'd
> To hoarce or mute, though fall'n on evil dayes.[142]

The opening of *Paradise Regain'd* is far more typical of the classical epic formula: a mere identification of the singer, a brief statement of the topic of the new song, and a short invocation. There is no mention of blindness or evil days. *Samson Agonistes,* inasmuch as it is a drama, is completely free from direct personal utterance except for the wholly objective explanation of an unfamiliar type that precedes the play proper. The intense subjective element has been completely assimilated and incorporated into the art form.

Of all the men who sought to achieve the epic goal in English, Milton alone fully succeeded. Spenser's epical romance was left only half finished; Drayton was led by his dominant nationalism into an entirely different kind of long poem; the accomplishment of Giles Fletcher was too brief, that of his brother too allegorical; Browne abandoned his project abruptly; Wither lost all consideration of style in performing his role as remembrancer; Cowley, too servile in his imitation of Vergil, after four books bored himself to the point where he could write no more. Milton's art was founded upon a rock, the passion to teach his countrymen high matter through forms that had proven their worth. He deliberately absorbed all the strength of previous tradition and converted it to his own purpose. In part, Milton's greater success was the measure of his greater gift of song, but that alone would have been of little avail. Much of the secret of his genius lay in the power to accept the seventeenth-century theory of poetry in its purest, broadest, and highest form and to consecrate himself to the discipline and toil that such a theory demanded.

---

142 *Paradise Lost,* Works, Columbia ed., II, 212.

CHAPTER X

JOHN DONNE

IT IS GENERALLY more difficult to formulate the poetic princi-
ples of the minor group than of the major writers. The minor poet
is usually not primarily concerned with poetry. He has little or no
occasion to write explanatory prefaces or notes; neither is he likely
to introduce into his works revealing digressions. Frequently it is
impossible to determine whether the sentiment he advances in a
poem is real or feigned. No case, perhaps, is more disappointing
than that of Donne. The man whom Ben Jonson regarded as his
peer in criticism nowhere professed a positive and comprehensive
theory of poetry. The man who broke the smooth, sweet, singing
tradition of the lyric and substituted for the "stuff of the Meta-
morphoses"

images drawn from all the sciences of the day, from the definitions and dis-
tinctions of the Schoolmen, from the travels and speculations of the new
age, and . . . from the experiences of everyday life,[1]

had very little to say about his reforms. He could and occasionally
did write in the traditional fashion. There is little to indicate a con-
sistent or progressive plan, much to show that his works were what
the whim of the poet dictated at the time. Such of his verses as were
published during his lifetime were published for reasons of ex-
pediency, ulterior to true poetic purpose. Poetic principle was not a
matter of great importance in his hectic and troubled career:

He speaks, in a letter, of "descending to print anything in verse"; and it is
certain that he was never completely absorbed by his own poetry, or at all
careful to measure his achievements against those of others. He took his own
poems very seriously, he worked upon them with the whole force of his
intellect; but to himself, even before he became a divine, he was something
more than a poet. Poetry was but one means of expressing the many-sided
activity of his mind and temperament.[2]

---

[1] The Poems of John Donne, ed. by Grierson, II, xxxviii.

[2] Symons, *John Donne*, from "The Library of Literary Criticism," by Charles W.
Moulton.

In addition to such theories as have been deduced by various critics
from his practice, we have only meager and scattered comment by
Donne himself:

> To know and feel all this, and not to have
>   Words to expresse it, makes a man a grave
> Of his own thoughts.[3]

Taken in the light of supporting facts, this quotation is the
epitome of Donne's poetic creed. The poets of the minor group
tend to regard their poetry more from the point of view of the
effect on the writer than from the point of view of the audience,
and they count as one of the great values of their gift the relief
self-expression affords their own pent-up emotions:

> But as a Lay Mans Genius doth controule
> Body and mind; the Muse beeing the Soules Soule
> Of Poets, that methinks should ease our anguish.[4]

The greater the stress on self-expression, the less necessity there is
for the author to consult tradition for topics and forms. Donne,
wishing to write of love, rejected the stereotyped sentiments and
conventional mold of previous amorist. He was contemptuous of
love poetry that proceeded from the muse rather than from man's
actual experience:

> Love's not so pure, and abstract, as they use
> To say, which have no Mistresse but their Muse.[5]

He was equally contemptuous of those whose poetry recorded only
the complaints of rejected passion:

> After a such fruition . . . I
>   shall to love more thankfull Sonnets Make,
> Then if more honour, teares, and paines were spent.[6]

He disliked "whining" love poetry.[7] Certainly the torments of love
should not be sung in pleasing verse if the writer desired relief. It
would take another type of writing to obtain that. The charm of
pleasing verse would only serve to augment the force of passion:

> I thought, if I could draw my paines,
> Through Rimes vexation, I should them allay,

---

[3] Poems, I, 134.   [4] Ibid., p. 207.   [5] Ibid., p. 33.   [6] Ibid., p. 95.   [7] Ibid., p. 16.

> Griefe brought to numbers cannot be so fierce,
> For, he tames it, that fetters it in verse.
>
> .   .   .   .
>
> To Love, and Griefe tribute of Verse belongs,
> But not of such as pleases when 'tis read,
> Both are increased by such songs.[8]

His dissatisfaction with the drama,[9] for which he assigns no reason, is probably another illustration of his aversion to a form of art in which passion is objective and romanticized rather than subjective and realistic; the drama, too, was a form in which a conventional concept of love was thoroughly established and usually followed.

Donne reacted particularly against the kind of direct "borrowing" that characterized the period. He was scornful of the imitative exercises, the modeling after successful patterns, which many of the poets considered a necessary foundation for their art:

> But hee is worst, who (beggarly) doth chaw
> Others wits fruits, and in his ravenous maw
> Rankly digested, doth those things out-spue,
> As his owne things.[10]

He scored the "wit pirates" [11] and was proud to assert in the preface to his "Progresse of the Soul": "Now when I beginne this booke, I have no purpose to come into any mans debt." [12] He could say in all honesty "I give to Nature, all that I in Ryme have writ." [13]

He extended the famous advice of Sidney; not only his subject matter but also his style was self-derived. His far more compact and difficult manner of expression was what might be expected of a poet who was trying to achieve a newly precise vehicle for communicating feeling, rather than to demonstrate his control over the "inchanting power of verse." In a few cases Donne goes so far as to excuse manifestly poor versification by calling attention to the excellence of what he has said:

> Now if this song be too 'harsh for rime, yet, as
> The Painters bad god made a good devill,

---

[8] Poems, I, 16.   [9] Ibid., p. 150. Cf. p. 187.   [10] Ibid., p. 150.
[11] Ibid., p. 173.   [12] Ibid., p. 295.   [13] Ibid., p. 57.

> 'Twill be good prose, although the verse be evill,
> If thou forget the rime as thou dost passe.[14]

His muse is essentially a giver of matter; form, though admittedly the criterion of poetry, is always minimized. He criticizes certain of his own verses because they lack substance and possess only rime.[15] The emphasis on matter and the chafing at "rimes vexation," carried to their logical conclusion, lead to Donne, the prose artist. And yet there was at least one respect in which verse possessed an enormous advantage over prose, namely, in its power of survival. Donne had been deeply impressed by the fact that slight verses lasted as long as weighty histories. He was reminded of it every time he looked at his own bookshelves:

> Here gathering Chroniclers, and by them stand
> Giddie fantastique Poets of each land.[16]

Immortality was not dependent upon bulk of work in any art:

> . . . a hand, or eye
> By Hilliard drawne, is worth an history,
> By a worse painter made.[17]

The same principle applied in literature:

> And if unfit for tombes and hearse
> Our legend bee, it will be fit for verse;
> And if no peece of Chronicle wee prove,
> We'll build in sonnets pretty roomes;
> As well a well wrought urne becomes
> The greatest ashes, as halfe acre tombes.[18]

He discusses the phenomenon most completely in anticipating the argument that the commemoration of Elizabeth Drury was "matter fit for Chronicle, not verse":

> Vouchsafe to call to minde that God did make
> A last, and lasting'st peece, a Song. He spake
> To Moses to deliver unto all,
> That song, because hee knew they would let fall
> The Law, the Prophets, and the History
> But keepe the song still in their memory.

---

[14] Poems, I, 204. Cf. *ibid*., p. 205.　　　　[15] *Ibid*., p. 213.　　　　[16] *Ibid*., p. 145.
[17] *Ibid*., p. 175.　　　　　　　　　　　　　[18] *Ibid*., p. 15.

Verse hath a middle nature: heaven keepes Soules,
The grave keepes bodies, Verse the Fame enroules.[19]

On the use of verse to preserve fame Donne is in complete accord
with the dominant poetic principle of his period. Such selections
as the following were written by most of the seventeenth-century
poets:

I would show future times
What you were, and teach them to'urge towards such.
Verse embalmes vertue; 'and Tombs, or Thrones of rimes,
Preserve fraile transitory fame, as much
As spice doth bodies from corrupt aires touch.[20]

The same note rings out in his valediction of his book:

How I shall stay, though she Esloygne me thus
And how posterity shall know it too.[21]

But he is not extreme in his theory of poetic fame. He never guar-
antees that it will last to eternity, only that it will affect posterity.
He qualified even his powerful argument in the poem on Elizabeth
Drury quoted above; her fame will last to the end of the world,
because, in his conceit, the world is even now in a decline owing to
her death. He suggests very reasonably

These Hymnes may worke on future wits, and so
May great Grand children of thy prayses grow.[22]

The service that Donne performed for the satire is akin to that
which he rendered the lyric. He was one of those who freed it
from the trammels of fable and pastoral innuendo. He tried to
catch the clever, stinging flavor, the sharp realism of the Roman
writers; his own brilliance and hatred of sham were deeply akin to
theirs. Dryden praises the wit but censures the style of Donne's
satires:

Would not Donne's satires, which abound with so much wit, appear more
charming, if he had taken care of his words, and of his numbers? But he
followed Horace so very close that of necessity he must fall with him.[23]

---

[19] Poems, I, 245.   [20] Ibid., p. 199.   [21] Ibid., p. 29.   [22] Ibid., p. 252.
[23] Essay on Satire, The Critical and Miscellaneous Prose Works of John Dryden, ed.
by Malone, III, 202.

Grierson, wiser in the ways of Donne, points out that "verse of this kind seldom is poetry in the full sense of the word; but, as Stevenson says . . . talk not song." [24] He recognizes the satirist as a "verse-talker." Donne's treatment was deliberately rough because satire was considered primarily a vehicle for thought, the poetic form that was and should be nearest prose. Dryden should have understood in part the reason for Donne's style:

> And this unpolish'd rugged verse I chose
> As fittest for discourse and nearest prose. [25]

The excessive irregularity, or as Taine calls it the "terrible crudeness," of early seventeenth-century satire sprang from an idea less understandable to a Dryden, the Renaissance concept of satire as satyr poetry, which should manifest something of the rude and untamed strength of a faun aroused to comment on human folly or vice. Although not so completely original in design and temper as his love lyrics, Donne's satires are by no means mere classical imitations. Grierson comments particularly on the unusual nature of the third satire, with its appeal for religious tolerance based on Donne's own experience in turning from the Roman to the Anglican church. [26]

At the other extreme from the sharp etching of the satires is the fulsome praise lavished on Lucy, Countess of Bedford; the impossible hyperbole, no matter how symbolic, heaped upon an unknown child, Elizabeth Drury; and the courtly adulation of the "Eclogue" of 1613. Donne had already rendered a verdict on this type of poetic activity:

> And they who write to Lords, rewards to get
> Are they not like singers at doores for meat? [27]

These works were not the result of free composition, but were written to serve various purposes and were to be widely circulated. Donne knew "what lawes of Poetry admit." [28] The perfect "Eclogue" of 1613 shows how smoothly he could write in the traditional strain when he chose. But he also made a bold effort to graft his own style on occasional verse, and the resulting hybrid was not

---

[24] Poems, II, xiv (Introduction).
[25] Religio Laici, The Works of John Dryden, ed. by Scott and Saintsbury, X, 53.
[26] Poems, II, xiv (Introduction).   [27] Ibid., I, 150.   [28] Ibid., p. 266.

particularly successful. His extravagance of thought in conventional settings was a sort of new wine in old bottles. It out-Heroded Herod. His Petrarchan compliments to Lucy were so fantastic that even he thought he had somewhat overshot the mark:

> But these . . .
> Tast of Poetique rage, or flattery.[29]

> So, my verse built of your just praise, might want
> Reason and likelihood.[30]

As Donne explained to Sir Robert Carr in reference to the matter of writing him an epithalamion, he was far better on subjects where his imagination might roam without check, where no one could raise the question of truth:

you know my uttermost when it was best, and even then I did best when I had least truth for my subjects. In this present case there is so much truth as it defeats all Poetry.[31]

This same quotation makes it clear that in Donne's secular poetry his movement was directed away from imitation and toward self-expression; it was not essentially a movement toward truth. He objected to the old forms and attitudes, not because they were artificial and fanciful but because they were *clichés* and not the natural medium of the writer.[32] He preferred his own extravagances of idea and phrase to those of his predecessors. Gods and goddesses, fairies and metamorphoses meant nothing to him; he lived in an even stranger imaginative world, the world of philosophical paradoxes and postulates. His is a different and more startling style, and he prizes it for just that reason:

> . . . and to worthyest things
> (Vertue, Art, Beauty, Fortune,) now I see
> Rareness, or use, not nature value brings.[33]

It was not long, however, before Donne began to feel that although he had avoided the slough of imitation, his faculties had not been very nobly employed, that the vain use of art to exhibit his brilliance was barely legitimate in one who knew of higher ends that claimed his attention:

[29] *Poems*, I, 193.   [30] *Ibid.*, p. 199.   [31] *Ibid.*, p. 288.
[32] *Ibid.*, p. 224.   [33] *Ibid.*, p. 191.

> Like one who'in her third widdowhood doth professe
> Her selfe a Nunne, tyed to retirednesse,
> So'affects my muse now, a chaste fallownesse;
> Since shee to few, yet to too many'hath showne
> How love song weeds, and Satyrique thornes are growne
> Where seeds of better Arts, were early sown
> Omissions of good, ill, as ill deeds bee.
> For though to us it seeme, 'and be light and thinne,
> Yet in those faithfull scales, where God throwes in
> Mens workes, vanity weighs as much as sinne.

> There is no Vertue, but Religion: [34]

With the growing concentration on religion came the feeling that his earlier work had been a lamentable application of his passions and power, a feeling generalized thus in "The Litanie":

> That learning, thine Ambassador,
> From thine allegiance wee never tempt,
>   That beauty, paradises flower
> For physicke made, from poyson be exempt,
>   That wit, borne apt high good to doe,
>   By dwelling lazily
> On Natures nothing, be not nothing too,
> That our affections kill us not, nor dye,
> Heare us. [35]

This feeling culminated in a prayer for complete worldly self-effacement:

> Seale then this bill of my Divorce to All,
> On whom those fainter beames of love did fall
> Marry those loves, which in youth scattered bee
> On Fame, Wit, Hopes (false mistresses) to thee. [36]

Not the least of his problems was how to establish the sincerity of this change, since it was utterly inconsistent with his former attitude. He reiterates the fact that a "white sincerity" now dominates his muse, as different from the extravagant intensity of his earlier work as the love of God is different from the worship of idols, despite the fact that its manifestations are similar.

> How shall my mindes white truth . . . be try'd
> They see idolatrous lovers weepe and mourne. [37]

---

[34] Poems, I, 185.   [35] Ibid., p. 347.   [36] Ibid., p. 353.   [37] Ibid., p. 325.

In token of his truth of purpose, Donne, on entering this new field
of poetry, was very eager to avoid his old delight in the agility and
acuteness of his mind. It was hard to reform his style, hard not to
slip into spectacular composition:

> When wee are mov'd to seeme religious
> Only to vent wit, Lord deliver us.[38]

> So when thy braine workes, ere thou utter it,
> Crosse and correct concupiscence of witt,[39]

He very rightly feared his own capacity for ingenious excuses to be
ingenious:

> Those heavenly Poets which did see
> Thy will, and it expresse
> In rythmique feet, in common pray for mee,
> That I by them excuse not my excesse
> In seeking secrets, or Poetiquenesse.[40]

The reward for the kind of brilliance he had hitherto manifested
was at best an earthly immortality, but Donne was now expending
his skill to a different purpose. His new attitude was completely
neutral toward worldly renown:

> From thirst, or scorne of fame, deliver us.[41]

His later poems were written not to gain earthly glory but to hymn
the heavenly glory in the hope of achieving it:

> But doe not, with a vile crowne of fraile bayes,
> Reward my muse's white sincerity,
> But what thy thorny crowne gain'd, that give mee.[42]

Donne is the first of a group of poets who, having cultivated
poetry casually in their youth, discovered that it was the perfect
medium for expressing the powerful religious emotions that pos-
sessed them during their later years. Under them the lyric was re-
leased from the old artificial, imitative bounds of the Renaissance
and the preoccupation with a Roman style that possessed the sons
of Ben. It emerged as a type capable of treating the most important
human convictions and clothing them in a fresh beauty of figure
and form. Having broken the dam of Petrarchan tradition, Donne

---

[38] *Ibid.*, p. 345.   [39] *Ibid.*, p. 333.   [40] *Ibid.*, p. 341.
[41] *Ibid.*, p. 344.   [42] *Ibid.*, p. 318.

most unexpectedly diverted the lyric stream into the channel of religion, where it was kept by his followers. Thus the lyric met at once with a remarkable development and an absolute check. Ben Jonson, it will be remembered, had cautioned the poet against entering the province of things unknowable and divine. His fear was well-founded. The poets who enter there are indifferent to a theory that hopes to elevate mankind by the spreading of demonstrable truth. They, too, teach virtue by means of poetry, but for them

There is no Vertue, but Religion.

CHAPTER XI

GEORGE HERBERT, RICHARD CRASHAW, AND HENRY VAUGHAN

DONNE'S LATER LYRICS provided the corner stone for the theory of Herbert, Crashaw, and Vaughan, each of whom felt that there was but little virtue in the poetry that was not religious. The main tenet of Herbert's poetic creed was that the gift of song was divine and should therefore be used in the service of God. The very first lines of his book are

> Lord, my first fruits present themselves to Thee;
> Yet not mine neither; for from Thee they came,
> And must return.[1]

This is merely a special application of his general philosophy, the broader view being

> Indeed, man's whole estate
> Amounts, and richly, to serve Thee.[2]

Poetry happened to be his particular "estate" and therefore his proper employment:

> To write a verse or two is all the praise
> That I can raise
> Mend my estate in any wayes
> Thou shalt have more.[3]

He says the same thing in more detail in another poem, promising the Lord the return of such honor, music, and wit as He shall choose to bestow.[4] In a third poem on the same subject, however, he realizes that if he were to receive more honors, he might, in his preoccupation with them, give less praise.[5] Thus he is reconciled to his state; for he considered it the glory of man that he alone could recognize and praise God's providence; especially did he consider it the sacred duty of those on whom the gift of writing had been conferred, to create fitting songs for their inarticulate fellows:

---

[1] The Complete Works of George Herbert, ed. by Grosart, I, 8.   [2] Ibid., p. 70.
[3] Ibid., p. 68.   [4] Ibid., p. 41.   [5] Ibid., p. 107.

Onely to man Thou hast made known Thy wayes,
And put the penne alone into his hand,
And made him secretarie of Thy praise.

Man is the world's high priest: he doth present
The sacrifice for all
He that to praise and laud Thee doth refrain
. . . robs a thousand who would praise Thee fain.[6]

In addition to the relief from pent-up emotions that expression affords the subjective writer, the religious poet enjoys the sense of performing a grave and high commission. From this knowledge proceeded a kind of glorious ecstasy, which Herbert described in "To God," a splendid uprush of inspiration during which the poet felt "the fecund strength of Poesy" sweep through him and give him new health of body and mind.[7]

If, like the other minor poets, Herbert was well aware of the value of poetry to the writer, he was by no means indifferent to the benefits it might confer on an audience. He hoped to have for readers those who would "make a gain" from their perusal of his works.[8] In "Obedience" he represented his writings as a contract, selling himself to God in return for God's sacrifice, and his hope that others might be moved thereby to do the same.[9] Especially did he wish to interest the young by using the attractive force of poetry:

Hearken unto a Verser who may chance
Ryme thee to good, and make a bait of pleasure.[10]

Among those who read with extraordinary interest Herbert's *The Temple* was the young Cambridge student, Richard Crashaw, who himself published in 1634 *Epigrammatum sacrorum liber,* as the name suggests, a book of religious verse in Latin. The titles of Crashaw's books are a helpful index to his development. Twelve years later, he showed his indebtedness to Herbert very clearly by calling his major work *Steps to the Temple;* yet he exhibited a certain independence in his poetic theory, since he included in the same volume the largely secular *Delights of the Muses.* The posthumous volume, *Carmen Deo nostro,* which includes most of his

---

[6] Herbert, Complete Works, I, 132.   [7] *Ibid.,* II, 156.
[8] *Ibid.,* I, 8.   [9] *Ibid.,* p. 117.   [10] *Ibid.,* p. 9.

early works, epitomizes in its title the general trend of his muse.

In the case of most of the minor poets, secular lyrics preceded their religious work. The secular works of Crashaw were apparently interpolations and by their innocuous nature reassert his dominantly religious interests. There is little of love, and that little is mainly translation, with the notable exception of the "Wishes. To his (supposed) Mistresse." There is the usual proportion of adulatory and elegaic verse, and there are several translations and imitations, the most important being "Musicks Duell." From the type of subject matter and the high percentage of translation, it is fair to deduce that Crashaw probably used his secular poetry for occasional verses or exercises. In one of the best of his secular pieces he pays tribute to the eternizing power of such art. This poem, "To the Morning," pictures him as having overslept. Apollo, angry at his disciple's conduct, bids him take Morpheus as his inspiring god, and Crashaw describes the consequences:

> Hence 'tis my humble fancie findes no wings,
> No nimble rapture starts to Heaven and brings
> Enthusiastic flames, such as can give
> Marrow to my plumpe Genius, make it live
> Drest in the glorious likeness of a Muse,
> . . . whose holy heats can warme
> The grave, and hold up an exalted arme
> To lift me from my lazy Urne, to climbe
> Upon the stooping shoulders of old Time,
> And trace Eternity.[11]

This is a brilliant statement of the power of poetry to immortalize its writer after his death; yet he shows a sense of the futility of such immortality in the couplets of his "In Memoriam":

> So while these lines can but bequeath
> A life perhaps unto his death
> His better Epitaph shall be
> His life still kept alive in thee.[12]

Evidently, although Crashaw thought secular poetry worth practicing and publishing, he had not fallen under the spell of poetic immortality. In the field of religious poetry, Crashaw's purpose

[11] Poems by Richard Crashaw, ed. by Waller, p. 146.
[12] English Poems by Richard Crashaw, ed. by Tutin, p. 29.

was the same as Herbert's. The dedication of *Epigrammatum sacrorum liber* to the Rev. Benjamin Lany assures him that "in it without doubt the very substance of theology being overlaid with a poetic grace, sets off its grandeur by loveliness." [13] He presents his purpose to the reader more simply. He will attempt to portray the events in the life of Christ so that the reader will say,

> O, not enough these things I love;
> But they are sweet all things above;
> And certainly the love of Him
> Deserves all other loves to dim.[14]

His concept of the supremacy of religious subject matter is expressed even more strongly in his poem "To the Name Above Every Name—Jesus":

> take from us
> All force of so Prophane a Fallacy
> To think ought sweet but that which smells of Thee.[15]

An even more striking conversion to the theory of Herbert was experienced by Henry Vaughan. He had already published two books of secular verse before reading *The Temple*. There was little in either the theory or practice of these early works to suggest the powerful mystic poet that later emerged. Such theories as he expressed were in no way original and were largely negative. He wanted to join the ranks of the poets, but he did not seem to be drawn toward any special topics or technique. Like Carew and Herrick, he was thoroughly subjective, centering the universe quite frankly in himself. The dedication of his early poems expresses the instinctive assurance of the lyric poet that his slight fancies outweigh the "durty Intelligence" of the times. Long before a climax in his own life supplied him with all-absorbing subject matter, while he had as yet no theme that really attracted him, he had developed far enough to reject certain topics. Thus he knew that the hymning of great events was not his function:

> let us
> 'Midst noise and War, of Peace and mirth discuss.

---

[13] The Complete Works of Richard Crashaw, ed. by Grosart, II, 12.
[14] *Ibid.*, p. 31.   [15] Poems by Richard Crashaw, ed. by Waller, p. 197.

> This portion thou wert born for: why should wee
> Vex at the times ridiculous miserie? [16]

Again, in another passage, he expresses the characteristic tendency of the minor poet to reject the macrocosm for the more secure ground of the microcosm:

> and, while this world
> In wild Excentricks now is hurld,
> Keep wee, like nature, the same Key,
> And walk in our forefathers way.
> Who into future times would peer
> Looks oft beyond his term set here. [17]

The exclusion of current events on the part of a secular poet would seem to lead most naturally to love as a theme, but Vaughan early assures the reader that his is a "Flame bright only in its own Innocence, that kindles nothing but a generous Thought." He apparently feared that someone would mistake the half dozen love poems to Amoret for the promptings of passion. If he paid little attention to the primary theme of the secular lyric poet, he paid less to the other popular subject, poetic immortality. His elegies are mild in their claims of preserving memory:

> yet as man
> Subject to Envy, and the common fate
> It may redeem thee to a fairer date. [18]

A jesting poem of thanks for the loan of a cloak suggests that

> (perhaps) thy love paid thus
> Might with my thanks out-live thy Cloke, and Us. [19]

What current events, love, and fame could not do, sack could. To that liquor he pays full homage for its power to release his fancy. He speaks of "royall, witty, Sacke, the Poets soule": [20]

> So, if a Nap shall take us, we shall all,
> After full Cups have dreams Poeticall. [21]

A poem to his retired friend urges him to return and drink sack:

[16] The Works of Henry Vaughan, ed. by Martin, I, 47.
[17] Ibid., p. 61.   [18] Ibid., p. 51.
[19] Ibid., p. 52.   [20] Ibid., p. 10.   [21] Ibid., p. 12.

> I have reserv'd 'gainst thy approach a Cup
> That were thy Muse stark dead, shall raise her up,
> And teach her yet more Charming words and skill
> Than ever Cœlia, Chloris, Astrophil,
> Or any of the Thredbare names Inspir'd.
> Poore riming lovers with a Mistris fir'd.[22]

He chose to translate from Ovid the passage in which the poets celebrate the birthday of Bacchus, "Blith god of Sack." [23]

One of Vaughan's lighter poems indicates that he, like Donne, was weary of certain time-worn poetic machinery. In an attempt to induce a money lender to cancel a debt, he promises him all the kingdom of poetry; the latter, itemized, proves to include Parnassus, Tempe, Pegasus, nymphs, roses, springs, and so forth. He approved the interweaving of fable and truth, "that commended mixture wished of old," [24] but he heartily disliked the rich Elizabethan excess of fancy, and he praised D'Avenant for correcting it.[25]

A reading of Vaughan's secular poetry leaves the unmistakable impression that his main object in writing was to be known as an author. That he had very little to say is evident from the large proportion of occasional verse and translation. The avowed purpose of the best of his early efforts, the translation of the tenth satire of Juvenal, was merely "to feather some slower Houres." [26] A very accurate self-portrait of the author at this period is given in the preface to *Silex Scintillans,* where he describes those wits who have spent their time in "a deliberate search or excogitation of idle words, and a most vain, insatiable desire to be reputed Poets." There seems to have been no other motive that impelled Vaughan to publish his first book of poems.

In this early period, Vaughan's conception of poetry was largely influenced by the practice of those whom he admired. Ben Jonson was the god of his idolatry,[27] flanked by such lesser figures as Randolph, Fletcher, Cartwright, D'Avenant, and Orinda. There is imitation of Donne in one poem [28] and borrowing from Browne in another,[29] and, in general, a dilettante and unfocused experimentation. His high regard for Jonson is, however, the principal deter-

---

[22] Vaughan, Works, I, 47.   [23] *Ibid.,* p. 65.   [24] *Ibid.,* p. 49.   [25] *Ibid.,* p. 64.
[26] *Ibid.,* p. 2.   [27] *Ibid.,* pp. 3, 55.   [28] *Ibid.,* p. 12.   [29] *Ibid.,* p. 12.

mining factor in his early theory; it accounts for the credit given
to sack as a source of inspiration, the slight emphasis on love, the
high percentage of occasional poems, complimentary verses, trans-
lations, and the moderate tone and style of his writing. It is note-
worthy that during this early period Vaughan himself has nothing
to say concerning the technique of poetry.

Vaughan's later theory of poetry was as positive and clear as his
early ideas were groping and negative. As the result of a miraculous
recovery from extreme illness, he turned completely to religious
verse. Of course he deprecated his early work, but not too strongly,
since he had not, after all, continued in such vanity. He did not
condemn the folly of young poets, but the persistence in light,
secular themes of those who, he considered, should know better,
especially those who lavished their art on the writing or translating
of romantic fiction. On them he urged the exchange of "vain and
vitious subjects for divine Themes and Celestial praise." [30] But the
mere writing on religious topics was not enough. Here, too, there
were pitfalls. Some of the most learned writers of English verse had
been guilty of impious conceits concerning the Scriptures and God.
Worse still, some had merely followed the fashion of religious verse
and had written that, as they would have written any type popular
at the moment, purely for the sake of being seen in print.

It was through the works of Herbert that Vaughan realized the
possibility of sincerely expressing his altered attitude toward life
and God through the familiar medium of poetry. From trifling
with verses to gain a reputation, he sprang at once to the tremen-
dous concept of his gift as a divine loan, a part of the scheme of
things, a talent that would be required in an ultimate accounting.
In the dedicatory stanzas to Jesus, he says in the manner of Her-
bert,

> 'Twas thine first, and to thee returns.

What more logical than to employ his gift on divine subjects?

Having chosen a single great theme, the religious poets were
faced by the question of what style to use in presenting it. Herbert

30 Vaughan, Works, II, 391.

found the pastoral too fictitious and artificial, too curious and conventional:

> Who sayes that fictions onely and false hair
> Become a verse? Is there in truth no beautie?
> Is it not verse, except enchanted groves
> And sudden arbours shadow coarse spunne lines?
> Must purling streams refresh a lover's loves?
> Must all be vail'd while he that reades divines,
>   Catching the sense at two removes?

> Shepherds are honest people, let them sing:
> Riddle who list, for me, and pull for prime,
> I envie no man's nightingal or spring;
> Nor let them punish me with loss of rhyme,
>   Who plainly say, My God, my King.[31]

The insistence on directness and the avoidance of the pastoral mechanism undoubtedly show the influence of Donne. Herbert had no wish to worship Pan in the groves of Arcady. But neither had he any desire to write the plainest of styles. Only in his satire, the stripped and forthright counter-attack on Melville, did he consider simplicity a virtue, since it indicated the restraint and impersonality with which he wrote, whereas he could have piled up "a lexicon of reproachful words." [32]

Like Donne, Herbert found that the technique best suited to his needs was that of the singers of secular love—a bringing of his best invention to adorn a dear subject. In "Jordan" he relates how his early attempts to do justice to his great theme resulted in a florid and confused style:

> When first my verse of Heav'nly joyes made mention
> Such was their lustre, they did so excell,
> That I sought out quaint words and trim invention;
> My thoughts began to burnish, sprout, and swell,
> Curling with metaphors a plain intention,
> Decking the sense as if it were to sell.

> As flames do work and winde when they ascend
> So did I weave myself into the sense.[33]

---

[31] Herbert, Complete Works, I, 63.   [32] Ibid., II, 149.
[33] Ibid., p. 115.

In "A True Hymn" he has come to realize that sincerity and not decoration is the touchstone:

> The finenesse which a hymne or psalme affords
> Is when the soul unto the lines accords.[34]

Ideally, there would be excellence of style as well, for Herbert thought it an almost incredible profanation for poets to lavish all their ingenuity upon the theme of earthly love and pay no tribute of skill to the far greater wonder of divine love:

> Doth poetrie
> Wear Venus' liverie, onely serve her turn?
> Why are not sonnets made of Thee, and layes
> Upon Thine altar burnt? Cannot Thy love
> Heighten a spirit to sound out Thy praise
> As well as any she?
> Or, since Thy wayes are deep, and still the same,
> Will not a verse runne smooth that bears Thy Name? [35]

Herbert did not decry the theme of earthly love nor the efforts of those poets who treated of it; he used them as a model for his own greater design. The lover's concentration and inspiration were his standard of comparison. It was his ambition to sing the praises of spiritual love with the same power and ingenuity that other poets had displayed in handling the lesser subject of earthly passion:

> O, give me quicknesse
>
> The wanton lover in a curious strain
> Can praise his fairest fair,
> And with quaint metaphors her curléd hair
> Curl o're again
>
> Where are my lines, then? my approaches, views?
> Where are my window songs? [36]

But while he admired the artistic accomplishments of amorous devotion, Herbert deeply resented the monopoly that mortal love exercised over poetry. In "Love" he voices his dissatisfaction with the limitation of that word to earthly passion, and his hope that poets will eventually rise to use their wit more worthily in the grateful praise of God's love without which nothing would exist:

[34] Ibid., p. 193. [35] Ibid., II, 45.
[36] Ibid., I, 131.

Immortall Love, author of this great frame,
  Sprung from that beauty which can never fade,
  How hath man parcel'd out Thy glorious name,
And thrown it in that dust which Thou hast made,

While mortall love doth all the title gain!
  Which siding with Invention, they together
  Bear all the sway, possessing heart and brain—
Thy workmanship—and give Thee share in neither.

.   .   .   .

II

Immortall Heat, O let Thy greater flame
  Attract the lesser to it;

.   .   .   .

Then shall our hearts pant Thee, then shall our brain
All her invention on Thine altar lay,
And there in hymnes send back Thy fire again.[37]

Much as he desired to beautify the praise of God by every means
at his command, Herbert never confused the means with the end.
The perfect and artistic expression of his feelings was very dear to
him, but still more important were those feelings in their simplest
form. He longs to give his subject matter the aid of a rich tech-
nique, but he unmistakably gave style second consideration:

. . . if th' heart be mov'd,
  Although the verse be somewhat scant,
    God doth supplie the want.[38]

The problem is more fully presented in the stanzas which fol-
low:

Farewell, sweet phrases, lovely metaphors:
But will ye leave me thus? when ye before
Of stews and brothels onely knew the doores,
Then did I wash you with my tears, and more,
Brought you to Church well drest and clad:
My God must have my best, ev'n all I had

.   .   .   .

Beautie and beauteous words should go together.
Yet if you go, I passe not; take your way:

[37] Herbert, Complete Works, I, 60.   [38] Ibid., p. 193.

For 'Thou art still my God' is all that ye
Perhaps with more embellishment can say.[39]

Herbert took a deep delight in the beauty of words and in the control of them. He found English especially congenial and commented with some asperity on the intelligence of those who could not handle it:

Let forrain nations of their language boast
What fine varietie each tongue affords;
I like our language, as our men and coast
Who cannot dresse it well, want wit, not words.[40]

It was particularly the opportunities for conceits based on punning that made him prefer English.

Herbert's writing was so sincere a reflection of his life as to be an index to his physical and spiritual health.[41] His disppointments and discouragements were mirrored in a ragged technique very different from the smoothness of expression which he strove to attain. Describing his mood after he felt that God had denied him a request, he says most anticlimactically,

Then was my heart broken, as was my verse.[42]

Still gravely anticlimactic, he asks favors of God in order that

They and my soule may chime,
And mend my ryme.[43]

In "Grief" he sets forth the sound artistic principle that excessive sorrow is not the stuff of which verses are made; there must be enough control to consider "measure, tune, and time." [44] Poets accomplished their end through smoothness:

Bellarmine and stern schools could naught effect,
But more from the smooth poets we expect.[45]

Herbert was not interested in his art as a means of furthering his earthly fame. He pointed out that fame is not based directly on a man's deeds, but on those deeds as interpreted and expressed by others.[46] It is, furthermore, an uncertain, uncontrollable commodity, concerning which his advice was

[39] Herbert, Complete Works, I, 203.   [40] Ibid., p. 193.
[41] Ibid., p. 191.   [42] Ibid., p. 89.   [43] Ibid., p. 90.
[44] Ibid., p. 188.   [45] Ibid., II, 214.
[46] Ibid., I, 77.

> Nor suck in fame, nor blow it to the gales.[47]

Crashaw, like Herbert, sought an eloquence proper to divine poetry. The versified preface to the reader in his earliest book lists those qualities which will not be found in his work. There will be no jest or sport, nothing pertaining to Venus or Cupid, for, though he is capable of writing love poetry, he feels that the praise of holy subjects is a far better thing than the further extension of Love's tyranny. He presents "no Circe-cup," "no draft of Lethe," no spleen or melancholy, nothing wine-inspired, nothing immodest, nothing foul:

> Rarely do I raise a smile,
> Ne'er merge my wit in wanton wile;
> Never quicken Passion's pulse.[48]

Just as Crashaw felt that no secular subject could be truly "sweet," so he argued conversely that the love of God easily became poetry. It was from St. Theresa that Crashaw "learn't to know that love is eloquence." [49] True poetry should result when a soul burning with the love of God tries to manifest its experience in words:

> Soul . . .
>   Awake and sing
>   . . . and let me see
> What of thy Parent Heavn yet speakes in thee.[50]

To Crashaw, brought up in the richest Christian traditions, religious poetry required no simple eloquence. He wished to mingle nature and art, to combine beautiful sounds and words; he bade his soul fit itself with wings of song, employ all "vessells of vocall Joyes":

> Then rouse the nest
> Of nimble Art, and traverse round
> The Aiery Shop of soul-appeasing Sound [51]

He longed to set forth with full embellishment all the passion and the pity, all the intensity and all the tenderness of his faith.

[47] Herbert, Complete Works, II, 207.
[48] Crashaw, Complete Works, ed. by Grosart, II, 24.
[49] Poems by Richard Crashaw, ed. by Waller, p. 272.
[50] Ibid., p. 193.   [51] Ibid., p. 194.

Crashaw had a deep-lying desire to reproduce in English the excellences of foreign religious poetry. Naïvely he explains how St. Theresa's statement that love is eloquence gave him hope that his adoration of her would heighten his poetic power:

> That hopefull maxime gave me hart to try
> If, what to other tongues is tun'd so high
> Thy praise might not speak English too.[52]

In prose, too, he expressed the hope that he might be a contributor to the building up of an insular culture:

Yet still, how I do wish that I were of service whenever my Country desires to cast aside its own particular custom . . . by which, all her own things being despised, she only prizes those things to which having crossed the Alps and lived over the sea has given a value.[53]

Yet he himself was thoroughly English in his prizing of foreign products as the great amount of translation in his work shows.

In Crashaw's development there was no sudden turning to religious interests; they had been dominant from the first. He had no dark moments of doubt and uncertainty. He could digress and treat a secular subject with no sense of defection. He experimented with translating and in various ways tried to enrich his technique. It was his great aim to apply the full richness of poetic art to expressing the consummate "sweetness" of divine love. There was no conflict between his love of art and his love of God, nor did he ever question the sincerity of his most florid figures.

Vaughan, changing sharply from secular to divine poetry, found it no such easy matter to write now as it had been before:

> O! 'tis an easie thing
> To write and sing;
> But to write true, unfeigned verse
> Is very hard! [54]

Less consciously and more simply than Donne, he recognized the difficulty of preserving sincerity in poetry, and realized the high accomplishment of an artist who succeeds in transmitting an undistorted picture of a genuine emotion:

[52] Poems by Richard Crashaw, ed. by Waller, p. 272.
[53] Crashaw, Complete Works, ed. by Grosart, II, 32.   [54] Vaughan, Works, II, 526.

> And sweeter aires streame from a grone,
> Than any arted string.[55]

The vanities of the world and in particular the adventitious elements of poetry still attracted him strongly:

> Mans favorite sins, those tainting appetites
> Which nature breeds, and some fine clay invites,
> With all their soft, kinde arts and easie strains
> Which strongly operate, though without pains,
> Did not a greater beauty rule mine eyes,
> None would more dote on, nor so soon entice.[56]

It was one thing to renounce the "pois'nous ware" of youth and folly, but old interests died hard and the new inspiration came only fitfully.[57] In "Idle Verse" he stops the siren call of his old type of writing with the realization that he has had his term of such dangerous pleasures:

> Go, go, queint folies, sugred sin,
>   Shadow no more my door;
> I will no longer Cobwebs spin,
>   I'm too much on the score.
>
>   .   .   .   .
>
> Blind, desp'rate fits, that study how
>   To dresse, and trim our shame,
> That gild rank poyson, and allow
>   Vice in a fairer name;
>
>   .   .   .   .
>
> Let it suffice my warmer days
>   Simper'd and shin'd on you.
> Go, go, seek out some greener thing,
>   It snows and freezeth here;
> Let Nightingales attend the spring,
>   Winter is all my year.[58]

Here is nostalgic yearning for the fleshpots of Egypt, the implication that idle verse is the prerogative of the youthful poet and no longer has a proper place in Vaughan's life. He held to the course he had set himself, despite frequent temptations to drop back into

[55] Vaughan, Works, II, 418.
[57] Ibid., pp. 444, 445.
[56] Ibid., p. 520.
[58] Ibid., p. 446.

an easier type of writing. Sometimes the conflict resulted in a powerful, almost despairing, plea for help:

> give wings to my fire
> And hatch my soul, untill it fly
> Up where thou art . . .
> Let not perverse,
> And foolish thoughts adde to my Bil
> Of forward sins, and Kil
> That seed, which thou
> In me didst sow.
>
> . . . tune to thy will
> My heart, my verse.[59]

Insofar as it was consciously possible, he abandoned the desire for recognition as a poet. Ironically enough, he thought it was by the sacrifice of his coveted poetic fame that he would gain a now far dearer immortal reward:

> Flowres gather'd in this world, die here; if thou
> Wouldst have a wreath that fades not, let them grow,
> And grow for thee; who spare them here, shall find
> A garland, where comes neither rain, nor wind.[60]

His attitude toward poetic technique was divided. Like Herbert, he wanted to see divine subjects treated with some of the art so wastefully lavished on worldly things:

> Mount of Olives
>
> Sweete, sacred hill! on whose fair brow
> My Saviour sate, shall I allow
> Language to love
> And idolize some shade, or grove,
> Neglecting thee? such ill-plac'd wit,
> Conceit, or call it what you please
> Is the braines fit
> And meere disease; [61]

But the poet had to take great care lest he beguile himself, even in religious verse, by the mere exercise of his art:

> Be dumb course measures, jar no more; to me
> There is no discord, but your harmony.

---

[59] Ibid., p. 445.   [60] Ibid., p. 493. Cf. p. 462.   [61] Ibid., p. 414.

> False, jugling sounds; a grone well drest, where care
> Moves in disguise, and sighes afflict the air:
>
> .   .   .   .
>
> Such numbers tell their days, whose spirits be
> Lulled by those Charmers to a Lethargy.[62]

Furthermore, truth could easily be lost, twisted, or at the least sub-ordinated, if the poet began to concentrate on beauty; this was a special danger in the elaboration of conceits:

> And likelines doth but upbraid,
> And mock the Truth, which still is lost
> In fine Conceits, like streams in a sharp frost.[63]

Vaughan was particularly opposed to conceited translations of the Scriptures:

> and thy dear word,
> As thou hast dress't it: not as Witt
> And deprav'd tastes have poyson'd it:
> Shall in the passage be my meat
> And none else will thy Servant eat.[64]

Thus, by a not uncommon psychological process, Vaughan developed a theory of poetry in which his very deficiencies were desirable:

> O thou! who dids't deny to me
> This world's ador'd felicity,
> And ev'ry big, imperious lust,
> Which fools admire in sinful Dust;
> With those fine, subtile twists, that tye
> Their bundles of foul gallantry.[65]

In her book, *Four Metaphysical Poets*, Joan Bennett says, "It would not be wide of the mark to describe metaphysical poetry as poetry written by men for whom the light of day is God's shadow." [66] Herbert, Crashaw, and Vaughan all longed to share their sense of the imminence of God, to set forth his love and power, his glory and his mercy as they had experienced it. Their esthetic, then, is necessarily that of a limited field:

> For 'Thou art still my God' is all that ye
> Perhaps with more embellishment can say.

---

[62] Vaughan, Works, II, 491.
[63] *Ibid.*, p. 649.   [64] *Ibid.*, p. 651. Cf. p. 531.
[65] *Ibid.*, p. 647.   [66] Bennett, *Four Metaphysical Poets*, p. 7.

It was their aim to divert some of the beauty of poetry to the praise of its great Creator. Grierson has defined metaphysical poetry in its widest sense as "poetry which . . . has been inspired by a philosophical conception of the universe and the rôle assigned to the human spirit in the great drama of existence." [67] Like Donne in his later work, these religious poets had a simple, direct, personal interpretation of the function of art as an element in that dimly guessed formula which attempts to establish a relationship between the powers conferred on man and the way in which they are to be used in the performance of God's will. The didactic poet uses them to direct mankind toward an idea of well-rounded human development. The divine poet assumes more the function of a priest. He speaks for mankind in his own person, or he exhorts men to believe that of which he has inner assurance. Like the major poet, he uses his art for the loftiest of purposes, but he has not the same attitude toward that art. Compared to the miracle of individual salvation, the broader, slower, more tangible miracle of human evolution through art goes unnoticed. The religious poet has not the same sense of unity with the classical poets; he has not the major poet's reverence for them as men who have best solved the eternal problems of human art. The theory of poetry contracts to almost medieval devotional limits as the focus of interest shifts from man to God.

[67] Grierson, *Metaphysical Lyrics and Poems of the Seventeenth Century*, p. xiii.

CHAPTER XII

ROBERT HERRICK AND THOMAS CAREW

THERE WERE in the seventeenth century at least two minor poets who found the altar of Apollo a more congenial spot than the high altar of God. Although both were definitely affected by the fervent religious poetry that had preceded their writing, they knew themselves for what they were: men of unexalted spirit and slight stature, who dwelt by preference in the secular world, delighting especially in its *trivia*. The abysses and heights of the vacillating soul were not their foremost preoccupation, but rather lyric lightness, polish, and perfection—a wondrous neatness of design and execution. Sons of Ben both, Herrick and Carew were devoted primarily to their art and sought the artist's reward of earthly fame and recognition for their smooth and musical verses. Love returns as the dominant theme for Carew and as a major theme among the several secular favorites of Herrick. Passionate intensity and difficult conceit give place to a gallant, patronizing tone and smooth clarity. No matter whether Herrick sings of Julia or Carew of Celia, in reality both are openly wooing the lyric muse.

Yet even these light-hearted singers dwelt within the shadow of a great faith; they respected, although they did not observe, the principle of devoting the poetic gift to God. Each in his own way manifested his interest in the religious lyric. A section of Herrick's book was given over to "Noble Numbers." Carew wrote feelingly in praise of religious verses and was apparently about to essay that type of writing when death cut him short.

Their obvious love of the poetic art for itself and its secular possibilities is, however, their most significant common quality. Their methodical approach, restraint, clarity, and faith in the self-sufficiency of art all herald the later half of the century. The shift from emphasis on subject to emphasis on style has already been accomplished in the work of these two artists, who had no deeper purpose than to create delectable lyrics by "tickling the Citterne with a quill."

ROBERT HERRICK

Although Herrick twice indicated the scope of his muse, once at the beginning of *Hesperides* [1] and once in the midst of *Noble Numbers*,[2] he nowhere made a statement as to any principle that determined his selection of topics. His subjects were drawn largely from his daily life: sack, a flower, a mistress, a friend, an unsavory parishioner, his possessions, country festivals, current events, a bit of advice, a litany. This assortment was unified only by the underlying desire, instinctive in those who are sensitively aware of the enjoyment of living, to preserve the transient thought or sensation and to fix the evanescent mood. His compositions were written to add enjoyment to the life of an epicure and were published for the delight of other epicurean souls. Herrick's philosophy of enjoyment is shown in his "advisive verse" to John Wicks: really to live is to "feast and frolick, sing and play." [3] He loved to picture himself as a second Anacreon and rejoiced in the title that his convivial comrades had bestowed upon him, "The musick of a Feast." [4] In keeping with this, his last introductory poem advises the reader "When he would have his verses read":

> In sober mornings, doe not thou reherse
> The holy incantation of a verse;
> But when that men have both well druncke, and fed,
> Let my Enchantments then be sung, or read.

His verses are not impure, but they do possess a debonair quality, a "cleanly wantonness." They require a kind of *camaraderie* and relaxation as their proper background.[5] He planned to leave the world a legacy of delight,[6] but, aside from this broad intention, no general aim controlled the choice of his material.

Upon the matter of poetic style, Herrick had much more to say. He wrote a request to Julia to burn his work if he died before printing it, preferring to leave nothing rather than to have his book "live not perfected." [7] The perfection about which Herrick was so

---

[1] Poetical Works of Robert Herrick, ed. by Moorman, p. 1. [2] *Ibid.*, p. 225.
[3] *Ibid.*, p. 229. [4] *Ibid.*, p. 144. [5] *Ibid.*, pp. 5, 7.
[6] *Ibid.*, p. 89. [7] *Ibid.*, p. 21.

concerned was that of the sound or music of his verse for he mentions no other characteristic of poetry whereas he refers to the problem of metrical smoothness several times:

> Phoebus! when that I a Verse
> Or some numbers more rehearse;
> Tune my words that they may fall,
> Each way smoothly Musicall: [8]

Again, in the vow to Minerva, he pleads,

> . . . make the Texture lye
> Each way smooth and civilly.[9]

In the poem to Prince Charles we find

> That done, our smooth-pac't Poems all shall be
> Sung in the high Doxologie of Thee.[10]

Herrick was a lyrist in the original sense of the word, strongly conscious that many of his poems would be sung rather than said, and well pleased when they were set to music by Lawes and other composers. He wanted sweetness and smoothness in all his lines and he labored to obtain an ease and grace in the very run of a verse which should give his poetry an appeal as fundamental as that of lofty subject matter or magnificent structure:

> A Request to the Graces

> Ponder my words, if so that any be
> Known guilty here of incivility:
> Let what is graceless, discompos'd and rude,
> With sweetness, smoothness, softness, be endu'd.[11]

No one realized better than Herrick that he had succeeded in achieving an extraordinary sweetness. He addresses a skillful reader of verses:

> Thy mouth will make the sourest numbers please;
> How will it drop pure hony, speaking these? [12]

The secret of his limpid ease was constant practice within a limited field:

> Oft bend the Bow, and thou with ease shalt do,
> What others can't with all their strength put to.[13]

---

[8] Herrick, Poetical Works, p. 122.   [9] Ibid., p. 193.   [10] Ibid., p. 249.
[11] Ibid., p. 283.   [12] Ibid., p. 320.   [13] Ibid., p. 241.

Concerning the inspiration of his poetry, Herrick found that the "good Daemon" was fitful:

> 'Tis not ev'ry day that I
> Fitted am to prophesie:
> No, but when the Spirit fills
> The fantastick Pannicles:
> Full of fier; then I write
> As the Godhead doth indite.
> Thus inrag'd my lines are hurl'd
> Like the Sybells through the world
> Look how next the holy fier
> Either slakes or doth retire;
> So the Fancie cooles, till when
> That brave Spirit comes agen.[14]

The best way to assure its return was to drink deeply of sack. His liking for this drink was unusually strong, and when poor health compelled him to do without it for awhile, the earnestness of his poetical farewell to sack put to shame his protestations to his mistresses:

> 'Tis thou, alone, who with thy Mistick Fan,
> Work'st more then Wisedome, Art, or Nature can,
> To rouze the sacred madnesse; and awake
> The frost-bound-blood and spirits; and to make
> Them frantic with thy raptures, flashing through
> The soule, like lightening, and as active too.
> 'Tis not Apollo can, or those thrice three
> Castalian Sisters, sing if wanting thee.
>
> .   .   .   .
>
> Let my Muse
> Faile of thy former helps; and onely use
> Her inadult'rate strength: what's done by me
> Hereafter, shall smell of the Lamp, not thee.[15]

We are glad to read the title, "The Welcome to Sack," a few pages further on, although the poem itself is not nearly so powerful. At the end of it, however, Herrick once more links wine and poetry. If ever again he deserts sack

> Let Wine
> Ne'er shine upon me; May my Numbers all
> Run to a sudden Death and Funerall.

---

14 Herrick, Poetical Works, p. 132.   15 Ibid., pp. 45, 46.

> And last, when thee (dear Spouse) I disavow,
> Ne'r may Prophetique Daphne crown my Brow.[16]

He laments the lack of this English Hippocrene in his poem to Sir Clipseby Crew:

> Since to th' Country first I came,
> I have lost my former flame:
> And, methinks, I not inherit,
> As I did, my ravisht spirit.
> If I write a Verse, or two,
> 'Tis with very much ado;
> In regard I want that Wine
> Which sho'd conjure up a line.[17]

In a second poem to the same gentleman and in another to a Mr. Kellam, he asked openly for his source of inspiration.[18]

Herrick's isolation in Devonshire removed him from unlimited sack and from the headier wine of the choice spirits that gathered about Ben Jonson; it set him, an alien urban spirit, among the rustics of the west. The change was bound to be distasteful in many respects:

> Come, leave this loathed Country-life and then
> Grow up to be a Roman Citizen.
> Get their comportment and the gliding tongue
> Of those mild Men, thou art to live among: [19]

Yet he was honest enough to balance the benefits of the new environment against its deficiencies:

> More discontents I never had
> Since I was born, than here [Devonshire]
>
> .   .   .   .
>
> Yet justly too I must confesse;
> I ne'r invented such
> Ennobled numbers for the Presse,
> Then where I loath'd so much.[20]

To be sure, this transplanted "Roman citizen" had moments of intense homesickness in rough Devonshire, but he also had hours of great happiness and tranquillity. He was not long in discovering

---

[16] Herrick, Poetical Works, p. 79.   [17] Ibid., p. 180.
[18] Ibid., pp. 214, 284.   [19] Ibid., p. 170.   [20] Ibid., p. 19.

that the music of life could be heard at country festivals as well as at city feasts:

To his Closet-Gods

When I goe Hence ye Closet-Gods, I feare
Never againe to have ingression here:
Where I have had, what ever thing co'd be
Pleasant, and precious to my Muse and me.[21]

His Grange

How well contented in this private Grange
Spend I my life (that's subject unto change:)
Under whose Roofe with Mosse-worke wrought, there I
Kisse my Brown wife, [Sack] and black Posterity [Poems].[22]

"His returne to London" tells of the satisfaction of the man, but says nothing of the poet. On the whole, he seems to have looked to the country for inspiration and to the city for appreciation.

As a result of his Devonshire situation, Herrick became interested in rural poetry, writing naturally on themes suggested by his environment. He also felt some kinship with the pastoral school and experimented with works entitled "Eclogues" and "Beucolicks." Thus he sometimes employed the Arcadian vocabulary and referred in idyllic fashion to "my puling pipe," "my Reed," or "My wearied Oat." [23] In evaluating the pastoral type, he deferred to the theory that it was a lesser, smaller, meaner class of poetry.[24] He adopted the convention of pastoral humility; but, like the other "shepherds," did not mean to be taken too seriously in such lines as:

But for the Court, the Country wit
Is despicable unto it.[25]

Like his fellows, Herrick used a pastoral to celebrate the birth of Charles, a piece obviously intended for court consumption.

Despite his simple subject matter, Herrick was not, as was Wither, a writer of poetry for the people. His poetry would not be poetry unless read by an educated person:

To My Ill Reader

Thou say'st my lines are hard;
And I the truth will tell;

---

[21] *Ibid.*, p. 79.   [22] *Ibid.*, p. 180.   [23] *Ibid.*, pp. 17, 202, 244.
[24] *Ibid.*, p. 5.   [25] *Ibid.*, p. 5.

> They are both hard, and marr'd,
> If thou not read'st them well.[26]

He desired noble patronage [27] and looked to the courtiers, not to his Devonshire parishioners, for a fit audience:

> Though Granges do not love thee, Cities shall.[28]

He dedicated his book to Charles, Prince of Wales, and included several bids for royal and noble attention.

Herrick seems to have been a man of delicate rather than deep sensitivity. This is manifest in his attitude toward the stern march of events. He had a small and insistent strain "of Times trans-shifting" and he wrote some charming laments:

> To his friend on the untuneable Times
>
> Play I co'd once; but (gentle friend) you see
> My Harp hung up, here on the Willow tree.
> Sing I co'd once; and bravely too enspire
> (With luscious Numbers) my melodious Lyre.
>
> .   .   .   .
>
> I feele in me this transmutation now
> Griefe, (my deare friend) has first my Harp unstrung;
> Wither'd my hand, and palsie-struck my tongue.[29]
>
> Aske me, why I do not sing
> To the tension of the string,
> As I did not long ago,
> When my numbers full did flow?
> Griefe (ay me! hath struck my Lute,
> And my tongue at one time mute.[30]

Thus Herrick in impeccable verses, obviously variations on the same theme, tells how sorrow has silenced his muse! In his poem "The bad season makes the Poet sad," he calls himself "lost to all musick" now that Charles has been deprived of his power,[31] yet the cataclysmic years 1648–49 were perhaps principally marked in his mind by the events of his return to London and his publication of *Hesperides:*

[26] Herrick, Poetical Works, p. 138. Cf. p. 209.
[27] *Ibid.*, pp. 268, 40, 41, 141, 215, 317.   [28] *Ibid.*, p. 170.   [29] *Ibid.*, p. 84.
[30] *Ibid.*, p. 131.   [31] *Ibid.*, p. 211.

> Give me a man that is not dull,
> When all the world with rifts is full:
> But unamaz'd dares clearly sing,
> When as the roof's a tottering;
> And though it falls, continues still
> Tickling the Citterne with his quill.[32]

The majority of Herrick's references to poetry occur in those pieces which are dedicated to his kinsmen and friends and have to do with what was for him a most important function of poetry, its immortalizing power.[33] First, as a just debt, he confers on his father life everlasting.[34] In the next three references he is concerned with his own immortality. He has been pledging the great classical poets and concludes:

> Trust to good Verses then;
> They onely will aspire,
> When Pyramids, as men,
>   Are lost, i' th' funerall fire.
> And when all Bodies meet
> In Lethe to be drown'd;
> Then onely Numbers sweet,
>   With endless life are crown'd.[35]

The personal application is developed at length in "His Poetry His Pillar."[36] He considered that fame, the breath of popular applause, was the general incentive for printing poetry.[37] No wonder, then, that Herrick, weighing enduring values and seeing truly down the long perspective of time, continued to "tickle his Citterne" through all the disturbance of civil war:

On Himselfe

> Live by thy Muse thou shalt; when others die
> Leaving no Fame to long Posterity:
> When Monarchies trans-shifted are, and gone
> Here shall endure thy vast Dominion.[38]

Upon Himself

> Thou shalt not All die; for while Love's fire shines
> Upon his Altar, men shall read thy lines;

---

[32] *Ibid.*, p. 311.

[34] *Ibid.*, p. 28.

[36] *Ibid.*, p. 85.

[33] *Ibid.*, pp. 259, 260.

[35] *Ibid.*, p. 81.

[37] *Ibid.*, p. 168.

[38] *Ibid.*, p. 208.

> And learn'd Musicians shall to honour *Herricks*
> Fame, and his Name, both set and sing his Lyricks.[39]

Herrick did not expect this fame to come during his lifetime. It would develop slowly as a result of printing his work. He was resigned to the idea of posthumous glory:

> I make no haste to have my Numbers read
> Seldom comes Glorie till a man be dead.[40]

The idea of becoming utter nothingness in this world appalled him. It would not happen to him; it should not happen to his friends. Therefore one by one he worked up little poems that should forever preserve their memories. Typical are the eight lines to Sir Edward Fish:

> Since for thy full deserts (with all the rest
> Of these chaste spirits, that are here possest
> Of Life eternall) Time has made thee one
> For growth in this my rich Plantation:
> Live here: But know 'twas vertue and not chance,
> That gave thee this so high inheritance.
> Keepe it for ever; grounded with the good,
> Who hold fast here an endlesse lively-hood.[41]

Among those thus honored were Shapcott, who had been responsible for two of the fairy poems, and Selden, who, Herrick gracefully acknowledged, conferred more fame on the poem by lending it the prominence of his name than he received. Herrick thought of these poems collectively as a "White Temple of my Heroes, here Beset with stately figures"; these people were "Saints" in his "poetick Liturgie" or in his "Eternall Calender"; the generation of his just.[42] The lines "To a Friend" express his intention perfectly:

> Looke in my Book, and herein see
> Life endlesse sign'd to thee and me.
> We o're the tombes, and Fates shall flye;
> While other generations dye.[43]

It is strange that he did not, after the manner of the day, promise his mistresses immortality, unless he felt that he had sufficiently secured it to any who were real under their assumed names.

[39] Herrick, Poetical Works, p. 143.   [40] *Ibid.*, p. 215.   [41] *Ibid.*, p. 152.
[42] *Ibid.*, pp. 183, 187, 196, 228, 261, 306.   [43] *Ibid.*, p. 281.

The work of many scholars has shown that Herrick's lyric theory, both as to subject and style, is largely pragmatic; it represents an aggregation of certain practices of the various classical models he knew and loved best.[44] Pauline Aiken indicates the nature of Herrick's debt:

In general, it is evident that Herrick's borrowings from the Elegists are both extensive and intensive. Though he seldom directly imitates, his themes, his subjects, his moods and attitudes are those of the Augustan Elegists. Their phrases trip off his tongue so naturally that to the casual reader there is no suggestion of Latin influence. He echoes, he varies, he parodies; and the resulting verse usually seems entirely original and spontaneous.[45]

All the evidence confirms the statement of Moorman:

Indeed, the more carefully the Hesperides are studied, the more do they reveal the fact that Herrick carried with him to his vicarage at Dean Prior the best works of the great Roman authors, and that during the long winter evenings which he spent there, he pored over their writings with the eyes of a scholar and a lover.[46]

The idea of formulating a lyric style on selective imitation of the classics was sanctioned for Herrick by the example and approval of Ben Jonson,[47] "the rare Arch-Poet" and saint of art through whose good offices an inferior spirit could approach the godhead of poetry:

> When I a Verse shall make,
> Know I have praid thee,
> For old Religions sake,
> Saint Ben to aide me.[48]

Concerning the order in which Herrick wrote his poems very little is known. The chronology, even if established, would not shed much light on a theory of poetry that is almost static. When classified according to subject matter, the twelve hundred (approximately) poems of *Hesperides* and *Noble Numbers* fall into about fourteen separate and distinct types, but there is no reason

---

[44] McEuen, *Classical Influence upon the Tribe of Ben*, see bibliography.

[45] Aiken, *Influence of Latin Elegists on English Lyric Poetry, 1600–1650*, "University of Maine studies," Series 2, No. 22, p. 105.

[46] Moorman, *Robert Herrick*, p. 220.

[47] Herrick, Poetical Works, p. 282. Cf. p. 285.

[48] *Ibid.*, p. 209.

to suppose that he wrote all of one type at one time, and certainly he
did not wish the poems of one kind to be thought of as a group.
He could easily have put all the Julia poems together or could have
gathered the figures in his Hall of Fame, but to do so would have
lessened their individual effectiveness. Proximity would have made
the reader painfully conscious of how often the poet had repeated
a favorite formula. With true artistic instinct, moreover, Herrick
realized the importance of brevity in the lyric,

> Catullus, I quaffe
> To that Terce Muse of thine [49]

and the effect of brevity would have been ruined by grouping the
poems related in spirit or theme. He very carefully separated even
pieces originally meant to go together, such as "Oberon's Feast" and
"Oberon's Palace."

Particularly interesting in this connection is Herrick's use of
the sententious couplet and the epigram. The presence of these
throughout his work indicates the development in the field of
minor poetry of two strains, prominent in the Jonsonian tradition,
that were to reach their full flowering in the next century—com-
mon sense and satire. Major poets could very readily work senten-
tious and satirical passages into their long poems, but Herrick
wrote few poems through which he could properly scatter nuggets
of wisdom or splashes of vitriol. His delight in casting a good
thought or a telling caricature in the mold of a neat couplet found
its outlet in the separate form of the epigram. When the time came
to edit his work, he seems to have had on hand an accumulation of
these couplets which he interspersed so as to enhance the delicately
sensuous beauty of his lyrics by the proximity of a contrasting type
of verse. The rather gross specimens which have embarrassed many
lovers of his dainty lyrics are completely in the Renaissance tradi-
tion of the epigram, which Scaliger subdivided into one adulatory
type, the *mel* or honey, and several harsher varieties, the *fel, ace-
tum,* and *sal,* i. e., the gall, vinegar, and salt epigrams. The epigram
was necessarily condensed and witty; otherwise it was untrammeled.
The attack on individual deficiency, deformity, or depravity,

[49] Herrick, Poetical Works, p. 80.

barred from the satire, was here allowed full freedom. To be sure, Herrick's epigrams are frequently coarse and ugly. He was just as sensitive to foul impressions as to fair, and the epigram was the medium in which he might properly utilize unsavory details. Some of these couplets were deliberately included in his book for their very rankness, as one might add a small amount of civet to an exquisite perfume to make the result less cloying and monotonous, to stiffen the whole work:

> As in our clothes, so likewise he who looks,
> Shall find much farcing Buckram in our Books.[50]

That Herrick, too, had no respect for "toothless satires" is seen when he criticizes Prat's satires for having no "salt" in them.[51]

A second reason for the inclusion of these couplets and epigrams was Herrick's apparent unwillingness to leave even the least of his writings unpublished. One did not know, one could not guess, what would travel down the ages and preserve a man's name to posterity. Vergil had wanted his *Aeneid* destroyed; a few verses kept Anacreon's name immortal; Martial lived on in bitter comments; the great Ben Jonson himself had seen fit to publish his lyrics as well as his dramas. Herrick was well aware that he had included some poems that were little better than practice sketches for others:

> Say, if there be 'mongst many jems here; one
> Deservelesse of the name of Paragon:
> Blush not at all for that; since we have set
> Some Pearls on Queens, that have been counterfet.[52]

He could not bring himself to omit certain verses that were obviously inferior variations on a theme that he had finally brought to perfection. One poem out of all, and that perhaps the least regarded, would be enough to insure immortality. On the other hand, the more he improved his poetry, the better his chance for fame. This explains his many poems and few types. Herrick deliberately narrowed his scope and patiently repeated a subject or a verse form, in an attempt to achieve an occasional flawless specimen through his complete mastery of a small field.[53] Again and again he returns

[50] Herrick, Poetical Works, p. 199.   [51] *Ibid.*, p. 234.   [52] *Ibid.*, p. 76.
[53] *Ibid.*, p. 302.

to the idea of a "perfect" or "best" poem.[54] At least one must emerge from more than a thousand, and one would be enough. The idea is expressed in several places, but most completely in "To Cedars." The significance of these lines rests upon the fact that oil of cedar was an excellent preservative:

> If 'mongst my many Poems, I can see
> One, onely, worthy to be washt by thee
> I live for ever; let the rest all lye
> In dennes of Darkness, or condemn'd to die.[55]

The intense seriousness of this idea is shown by the fact that he introduces it only when addressing the highest hearers: the Lord Bishop of Exeter, the King, and God.

It is characteristic of Herrick that the last-mentioned poem to God should sound very like the one to the Lord Bishop; yet his *Noble Numbers* hardly deserves the severe criticism of Grierson, to wit:

Herrick does not approach God with the earnest pleading of Herbert, rapt love of Crashaw, or mystic awe of Vaughan, but artless frankness of a child confessing his naughtiness and asking to escape too severe a penalty.[56]

It would be much more to the point to suggest that his religious ideas are those of a man of the eighteenth century. The necessary logic of the universe interested him, and he proceeded on a very small scale to analyze the ways of God in couplets that might have come from Pope:

Gods Providence

> If all transgressions here should have their pay,
> What need there then be of a reckning day:
> If God should punish no sin, here, of men,
> His Providence who would not question then? [57]

Such reasoned aphorisms are a far cry from the passion of Donne or the emotion of Herbert.[58] Herrick seems to have experienced very little ecstasy in his religious verse. He complains,

> 'Tis hard to finde God, but to comprehend
> Him, as He is, is labour without end.[59]

---

[54] Herrick, Poetical Works, pp. 63, 107, 315, 329.   [55] *Ibid.*, p. 63.

[56] Grierson, *First Half of the Seventeenth Century*, p. 178.

[57] *Ibid.*, p. 333.   [58] Cf. *ibid.*, pp. 346, 377.

[59] *Ibid.*, p. 330.

The mysticism and ardor of the more fervent religious poets seemed
to him to verge on the frantic:

> To seek of God more than we well can find
> Argues a strong distemper of the mind.[60]

The God of Herrick was preëminently reasonable and tolerant; He
did not resent art for art's sake; He was concerned over a man's
life, not his innocent recreations:

> Poets
>
> Wantons we are; and though our words be such,
> Our Lives do differ from our Lines by much.[61]

Herrick had no real doubt of salvation, no sense that his gift as
well as his life should be dedicated to God. His conscience as to the
exercise of his art was clear and easy; he could echo Martial and
Ovid:

> To his Book's end this last line he'd have plac't
> Jocund his Muse was; but his Life was chast.[62]

In the opening of this chapter I have tried to establish that
Herrick's choice of subject matter in secular poetry was guided
largely by his desire to prolong enjoyable sensations, moods, and
thoughts. The same principle may be found underlying his re-
ligious themes. Among the pleasures of life was the consolation of
hoping for an even more wonderful hereafter by the grace of God.
As Herrick grew older and the thought of his death began to recur
more frequently, it was natural to turn to the subject of God:

> Il'e write no more of Love; but now repent
> Of all those times that I in it have spent.
> Ile write no more of life; but wish twas ended
> And that my dust was to the earth commended.[63]

Although Herrick saw fit to group his religious poems under a
separate heading, no new poetic principle was introduced. These
poems were very much like those of the *Hesperides,* except for their
subject matter. Lossing stresses the fundamental unity of all Her-
rick's work:

If his poetry is considered sympathetically and as a whole, the sensitiveness
to physical impressions which results in the "coarseness" of the epigrams will

---

[60] *Ibid.,* p. 346. [61] *Ibid.,* p. 215.
[62] *Ibid.,* p. 326. [63] *Ibid.,* p. 325.

be recognized as the very same quality which brings sensuous beauty into the lyrics, while the *Noble Numbers* will reveal the limitations inherent in the poet's reliance on sense impressions.[64]

Surveyed more broadly, the expository tone, undecorated simplicity, and minor importance of Herrick's *Noble Numbers* prefigures the age of reason in religious verse, even as his Roman allegiance, high subjectivity, predilection for satire, and concern over technique indicate coming trends in secular verse.

THOMAS CAREW

Carew, like Herrick, belongs to the bright galaxy of secondary seventeenth-century writers who professed no burning zeal and who left no impressive tomes, but live on imperishably in a few perfect lyrics. An examination of the work of Carew demonstrates on a smaller scale that which has already been shown in regard to Herrick, that the less voluminous writers were frequently very much concerned with a narrow range of poetic theory and very consciously chose to work within self-imposed limits. Like Herrick, Carew deliberately restricted himself to that type of poem in which he thought he could progress furthest toward perfection. Both poets obviously strove to gain complete mastery of form and music by sacrificing variety and scope of subject matter in order to concentrate their practice. Carew's preferred subject matter was more limited than Herrick's, but very similar, in that he, too, apparently endeavored to give artistic expression to his immediate interests.

The majority of Carew's poems deal with love; Celia is either directly addressed or she is the implied hearer. Although there is no definite cycle or story, the slight events commemorated and the sentiments expressed are such as suggest a real woman, who, as is the case with Herrick's "mistresses," regardless of her actual relationship to him, was invaluable artistically because she provided a suitable lay figure upon which to expend his stock of skill.

But whether Celia was real or fancied, in the poetry that Carew wrote about her he stands revealed as the consummate singer of Caroline courtly love. According to his philosophy, poetry was the

[64] Lossing, "Herrick: His Epigrams and Lyrics," *University of Toronto Quarterly*, II (Jan., 1933), 239.

great tool of the lover. In his first mention of poetry, in "Good Counsel to a Young Maid," he warns her to beware of those "nets of Passion's finest thread, Snaring poems." And the poet-lover had more to offer than the immediate attraction of his art. By means of his special gift he could not only charm temporarily but could also offer his mistress immortality in return for her favor. Of course his own immortality was also assured:

> "Thus are we both redeem'd from Time"
> "I by thy grace"—"And I
> Shall live in thy Immortal rhyme,
>   Until the Muses die." [65]

The reverse of this picture, which teaches the same lesson, follows:

> If she must still deny
>   Weep not, but die!
> And in thy Funeral fire
> Shall all her fame expire
> Thus both shall perish, and as thou, upon thy Hearse
> Shall want her tears, so she shall want thy Verse. [66]

When his mistress is proud, he threatens her with the withdrawal of his fame-conferring and magnifying power. If she wishes to remain glorified, she had best be kind to her poet:

Ingrateful Beauty Threatened

> Know, Celia, since thou art so proud,
>   'Twas I that gave thee thy renown.
> Thou had'st in the forgotten crowd
>   Of common Beauties lived unknown,
> Had not my verse extoll'd thy name,
> And with it ympt the wings of Fame.
>
> That killing power is none of thine:
>   I gave it to thy voice and eyes;
> Thy sweets, thy graces, all are mine;
>   Thou art my Star, shin'st in my skies:
> Then dart not from thy borrow'd sphere
> Lightning on him that fix'd thee there.
>
> Tempt me with such affrights no more,
>   Lest what I made I uncreate;

---

[65] The Poems and Masque of Thomas Carew, ed. by Ebsworth, p. 41.
[66] Carew, Poems and Masque, p. 41.

> Let fools thy mystic forms adore,
> I know thee in thy Mortal state.
> Wise poets that wrapt Truth in tales
> Knew her themselves through all her veils.

Thus an angry Pygmalion threatens a forgetful Galatea. But under normal circumstances, his pen was so completely dedicated to the celebration of Celia that he apologized to her for writing an elegy on another lady and even devoted a large part of that elegy to Celia:

> And pardon me, sweet Saint! whom I adore,
> That I this tribute pay out of the store
> Of lines and tears that were due unto thee.[67]

Love was to him the ideal subject for the lyric poet. Thus he pictures the poets whom he summons to write an elegy as interrupting their usual amorous versifying to respond:

> Let him who, banished far from her dear sight,
> Whom his soul loves, doth in that absence write,
> Or lines of passion, or some powerful charms,
> To vent his own grief or unlock her arms,
> Take off his pen, and in sad verse bemoan.[68]

Inevitably he tends to return to his theme proper:

> And having ended these sad obsequies
> My Muse must back to her old exercise,
> To tell the story of my martyrdom.[69]

Carew, even when very sincerely writing an elegy, could not keep from revealing how much he would have preferred his favorite theme:

> Seek him no more in dust, but call again
> Your scattered beauties home, and so the pen,
> Which now I take from this sad Elegy,
> Shall sing the Trophies of your conquering eye.[70]

He tried verse as a *remedium amoris* unsuccessfully:

> So I, that seek in verse to carve thee out
>   Hoping thy Beauty will my flame allay
> Viewing my lines impolish'd all throughout
>   Find my will rather to my love obey.[71]

---

[67] Carew, Poems and Masque, p. 18.   [68] *Ibid.*, p. 17.
[69] *Ibid.*, p. 19.   [70] *Ibid.*, p. 110.   [71] *Ibid.*, p. 75.

Like Donne, Carew is not interested in unrequited love as a source of poetic inspiration. He does not sing in the Petrarchan vein of reverent admiration for the unattainable, but rather in the assured and virile tone of the experienced lover. He warns a lady who had "desired that he would love her" but had no thought of returning the love, that a grief-stricken poet cannot write of her so well as a joyous one; nor, in the nature of things, can he depict her as so fair. One of his longest love poems, "The Rapture," portrays the felicity of the attainment of the physical objective of love much after the fashion of Donne in his "Elegies."

In an attempt to create an extraordinary type of poem in honor of the Countess of Carlisle, he considers the possibility of poetry that should arise not from sensual but from "divine" love, apparently a sort of Platonic love, for Lucinda is pictured as a type of beauty beyond all that poets had feigned. Perfect beauty purges love to reverence and therefore the poetry of sensual love would not be worthy and would have to be supplanted by a higher type. It makes a very pretty conceit, but Carew fully realized that perfect ladies were only "aery Creations" of the poet's mind; therefore his concluding question

> Must Love needs be a storm?
>
> Can there no way be given,
> But a true Hell, that leads to her false Heaven? [72]

must still be answered in the negative, and he goes back to celebrating Celia. He had, however, the greatest admiration for Aurelian Townshend's poetry, which dealt with "Love made all spirit."

In regard to the nature of poetry, Carew acknowledged loftier types, but preferred the lyric for himself. His preference was determined by the nature of his poetic gift. He quite rightly considered himself a master of "smooth, soft language," and light lyric meter. He wrote couplets with an excellent polish and gliding ease, but could not be persuaded to try sustained works. Suckling gives us a clue to his reluctance by pointing out that his smoothness was not natural, like Browne's for instance, but the result of much labor:

[72] Carew, Poems and Masque, p. 87.

His muse was hard bound and the issue of's brain
Was seldom brought forth but with trouble and pain.

Such a man, fastidious, critical, painful and not spontaneous in
creation, could not temperamentally try poetry of wider scope.
Carew considered his specialized technique as suited only to certain
subjects:

Alas, how may
My lyric feet—that of the smooth soft way
Of Love and Beauty only know the tread—
In dancing paces celebrate the dead
Victorious King, or his majestic Hearse
Profane with th' humble touch of their low verse?

Thus he declined the invitation of Townshend to write upon the
death of Gustavus Adolphus. A thorough courtier, he found it
natural to write in terms of the temper of the court:

But let us, that in myrtle bowers sit
Under secure shades, use the benefit
Of peace and plenty. . . .
Let us of Revels sing

harmless pastimes let my Townshend sing
To rural tunes; not that thy Muse wants wing
To soar a loftier pitch, for she hath made
A noble flight. . . .
But these are subjects proper to our clime.
Tourneys, Masques, Theatres, better become
Our Halcyon days.

At the royal command, he wrote one of the most successful Jaco-
bean masques, *Coelum Britannicum*, a typical court extravaganza.
He had no desire to abandon the light subject and measure and he
pleaded against letting foreign turmoil

Drown the sweet airs of our tuned violins.
Believe me, friend, if their prevailing powers
Gain them a calm security like ours,
They'll hang their arms upon the Olive bough,
And dance and revel then, as we do now.[73]

Had Carew lived to a riper age and to more troublous times,
there is good reason to believe that he might have turned to the

[73] Carew, Poems and Masque, p. 115.

religious lyric. The concluding lines of his powerful elegy on Donne show that he held religious poetry to be a co-equal province of "wit":

> Here lies a king who ruled as he saw fit
> The universal monarchy of wit
> Here lie two Flamens, and both these the best
> Apollo's first, at length the true God's priest.

Shortly before his death he wrote in a poem entitled "To my Worthy Friend Master George Sandys, on his Translation of the Psalms:

> I Press not to the Choir, nor dare I greet
>   The holy Place with my unhallow'd feet;
> My unwashed Muse pollutes not things divine,
> Nor mingles her profaner notes with thine:
>
>   Sufficeth her, that she a Lay-place gain,
>
> Though nor in tune nor wing she reach thy Lark,
> Her lyric feet may dance before the Ark.
>   Who knows, but that her wand'ring eyes, that run
> Now hunting Glow-worms, may adore the Sun;
> A pure flame may, shot by Almighty Power
> Into my breast, the earthly flame devour?
>   My eyes in penitential dew may steep
>   That brine, which they for sensual love did weep.
>
> Perhaps my restless Soul, tired with pursuit
> Of mortal beauty, seeking without fruit
> Contentment there—which hath not, when enjoy'd,
> Quench'd all her thirst, nor satisfied, though cloy'd:
>   Weary of her vain search below, above
>   In the first Fair may find th' immortal Love.
>
> Prompted by thy example then, no more
> In moulds of clay will I my God adore:
> But tear those Idols from my heart, and write
> What his blest Spirit not fond Love, shall indite.
> Then I no more shall court the verdant Bay,
> But the dry leafless trunk on Golgatha:
>   And rather strive to gain from thence one Thorn
>   Than all the flourish Wreaths by Laureats worn.

To substantiate the idea of his active interest in religious poetry, there are among his works several attempts at poetical versions of the Psalms.

Carew deserves a high rating as a critic, if only for his analysis
of the contribution of Donne to poetry:

> The Muses' Garden, with pedantic weeds
> O'er spread, was purged by thee; the lazy weeds
> Of servile Imitation thrown away,
> And fresh invention planted.

Carew raged against

> Licentious thefts, that make poetic rage
> A mimic fury, when our souls must be
> Possess'd—or with Anacreon's ecstasy,
> Or Pindar's, not their own.

A keen and generous critic, he lauds Donne for having written
from his own inspiration and in a natural English vocabulary, not
in one that aped the classical turns of thought. He praises him the
more since Donne had been handicapped by being born after the
mighty poets had exhausted so much material and made originality
almost impossible, and because Donne had conquered the added
difficulty of writing in a less poetical though more masculine lan-
guage. In consideration of these facts, he rated Donne highest
among poets, truly prognosticating that few could hold his pitch
and that after his death there would be a return of "the goodly
exiled train of Gods and Godesses" and "the silenced tales i' the
Metamorphoses" to help poets stuff lines "and swell the windy
page."

And yet Carew had no objection to true classicism. He had no
patience with the stupid rout who dared to criticize Jonson for
taking too much time over his writing or borrowing too much.[74]
Such pains were necessary and such borrowing justifiable. But the
critic in Carew could not bear to group a weak play like *The New
Inn* with a masterpiece such as *The Alchemist*. He could understand
differences in taste, such as a preference for comedy rather than
tragedy, but he insisted that true art would be recognized as such
by any competent critic; that is, he would prefer a good tragedy
to a poor one:

> Some have derived an unsafe liberty,
> To use their judgments as their tastes, which choose

[74] Carew, Poems and Masque, p. 61, 120.

Without controul this dish, and that refuse.
But Wit allows not this large privilege.

> Things are distinct, and must the same appear
> To every piercing eye or well-tuned ear.

In the above quotations from poems to Davenant there again appears the central doctrine of the second half of the seventeenth century—the insistence on absolute standards of art. The high development of the critical sense, which is apparent in Carew, is necessary in a poet aiming at perfection. The emphasis has shifted from subject matter to style. No longer is the spirit abroad that tempted men to soar beyond their control, to imp their wings with immortal feathers, to fail gloriously in overgrand undertakings, dismissing the possibility of greater success in smaller fields with Fletcher's comment,

> Your songs exceed your matter, this of mine
> The matter which it sings shall make divine.

Poetic theory has pivoted on the turn of the century and is now exactly reversed. The typical poet now sedulously avoids matter that is beyond his proper limits. Not to recognize those limits or to transgress them is a grave error:

> Virgil, nor Lucan, no, nor Tasso—more
> Than both; not Donne, worth all that went before—
> With the united labour of their wit,
> Could a just poem to this subject fit.[75]

The "just" poem requires that the capacity of the poet match the demands of the subject. As such a theory gains prominence, the subjects will necessarily diminish in grandeur. The doctrine of technical perfection, at first held paramount only by the minor group, began to be of prime importance to all poets and came to full power in the eighteenth century.

[75] Carew, Poems and Masque, p. 114.

CHAPTER XIII

ANDREW MARVELL AND
JOHN DENHAM

THE POETIC THEORY of Marvell and Denham illustrates the rise of reason, clarity, and metrical conservatism, and the growing interest in contemporary and didactic topics. Denham, the lighter in mentality, floated easily with the current trend of his art, while Marvell retained much of the older theory and advanced slowly and independently. Marvell accepted in much of his own poetry the Renaissance heritage of seriousness and didactic responsibility, whereas Denham regarded the art of writing more in the light of an interesting pastime. Having little of his own to say, Denham was deeply concerned over improving the art of translation; Marvell desired merely literal accuracy in presenting the thought of a foreign poet. The courtier held Roman Vergil and neo-Roman Cowley in high esteem; the Parliamentarian's favorite poets were the patriots Spenser and Milton.

Each contributed his peculiar share to the rise of translation and satire and the decline of lyrics on secular and religious love that mark the progress of the seventeenth century. The era of faith is well summarized and concluded in the theory of Marvell; the era of reason is consciously ushered in by Denham.

ANDREW MARVELL

Within the brief compass of his poetical works, Marvell exhibited the same keen, independent, well-balanced mentality that characterized his political career. He neither worshiped the old nor followed the new, but profited by past and present practice in molding his own expression.

Nowhere does Marvell explicitly give his concept of the nature of poetry, but quite obviously, in accepting Horace and Ben Jonson as models, he tacitly adopted their theories. Like Jonson, he pointed out that rime was not a necessary attribute of poetry. He deemed it a superfluous ornament, a mere fashion, which he, as a man of his time, followed. In his poem on *Paradise Lost* he writes:

> Well mightst thou scorn thy Readers to allure
> With tinkling Rhime, of thy own Sense secure;
> While the Town-Bays writes all the while and spells,
> And like a Pack-Horse tires without his Bells.
> Their Fancies like our bushy Points appear,
> The Poets tag them; we for fashion wear.
> I too transported by the Mode offend,
> And while I meant to Praise thee, must Commend.
> Thy verse created like thy Theme sublime,
> In Number, Weight, and Measure, needs not Rhime.[1]

In regard to the purpose of poetry, Marvell's most characteristic statement occurs in his poem on "Tom May's Death." Ben Jonson, who has supreme command over the poets in Elizium, will not permit May to join their circle, on the grounds that he has prostituted his muse. May had turned Parliamentary historian out of spite, after his failure to succeed Jonson as laureate. In powerful words Ben shows him the noble function of the true poet:

> When the Sword glitters ore the Judges head,
> And fear has Coward Churchmen silenced,
> Then is the Poet's time, 'tis then he drawes,
> And single fights forsaken Vertues cause.
> He, when the Wheel of Empire whirleth back,
> And though the World's disjointed Axel crack,
> Sings still of ancient Rights and better Times
> Seeks wretched good, arraigns successful Crimes.[2]

This was the theory in accordance with which Marvell wrote his bitter and daring satires of the reign of Charles II. Even when, under Cromwell's ideal administration, such outbursts concerning England had not been necessary, Marvell had considered poetry an effective medium for world betterment. Apparently he had planned a great didactic poem that should destroy the Roman church and hasten the coming of Christ's reign on earth. He would try to persuade other rulers to free their country from the grip of Rome, as Cromwell had freed his:

---

[1] The Poems and Letters of Andrew Marvell, ed. by Margoliouth, I, 132.
[2] *Ibid.*, I, 92.

> Unhappy Princes ignorantly bred
> By Malice some by Errour more misled
> If gracious Heaven to my Life give length
> Leisure to Time and to my Weakness Strength
> Then shall I once with graver Accents shake
> Your regal sloth and your long Slumbers wake:
> Like the shrill Huntsman that prevents the East
> Winding his Horn to Kings that chase the Beast
> Till then my Muse shall hollow far behind
> Angelique Cromwell who outwings the wind.[3]

Like most seventeenth-century poets, Marvell recognized the possibilities of poetry as a means of perpetuating fame and acknowledged the responsibility of the poet in this connection. He praised certain national heroes as

> True sons of Glory, Pillars of the State,
> On whose fam'd Deeds all tongues, all writers wait.[4]

In the poem used to preface the works of Lovelace, he comments on the degeneration of his own time, in which the object of poets has become the destruction rather than the creation of fame:

> Who best could praise had then the greatest prayse
>
> .   .   .   .
>
> [Now] He highest builds who with most art destroys
> And against others Fame his owne employs.[5]

In his otherwise vitriolic "Last Instructions to a Painter," he devotes fifty lines to commemorating the heroic end of young Captain Douglas, who burned to death with his ship rather than desert his command. He ends with the Vergilian promise:

> Fortunate Boy! if either Pencil's Fame,
> Of if my verse can propagate thy Name;
> When Oeta and Alcides are forgot,
> Our English youth shall sing the Valiant Scot.[6]

He similarly thought of the fame of Cromwell as being preserved in verse:

> Thee, many ages hence, in martial verse
> Shall th' English souldier, ere he charge, rehearse;[7]

---

[3] Marvell, Poems and Letters, I, 106.   [4] *Ibid.*, p. 189.   [5] *Ibid.*, p. 3.
[6] *Ibid.*, p. 157. Cf. p. 172.   [7] *Ibid.*, p. 130.

For Cromwell, too, he borrows a Vergilian device:

> As long as rivers to the seas shall runne,
> As long as Cynthia shall relieve the sunne,
>
> . . . . .
>
> As long as future times succeed the past,
> Always thy honour, praise, and name, shall last.

In brief, the noblest function of the poet was to attempt to get the times back into joint by scourging the bad and praising the good. The same convictions that made him write, might, in a crisis, force him to abandon poetry for more direct participation. The first lines of "An Horatian Ode upon Cromwell's Return" give a clew to the slightness of Marvell's poetic output, exclusive of trenchant political satire. The times demanded action, not art:

> The forward Youth that would appear
> Must now forsake his Muses dear
> Nor in the Shadows sing
> His numbers languishing
> 'Tis time to leave the Books in dust
> And oyl th' unused Armours rust.

Milton suspended the operation of a much greater talent to contribute a scholar's share to the great cause.

But what of the lesser, nonsocial types of poetry? Does a study of Marvell establish any specific attitudes regarding these? His love poems may, as Legouis suggests, be best accounted for by the theory of Cowley: "Poets are scarce thought Freeman of their Company without paying some duties and obliging themselves to be true to Love." [8] But whereas Cowley chose to pay his dues in a group of more or less related poems with a fairly unified tone, Marvell experimented broadly, seeking a congenial thought pattern. Sometimes, as in "Young Love" or "Mourning," the argument reminds the reader of Donne's strange and paradoxical twisting of ideas. "The Fair Singer" might be Carew's and "The Definition of Love," Cowley's. In fact, the only distinguishing characteristic of his love poetry is a sort of impassioned logic. This is particularly evident in the dialogues. Starting from any given premise, Marvell works

---

[8] Legouis, *André Marvell*.

through to an inevitable conclusion. Legouis points out that Marvell's most powerful love poem has a rigidly logical structure. Certainly Marvell had very little interest in the ordinary mistress-praising, lover-pitying type of writing. He thought that Flecknoe, the English priest who resided at the poetical sign of the sad Pelican, was making the best possible use of such verses when he employed them to swaddle his thin frame against the cold. He did not agree in sentiment with the young gallant who, having failed to secure some of Flecknoe's love verses,

> Wept bitterly as disinherited.
> Who should commend his Mistress now? Or who
> Praise him? both difficult indeed to do
> With truth.[9]

As Legouis suggests, Marvell's criticism of much previous and contemporary love poetry may be deduced from his description of "The Unfortunate Lover." This rather willing victim languishes

> with doubtful Breath
> Th'Amphibium of Life and Death.
>
> And Tyrant Love his brest does ply
> With all his wing'd Artillery
>
> And all he saies, a Lover drest
> In his own Blodd does relish best.
> Who though, by the Malignant Starrs,
> Forced to live in Storms and Warrs:
> Yet dying leaves a Perfume here,
> And Musick within every Ear:
> And he in Story only rules,
> In a Field Sable a Lover Gules.[10]

But Marvell's experiments in the conventional field of love poetry soon began to lose ground before his newer and deeper interest in nature. The leaven of the new influence is very apparent if one compares "The Picture of Little T.C. in a Garden of Flowers" with "Young Love." The perfect fusion of both love and nature themes is found in the Mower poems. But it is in "The Garden" that we get unmistakable evidence as to the relative importance of these themes to Marvell:

[9] Marvell, Poems and Letters, I, 87.   [10] Ibid., pp. 28, 29.

No white nor red was ever seen
So am'rous as this lovely green.
Fond Lovers, cruel as their Flame,
Cut in these Trees their Mistress name,
Little, Alas, they know or heed,
How far there Beauties Hers exceed!
Fair Trees! where s'eer your barkes I wound,
No Name shall but your own be found.

.   .   .   .

Such was that happy Garden-state,
While Man there walk'd without a Mate:
After a Place so pure, and sweet,
What other Help could yet be meet!
But 'twas beyond a Mortal's share
To wander solitary there;
Two Paradises 'twere in one
To live in Paradise alone.

An added importance is given to this poem by the fact that Marvell composed it in both Latin and English.

His choice of nature as a subject was not, as is often thought, a spontaneous one arising from his residence at Nunappleton, but was directly influenced by the work of Fairfax, who had completed a rough translation in verse of a French nature poet, Saint-Amand.[11] But whatever the reason for his choice of topic, from the time of his "discovery" of nature, gardens, hills, groves, fields, birds, and insects delighted him. Contrary to the pastoralists, Marvell did not use nature as a mere setting for love but rather as a substitute. It fitted his temperament admirably that the magic spell of growing things should possess him utterly, absorbing him in a mystical union,

Annihilating all that's made
To a green Thought in a green Shade.[12]

The less absorbing, less restful mystery of love was cheerfully abandoned:

Thus I, easie Philosopher,
Among the Birds and Trees confer

---

[11] Woledge, "St. Amand, Fairfax, and Marvell," *Modern Language Review*, XXV (Oct., 1930), 481–83.

[12] Marvell, Poems and Letters, I, 49.

> And little now to make me wants
> Or of the Fowles, or of the Plants
>
> Give me but Wings as they and I
> Streight floting on the Air shall fly:
> Or turn me but, and you shall see
> I was but an inverted Tree.
>
> Thrice happy he who, not mistook
> Hath read in Natures mystick Book.
>
> How safe, methinks, and strong, behind
> These Trees have I incamp'd my Mind;
> Where Beauty, aiming at the Heart,
> Bends in some Tree its useless Dart.[13]

Before his discovery of nature, Marvell had tried another sub-
ject more congenial than love. His definite leanings toward the
religious theme are evident in his moral debates and in the ele-
vated tone of his pastorals. Clorinda invites Damon to enjoy the
pleasures of the senses, but he has met Pan (Christ), who spoke
to him

> Words that transcend poor Shepherds skill
> But He ere since my Songs does fill
> And His Name swells my slender Oate.[14]

In his religious poetry, as in his love verses, Marvell was concerned
with logical exposition rather than with fervent appeal or praise.
Perhaps this explains his fondness for dialogue,[15] a form peculiarly
adapted to presenting a problem as economically and clearly as
possible, and endorsed by the triple authority of classical, medieval,
and pastoral practice. Thus we have "A Dialogue between the Re-
solved Soul, and Created Pleasure," which touches upon the very
material of *Paradise Regain'd,* for under "created pleasure" Mar-
vell treats of the same temptations that Jesus knew in the desert.
"On a Drop of Dew" is another exercise in exposition that draws
an elaborate comparison between a drop of dew and the human
soul. "The Coronet" reveals why we have so little religious poetry
from a man of Marvell's serious and earnest temperament. With

---

[13] Marvell, Poems and Letters, I, 76, 77.   [14] *Ibid.,* p. 18.

[15] G. C. Moore-Smith suggests that several of Marvell's poems, particularly those in
dialogue ending with a chorus, were written to be set to music. *Modern Language Re-
view,* XXIV (Jan., 1929), 79.

the same logical and honest approach that he used in other subjects, Marvell examined his own purpose in writing religious poetry and found that even his verses in praise of God had too strong an admixture of ulterior motive. He was too sincere a man to claim that his work was dedicated to God's glory when it had really been written for his own. He recognized the difference between a simple, surface change in subject matter and the much deeper and more profound change of purpose that would characterize truly devout poetry. To make God the subject was not sufficient:

> I gather flow'rs (my fruits are only flow'rs)
> Dismantling all the fragrant Towers
> That once adorn'd my Shepherdesses head.
>
> Alas I find the Serpent old
> That twining in his speckled breast
> About the flow'rs disguis'd does fold,
> With wreathes of Fame and Interest.[16]

It is in such a poem as "Bermudas" that Marvell completely succeeds in realizing his theory in his practice. This was the type of work he was preëminently fitted to write, the strong and manly praise of God in terms of nature—"an holy and a chearful Note."

Marvell obviously did not practice recognized forms of satire. He regarded the genre with distaste and used it only in desperation. His satires are little subject to considerations of art; they are the release of a pent-up torrent of disgust and righteous anger at the conduct of the Stuart regime. They are impassioned reasoning, subjected to the minimum of control. His apprenticeship to the craft of writing would not let him bring forth a mere catalogue of denouncements and scandals without some such device as making it "Last Instructions to a Painter" or a "Dialogue between Two Horses," but the crudity of the finished product shows that its only claim to be considered as poetry lies in its verse form and its fulfillment of the reforming purpose that Marvell had established in "Tom May's Death." In the satires he used the simplest and commonest meters, whereas in his freer art he was an experimenter and innovator in rhythms. He resorted to classical allusions, a practice that he did not follow in his more carefully worked out poems. To

[16] Marvell, Poems and Letters, I, 14.

force such stubborn and purely journalistic material into verse at all was a considerable feat, as Marvell ruefully recognized when he wrote concerning certain letters of state,

> The first instructs our (Verse, the Name abhors)
> Plenipotentiary Ambassadors.[17]

His most artistic satire, *The Rehearsal Transprosed*, acknowledges in its title the superiority of prose for the purpose of mockery. The model that he followed in verse satire was the bitter-tongued Cleveland, who "single did against a Nation write," [18] but whom Marvell pictured in Elysium as a milder spirit:

> Much had he Cur'd the Humor of his vein:
> He Judg'd more Clearly now and saw more plain.

The satirist must of necessity be extreme in his denunciation, and clear-headed, temperate Marvell could not have greatly enjoyed his coarse but effective broadsides. He was happier as a poet and a man when he could insert such a passage as the praise of the young Douglas.

Marvell's theory of translation is in complete opposition to Cowley's and Denham's, for Marvell desired the closest exactitude in rendering the text:

> He is Translations thief that addeth more,
> As much as he that taketh from the Store
> Of the first Author. Here he maketh blots
> That mends; and added beauties are but spots.[19]

> You have Translations Statutes best fulfil'd,
> That handling neither sully nor would guild.[20]

The complete eclecticism of Marvell is well illustrated by the two marriage songs that he wrote in honor of the marriage of Lord Fauconberg to Mary Cromwell. The first uses classical names and fable and presents Cynthia and Endymion and a chorus. The second is an English pastoral, with homely figures of speech strongly reminiscent of Suckling's "Ballad on a Wedding," and it presents characters with the Spenserian names of Hobbinol, Tomalin, and Phyllis. Marvell's poetic theory may fairly be said to represent a cross sec-

---

[17] Marvell, Poems and Letters, I, 152.   [18] *Ibid.*, p. 178.
[19] *Ibid.*, p. 94.   [20] *Ibid.*, p. 95.

tion of the various influences at play around him. His eclecticism arose from the balance of logic and passion in his nature. He is an almost perfect epitome of the transition period, an intermediary between the major and the minor groups, exemplifying by turns in his own work the divine, the didactic, and the purely delightful aim. His love poetry has the brilliance and verve of metaphysical wit; he thinks of religious poetry with the "white sincerity" of a Donne; he accepted that part of poetic theory, neglected by the divine poets, which regarded poetry as an adjunct of human virtue, as an aid to right thinking and noble living. Although he admired the great exponents of the social purpose of poetry, Spenser, Jonson, and Milton, he distrusted their method of teaching through "Fable and old Song." His theory is forward-looking in its simplicity of style, in its open treatment of contemporary problems, and in his preference for the straight-forward didacticism of the satire or the ode.

JOHN DENHAM

Like Cowley, Denham printed his works with the intention of terminating his avocation of poetry. He had already suspended his poetic activities for eighteen years, first because Charles I intimated that the writing of verses was hardly an aid to securing a responsible post; and second, because from 1649 on he was occupied with his duties as surveyor-general.[21] But in the summer of 1667 Denham, in retirement, was tempted "to divert those melancholy thoughts, which the new apparitions of Foreign invasion and domestic discontent gave us," and turned again to poetry. He justified this lapse into the "follies of youth" by the example of Socrates, Aristotle, and Cato; but promised his good behavior in the future, admitting that

when age and experience has so ripened mans discretion as to make it fit for use, either in private or publick Affairs, nothing blasts and corrupts the fruit of it so much as the empty, airy reputation of being *Nimis Poeta*, and therefore I shall take my leave of the Muses, as two of my Predecessors did saying
    Splendidis longum vale dico nygis,
    Hic versus and coetera ludicra pons

---

[21] The Poetical Works of Sir John Denham, ed. by Banks, pp. 59, 60.

[I bid a long farewell to brillant trifles
Here placing my verses and other toys].[22]

This attitude toward his art contrasts sharply with his retention of
the traditional ideas concerning the exalted office of the early
singers of the race. In "The Progress of Learning," he pictures
Moses, David, Musæus, and Orpheus as early civilizers and teachers,
bringing religion to their fellow men:

The eternal cause, in their immortal lines
Was taught, and Poets were the first Divines.[23]

More than that, he believed that the Divine One himself was the
first poet, a concept emphasized by Cowley too. Denham's attitude
is a strange compound of unreserved belief in the past glory and
disillusioned interest in the present status of his art.

An interesting review of Denham's ideas concerning the nature
of poetry occurs in his "Humble Petition of the Poets to the Five
Members of the Honourable House of Commons." In this he asserts
that the Parliamentarians have claimed many of the poet's priv-
ileges:

And first, 'tis to speak whatever we please
Without fear of a Prison or Pursuivants fees.
Next that we only may lye by Authority,

.   .   .   .

Next an old Custom, our Fathers did name it
Poetical license . . .
By this we have power to change Age to Youth,
Turn Non-sence to Sence, and Falsehood to Truth;
In brief to make good whatsoever is faulty
This art some Poet or the Devil has taught ye.

.   .   .   .

But that trust above all in Poets reposed
That Kings by them only are made and Deposed.
But when we undertake Deposing or Killing
They're Tyrants and Monsters, and yet then the Poet
Takes full Revenge on the Villains that do it.

The poet, then, was privileged to depart from truth, a freedom
given him not for wanton lying, but to enable him to paint more

---

[22] Denham, Poetical Works, p. 60. Translation by Leah Jonas.
[23] Ibid., p. 115.

ideal conditions than really exist, i. e., a world in which "poetic justice" functions. The "poems" of the Parliamentarians, he remarks ironically, lack only rime, wit, and sense;

> But for lying (the most noble part of a Poet)
> You have it abundantly.[24]

The idea of feigning as a customary feature of poetry appears again in the preface to "The Progress of Learning":

> My early Mistress, now my Antient Muse,
> That strong Circæan liquor cease to infuse,
> Wherewith thou didst Intoxicate my youth,
> Now stoop with dis-inchanted wings to Truth.[25]

In the "Prologue to his Majesty," he accuses the Cromwellian party of having outacted the players and outlied the poets. What he means by poetic "lying" he illustrates in "Cooper's Hill":

> This scene had some bold Greek or British Bard
> Beheld of old, what stories had we heard,
> Of Fairies, Satyrs, and the Nymphs their Dames,
> Their feasts, their revels, and their amorous flames:
> 'Tis still the same, although their aery shape
> All but a quick Poetick sight escape.[26]

The realism of Denham's original work bears evidence that he had very little personal interest in the art of feigning. Certainly he was not concerned over the doctrinal values of fiction. His translations were often from fictional material, but his own efforts were largely confined to versifying his direct observations. He showed no interest in developing the imaginary and fanciful. With sturdy good sense, he asserted the right of the poet to free himself from certain outworn subjects and conventions. Inspiration lay within the poet and could weave itself into concrete form about "Cooper's Hill" as truly as about Parnassus. Strongly he argued the case for the validity of contemporary subject matter:

> Sure there are Poets which did never dream
> Upon Parnassus, nor did tast the stream
> Of Helicon, we therefore may suppose
> Those made not poets, but the Poets those.
> So where the Muses and their train resort,

---

[24] Denham, Poetical Works, pp. 128, 129.   [25] Ibid., p. 114.   [26] Ibid., p. 79.

Parnassus stands; if I can be to thee [Cooper's Hill]
A Poet, thou Parnassus art to me.[27]

Though Denham made no statement as to the purpose of poetry, esteeming the whole art interesting rather than important, he has much to say about its nature. His experience as a translator had caused him to inquire into the essence of poetry, which he specially desired to retain in the new version, and his research had led him to believe that the *sine qua non* was a certain felicity of expression. He held it the duty of a poetic translator to convert the beauty of another era into the stylistic beauty typical of his own time:

for it is not his business alone to translate Language into Language, but Poesie into Poesie; and Poesie is of so subtile a spirit, that in pouring out of one Language into another, it will all evaporate . . . there being certain Graces and Happinesses peculiar to every Language, which gives life and energy to the words.[28]

Denham's own standard of poetic style is set forth in his famous lines on the Thames:

O, could I flow like thee and make thy stream
My great example as it is my theme
Though deep, yet clear, though gentle yet not dull
Strong without rage, without o'erflowing full.[29]

The perfect poem would exhibit a happy combination of nature and art. By "nature" he meant the instinctive, unmodified poetic impulse; by "art," the imitative and acquired element. In the proper balance of these lay the essence of the complete poetic gift:

None, this meer Nature, that meer Art can name:
'Twas this the Antients mean't; Nature and Skill
Are the two tops of their Parnassus Hill.[30]

It is this balance that he extols in "On Mr. Fletchers Works":

When Johnson, Shakespear and thy self did sit
And sway'd in the triumvirate of wit——
Yet what from Johnson's oyl and sweat did flow,
Or what more easie Nature did bestow
On Shakespear's gentler Muse, in thee full grown

---

[27] Denham, Poetical Works, p. 63.   [28] *Ibid.*, p. 159.   [29] *Ibid.*, p. 77.
[30] *Ibid.*, p. 142.

Their graces both appear, yet so, that none
Can say here Nature ends and Art begins.[31]

Later he found in Cowley an even better example of the perfect
fusion of nature and art:

Old Mother Wit, and Nature gave
Shakespear and Fletcher all they have;
In Spencer and in Johnson, Art,
Of slower Nature got the start;
But both in him so equal are,
None knows which bears the happy'st share.[32]

Denham had no patience with "fine" writing and even went so
far as to protest against the euphemistic phrases employed in deal-
ing with the subject of procreation:

What gives us that Fantastick Fit,
That all our Judgment and our Wit
To vulgar custom we submit?

Why is it then taught sin or shame,
Those necessary parts to name,
From whence we went, and whence we came?

Thus Reason's shadows us betray
By Tropes and Figures led astray,
From Nature, both her Guide and way.[33]

Even this light argument indicates the trend of the century away
from the intricate style with which it had begun. Denham followed
out his theory that nothing natural need be glossed over or sup-
pressed, with the result that he produced some stanzas that would
have been much better unwritten. Far from Denham's thought
was any taboo on immodest or obscene writing, such as Browne,
Wither, Drayton, and Cowley had observed.

The theory of poetic immortality was not greatly stressed by
Denham. He acknowledged it on several occasions, but the concept
was not sufficiently prominent in his mind for him to refer to it
very often. In "Cooper's Hill" he speaks of Waller as having im-
mortalized St. Paul's Cathedral.[34] He ascribed the Puritan closing

[31] *Ibid.*, p. 141.
[33] *Ibid.*, p. 106.
[32] *Ibid.*, p. 150.
[34] *Ibid.*, pp. 63, 65.

of the theaters to the fear the anti-Stuart faction felt at having the
people see the "Monuments of Fame" poets had raised to monarchs:

> by the art of conjuring Poets rear'd
> Our Harries and our Edwards long since dead
> Still on the Stage a march of Glory tread.[35]

At the end of his poem on Cowley, he made an extended compari-
son between Cowley and Vergil, concluding with the belief that
both had in their works achieved immortal fame.[36] But although
Denham occasionally ascribes to other poets the power of confer-
ring earthly immortality, he nowhere credits himself with such an
ability. Apparently he deemed his own talent insufficient to achieve
a lasting monument:

> Like him [Homer] in birth, thou should'st be like in fame,
> As thine his fate, if mine had been his Flame.[37]

For a Cavalier poet, he has remarkably little to say on the subject
of love. There is one rather poor specimen, "To His Mistress," re-
proaching a lady because she will

> Condemn my Love, and yet commend my Lays.[38]

His virtual omission of this universal theme is perhaps explained
by the argument in "Friendship and Single Life against Love and
Marriage."

Indifferent to the usual lyric themes and only moderately at-
tracted, as his sparse experimenting shows, to contemporary de-
scriptive and expository poetry, Denham was deeply interested in
the problem of translation. Here the element which least interested
him, subject matter, was supplied; and he was accordingly the freer
to devote himself to that aspect of poetry which was paramount to
him—style. He executed a version of the Psalms, translated two
poems from the Latin, and completed Mrs. Philips's translation of
Corneille. To quote one editor of his poetry, T. H. Banks, Jr., "over
half of his work, excluding 'The Sophy,' is translation," [39] prin-
cipally from the Latin. His theory of translation is expressed most
concisely in the lines "To Sir Richard Fanshaw," praising Fanshaw's
English rendering of "Pastor Fido"; the same ideas are given more

---

[35] Denham, Poetical Works, p. 94.   [36] Ibid., p. 152.   [37] Ibid., p. 67.
[38] Ibid., p. 121.   [39] Ibid., Introduction, p. 41.

expanded treatment in the preface to his own English version of part of the *Aeneid*. He comments first very justly that translation ought not to be attempted by anyone not capable of original poetry, for the object is not merely to be a "Fidus Interpres" of the thought but a translator of the artistic inspiration as well.[40] An ancient or foreign masterpiece must be re-created, in terms of contemporary, domestic poetic theory:

> That servile path thou nobly dost decline
> Of tracing word by word and line by line.
> Those are the labour'd births of slavish brains,
> Not the effects of Poetry, but pains:
> Cheap vulgar arts whose narrowness affords
> No flight for thoughts, but poorly sticks at words.

> They but preserve the Ashes, thou the Flame,
> True to his sense, but truer to his fame.
> Foording his current where thou find'st it low
> Let'st in thine own to make it rise and flow;
> Wisely restoring whatsoever grace
> Is lost by change of Times, or Tongues, or Place.
> Nor fetter'd to his Numbers, and his Times,
> Betray'st his Musick to unhappy Rimes,

> Yet after all (lest we should think it thine)
> Thy spirit to his circle dost confine.[41]

This is substantially the theory of Cowley.

Even the meager body of poetic theory which guided so inconsiderable a poet as Denham has its value to the student of trends. The tide of the century has already turned. Poetry is no longer a divine gift, carrying a serious obligation on the part of the possessor; it is a pleasant talent that may be developed into an interesting hobby. The two-handed engine of reform and worship has dwindled to a jeweled dagger, an ornament capable of an occasional lethal thrust. Subject matter is either appropriated, as in translation, or taken journalistically from life; invention is on the wane. Style is the chief concern, the proper compounding of nature and art, wit and judgment. The neoclassical movement is getting under way, and Cowley is the man of the hour. As the lyric and epic, both of which demand some kind of imaginative intensity, decline,

[40] *Ibid.*, p. 159. [41] *Ibid.*, p. 143.

those forms arise which require principally sharp realism and clear style—the expository poem and the satire. Indicative of the same trend toward a new and narrower theory is the increasingly critical spirit in art, which begins to have a negative effect as a few easily formulated tenets are substituted for the complex system of earlier times.

CONCLUSION

THE PREVAILING THEORY of the early seventeenth century was the fruit and fulfillment of the previous tradition. It continued to regard as peculiarly lofty types of writing the ode, the tragedy, and greatest of all, the epic.

The era was characterized by a group of poets who were working earnestly to instruct their audience in personal virtue, national enthusiasm, and Christian glorification of God by employing the attractions of poetic art. Each man sweetened his teaching according to his own taste, but from Wither, who thought it sufficient to employ the most elementary rime and meter, to Milton, who enriched his arguments by clothing them in all the majesty of classical epic and dramatic form, the principle is the same. Pleasure is subordinate to profit; poetry is conceived of as an instrument, as an art given by God for a specific social purpose. Closely connected with this purpose are the concepts of feigning and fame. Fiction is a source of delight; it is also more easily manipulated to point a moral than truth. Therefore the didactic poets desire to retain it, after carefully explaining that an invention is not a lie. Fame, too, is a powerful incentive toward virtue and accordingly the object of respect and cultivation to the teacher-poet. He fulfills the purpose of God by promoting virtue, through spreading the fame of real or fictitious worth by the exercise of his art.

The exceptions in the major group were Browne and Cowley, whose interest centered more strongly on the art itself, on the element of delight. Yet even they acknowledged the greatness of the didactic ideal and were obviously affected by it. The loftiness of the theory of the epic is the key to the early seventeenth century. It was their exaltation of that magnificent form which led the major poets to reduce lesser types to the rank of convenient stepping-stones, thus contributing to the eventual decay of the pastoral. It was the belief behind their exaltation of the epic—that the beautiful expression of lofty ideas was the ultimate purpose of God when he conferred the gift of poetry—which ennobled the whole art and made possible the application to religious subjects of the old lyric beauty of the sonnet and the new lyric forms developed by Jonson and Donne.

Fundamentally akin to the devoted major poet, in central purpose, is the religious lyrist. He, too, converts the sweetness of poetic art to the service of the Lord. But in him the strong religious feeling of the period asserts itself more directly. His is a smaller, more personal offering. The tone is often individual and mystical, narrow and intense. If the reader derives a lesson, that is well, but the primary purpose is to lay art on the altar, to enrich heavenly love with God-given loveliness. All earthly things were for the glory of God; certainly none could be used to magnify him more fittingly than poetry. And yet how many had sung a new song before the Lord since the days of the psalmist? Donne, Herbert, Crashaw, Vaughan began to use, in what seemed to them its true use, the lyric gift. As Herbert phrased it

> 'For thou art still my God' is all that ye
> Perhaps with more embellishment can say.

The century pivots on the point of "noble numbers" in minor as in major poetry. But even in the early seventeenth century there were among the minor poets those who practiced art for art's sake, who were absorbed principally by experiments in perfection of form. They desired to master the principles underlying poetic pleasure and they were not interested in the purpose poetry was intended to serve, considering the pleasure an end in itself. Many of the English lyrists followed Ben Jonson back to the classics; they began to work for exquisite finish and exact proportion, for unity of tone and unblemished smoothness, in short, for those poetic felicities that are beyond the scope of major poets, who have less time to lavish on detail. Music, charming, though not deeply meaningful, became the controlling element in their lyrics. Simultaneously, from the tortured, nervous brilliance of Donne came a new contribution, something that had hitherto appeared mainly in the satire or comedy, where it was applied to others rather than to one's self—a fierce concentration, an incandescence of passion that expressed itself not in familiar similes but in a vocabulary hitherto strange to poetry, the language of the scholastic. Aside from this iconoclastic revolt, no burning passion troubles the predominantly secular poets nor hurries their pens; yet it leaves its mark on men like Marvell. He is calmer and clearer than Donne, but there is a depth and richness of emotional tone in his work that does not flow from the "arted strings" of Herrick and Carew. These latter develop delicate and subtly perfect melodies, balanced beauty of structure, smooth fluency. Even when such poets practice "noble numbers," their best attention is devoted to the lyric feet.

Their absorption in form prefigures the second half of the century, when England, having passed through the throes of attempted reform in government and church, reacted violently against high enthusiasms and burning convictions and was content at the Restoration to have no illusions and make no great essays, but to aim at an immediate practical objective, to use more circumscribed and pertinent topics, to try for an attainable perfection within narrower limits of style. England had lost interest in the Renaissance dreams of man's growth through virtue and Christian faith. Man and art had been full grown in the days of Augustus. Here was a concrete goal to reach, an achievement to be reproduced. Instead of regarding the past as a stage in artistic evolution, the poets now took a certain period, with which they were in sympathy, as an absolute model, even to the extent of reproducing its subject matter. Translations once again loomed large in importance, with the emphasis now heavily on the classics. The great works of the past were regarded as embodying a kind of mortal perfection to which the nearest contemporary approach was a worthy re-rendering. Poets now thought of their gift as involving a duty to art rather than to God. God became less a subject for mystical inspiration and more a source of philosophical inquiry. It was evident that he could and did run the universe without any need of help or praise. The universe was so constructed that the individual would be using his gift to serve God's purpose, whether he did so consciously or unconsciously. Thus the latter half of the seventeenth century rationalized its desire to return to secular poetry. The rising group of poets read a new meaning into the glory of Augustan art, that the proper study of mankind was man and the proper goal of art was an internal aim of perfection.

Thoroughly characteristic of the approaching eighteenth century was the decline of the lyric. The sonnet was temporarily exhausted. The variety and individuality of the metaphysical lyrics were largely responsible for their loss of favor, as the coming era was one of clarity, precision, and regularity, and these brief, passionate, deeply personal utterances could not readily be regimented. The later seventeenth century was not interested in the deeply serious lyric tradition; it was skillful in song, but preferred the ode, the satire, the epistle, and other minor types that were more amenable to neoclassical principles.

Particularly noteworthy is the rise of the satire. The interest in journalistic subject matter gave great impetus to its development. The form, which had hitherto been considered low because it had been deliberately left roughhewn, was now elevated by having as careful treatment accorded to it as to any other type. As the fame of Martial, Horace, and Juvenal attested, satire was of worthy lineage and not without immortality. It had always been the chosen kind of poetry for general complaints or critical comments; it now added a personal element previously found mainly in the epigram, becoming an individual as well as a social instrument. The satire would naturally be the favored form in an age of cynical disillusionment. Just as the epic, with its effort to elevate the moral stature of man by setting a heroic model before his eyes, characterizes the desire of the early seventeenth-century poet to progress, to evolve, to get men nearer to what God desired them to be; and as the religious lyric reflected the passionate individual desire to become more worthy of the divine mercy by unremitting concentration upon it, so translations and satires characterize the age of reason as opposed to the age of faith. Man is doing as well as can be expected, in the best of all possible worlds. He has reached again that peak of complacent culture upon which the Romans stood in the Augustan age. Life and poetry have at last some fixed standards, and it is possible to excel in both by conforming to these. And the typical product is the satire, which, with the aid of invention and polished style, has now begun to put individuals in a pillory, just as the epic formerly placed imaginary heroes on a pedestal. Feigning becomes an engine of destruction in the characteristic original work of Pope and Dryden, and Fame yields her scepter not to merciful Oblivion but to Obloquy. God is now justified by an *Essay on Man,* which, while praising virtue, recognizes philosophically the function of vice, and concludes with the easy assurance that whatever is, is right, rather than with the early seventeenth-century heroic resolve that whatever is must be made better and that art has her role to play in that reform.

BIBLIOGRAPHY

Aiken, Pauline, Influence of the Latin Elegists on English Lyric Poetry, 1600–1650, "University of Maine Studies," Series 2, No. 22 (1932), 1–115.

Alden, R. M., "Lyrical Conceits of the Elizabethan Poets," *Studies in Philology*, XIV (April, 1917), 129–52.

——— "Lyrical Conceits of the Metaphysical Poets," *Studies in Philology*, XVII (April, 1920), 183–98.

Ball, Lewis F., "The Background of the Minor English Renaissance Epics," *Journal of English Literary History*, I, No. I (April, 1934), 63–89.

Banks, T. H., "Cooper's Hill," *Modern Language Review*, XXI (July, 1926), 269–77.

——— "Supposed Authorship of Directions to a Painter," *Modern Language Notes*, XLI (December, 1926), 502–5.

Baskervill, C. R., English Elements in Jonson's Early Comedy, *Bulletin of the University of Texas*, No. 178 (1911).

Beeching, H. C., "The Poetry of Herrick," *National Review*, XL (December, 1902–February, 1903), 788–99.

Bennett, Joan, Four Metaphysical Poets. Cambridge, 1934.

Boas, F. S., Note, *Modern Language Review*, XI (January, 1916), 93.

Brinkley, Roberta F., Arthurian Legend in the Seventeenth Century, Baltimore. 1932.

Browne, William, Poems of William Browne of Tavistock, edited by Gordon Goodwin. 2 vols., London, 1893.

——— The Whole Works of William Browne, edited by W. C. Hazlitt. 2 vols., printed for the Roxburghe Library, London, 1869.

Campbell, Lily B., "The Use of Historical Patterns in the Reign of Elizabeth," *Huntington Library Quarterly*, I, No. 2 (January, 1938), 135–67.

Campbell, Oscar James, Comicall Satyre and Shakespeare's Troilus and Cressida, "Huntington Library Publications," San Marino, California, 1939.

Carew, Thomas, The Poems and Masque of Thomas Carew, edited by J. W. Ebsworth. London, 1893.

Castelain, Maurice, Discoveries, a critical edition. Thèse présentée, Paris, 1906.

——— Ben Jonson, l'homme et l'oeuvre. Paris, 1907.

Cawley, R. R., "Drayton and the Voyagers," PMLA, XXXVIII (September, 1923), 530–56.

——— "Drayton's Use of Welsh History," *Studies in Philology*, XXII (April, 1925), 234–55.

Cory, Herbert E., "The Golden Age of the Spenserian Pastoral," PMLA, XXV (April, 1910), 241–67.

———— "Spenser, the School of the Fletchers, and Milton," *University of California Publications in Modern Philology*, II (June, 1912), 311–73.

Cowley, Abraham, Essays, Plays and Sundry Verses of Abraham Cowley, edited by A. R. Waller. Cambridge, 1906.

———— Poems of Abraham Cowley, edited by A. R. Waller. Cambridge, 1905.

———— The Works of Mr. Abraham Cowley. 7th edition, London, Herringman, 1681.

Crashaw, Richard, The Complete Works of Richard Crashaw, edited by A. B. Grosart. "Fuller Worthies' Library," 2 vols., London, 1872–73.

———— English Poems of Richard Crashaw, edited by J. R. Tutin. Great Fencote, Yorkshire, 1900.

———— Poems by Richard Crashaw, edited by A. R. Waller. Cambridge, 1904.

———— The Poems, English, Latin and Greek, of Richard Crashaw, edited by L. C. Martin. Oxford, 1927.

Davenant, William, Gondibert. London, Newcomb, 1651.

———— The Dramatic Works of Sir William Davenant, edited by James Maidment and W. H. Logan. 5 vols., Edinburgh, 1872–74.

———— The Works of Sʳ William D'avenant Kᵗ. Printed by T.N. for Henry Herringman, London, 1673.

Delattre, Floris, Robert Herrick. Paris, 1911.

Denham, John, The Poetical Works of Sir John Denham, edited by Theodore H. Banks, Jr. New Haven, 1928.

Dixon, W. M., English Epic and Heroic Poetry. London, 1912.

Donne, John, Complete Poetry and Selected Prose of John Donne, edited by John Hayward. New York, 1936.

———— The Poems of John Donne, edited by H. J. C. Grierson. 2 vols. Oxford, 1912.

Dowlin, Cornell, Sir William Davenant's Gondibert, Its Preface and Hobbe's Answer—A Study in English Neo-Classicism. University of Pennsylvania, Philadelphia, 1934.

Drayton, Michael, Works of Michael Drayton, edited by J. William Hebel. Oxford, 1931, Vols. I–IV.

Dryden, John, The Critical and Miscellaneous Prose Works of John Dryden, edited by Edmund Malone. London, 1800.

———— The Works of John Dryden, ed. by Sir Walter Scott and George Saintsbury. Edinburgh, 1885.

Dunn, Esther C., Ben Jonson's Art. Northampton, Mass., 1925.

Eliot, T. S., "A Note on Two Odes of Cowley," Seventeenth Century Studies Presented to Sir Herbert Grierson, pp. 235–42. Oxford, 1938.

———— For Launcelot Andrews. London, 1928.

Eliot, T. S. (*Cont.*) Homage to John Dryden. London, 1927.

———— Selected Essays, 1917–1932. New York, 1932.

Elton, Oliver, "Literary Fame: A Renaissance Study." *Otia Merseiana,* Publication of Arts Faculty of the University of Liverpool, London, 1904, IV, 24–52.

———— Michael Drayton. London, 1905.

Emperor, J. B., "Catullian Influence in English Lyric Poetry 1600–1650," *University of Missouri Studies,* III, No. 3 (July, 1928), 1–133.

Fletcher, Giles, and Phineas Fletcher, Poetical Works, edited by F. S. Boas. 2 vols., Cambridge, 1908–9.

Fletcher, Phineas, The Poems of Phineas Fletcher, edited by A. B. Grosart. "Fuller Worthies' Library," 4 vols., Blackburn, 1869.

Fletcher, Jefferson B., "Areopagus and Pleiade," *Journal of Germanic Philology,* II (1898–99), 429–53.

French, J. M., "George Wither," *Harvard University Summaries of Theses,* 1928, pp. 130–33. Cambridge, 1931.

———— "George Wither in Prison," PMLA, XLV (December, 1930), 959–66.

———— "Milton as a Historian," PMLA, L (June, 1935), 469–79.

———— "Milton as a Satirist," PMLA, LI (June, 1936), 414–29.

Gilbert, A. H., "The Cambridge Manuscript and Milton's Plans for an Epic," *Studies in Philology,* XVI (1919), 172–76.

Godolphin, F. R. B., "Milton, 'Lycidas,' and Propertius, 'Elegies,' III, 7," *Modern Language Notes,* No. 49 (March, 1934), 162–66.

Gourvitch, I., "Drayton's Debt to Geoffrey of Monmouth," *Review of English Studies,* IV (October, 1928), 394–403.

Gray, F. C., "Milton's Counterpoint," *Sewanee Review,* No. 43 (April, 1935), 134–43.

Greg, W. W., Pastoral Poetry and Pastoral Drama. London, 1906.

Grierson, Herbert J. C., Cross Currents in English Literature of the XVIIth Century. London, 1929.

———— First Half of the Seventeenth Century. New York, 1906.

———— Metaphysical Lyrics and Poems of the Seventeenth Century. 2d edition, Oxford, 1925.

———— Milton and Wordsworth, Poets and Prophets. New York, 1937.

Hale, Edward E., Poems of Herrick. "Athenaeum Press Series," Boston, 1895.

Hanford, J. H., A Milton Handbook. Revised edition, New York, 1933.

Harbage, Alfred, Sir William Davenant, poet venturer, 1608–1668. Philadelphia, University of Pennsylvania, 1935.

Harrison, J. S., Platonism in English Poetry of the Sixteenth and Seventeenth Centuries. New York, 1903.

Harrison, T. H., Jr., "The Latin Pastorals of Milton and Castiglione," PMLA, L (June, 1935), 480–93.

Hebel, J. William, "Drayton's Sirena," PMLA, XXXIX (December, 1924), 814 ff.

Herbert, George, The Complete Works of George Herbert, edited by A. B. Grosart. "The Fuller Worthies' Library," 3 vols., London, 1874.

Herford, C. H., and Percy Simpson, Ben Jonson: The Man and His Work. Oxford, Vol. I, 1925.

Herrick, Robert, Poetical Works of Robert Herrick, edited by F. W. Moorman. London, Humphrey Milford, 1921.

Jenkins, Raymond, "Drayton's Relation to the School of Donne as Revealed in the Shepheards Sirena," PMLA, XXXVIII (September, 1923), 557–87.

———— "Drayton's Sirena Again," PMLA, XLII (March, 1927), 129–39.

———— "Sources of Drayton's Battaile of Agincourt," PMLA, XLI (June, 1926), 280–94.

Jones, P. F., "Milton and the Epic Subject from British History," PMLA, XLII (December, 1927), 901–9.

Jonson, Ben, The Complete Plays of Ben Jonson, introduction by Felix Schelling. London, 1910.

———— The Works of Ben Jonson, edited by Peter Whalley. 7 vols., London, 1756.

———— The Works of Ben Jonson, edited by W. Gifford; introduction and appendices by F. Cunningham. 9 vols., London, 1875.

Judson, A. C., "Robert Herrick's Pillar of Fame," Texas Review, V (October, 1919–January, 1920), 262–74.

Jusserand, J. J., "Ben Jonson's Views on Shakespeare's Art," in Shakespeare's Works (1907), Stratford-on-Avon X, 297–319.

Kirsten, Rudolph, Studien über das Verhaeltniss von Cowley und Milton. Leipzig, 1899.

Klein, David, Literary Criticism from the Elizabethan Dramatists. New York, 1910.

Knights, L. C., Drama and Society in the Age of Jonson. London, 1937.

Knowlton, E. C., "The Plots of Ben Jonson," Modern Language Notes, XLIV (February, 1929), 77–86.

Laing, David, editor. Notes of Ben Jonson's conversations with William Drummond of Hawthornden. "Shakespeare Society Publications," Nos. 8–10, London, 1842.

Langdale, A. B., Phineas Fletcher. New York, 1937.

Langdon, Ida, Milton's Theory of Poetry and Fine Art. New Haven, 1924.

Legouis, Pierre, André Marvell (poète, puritan, patriote). London, 1928.

Leishman, J. B., The Metaphysical Poets. Oxford, 1934.

Lodge, Thomas, A Fig for Momus, Boswell, Frondes Caducae. Reprinted at the Auchinleck Press, 1817, Vol. XXI.

Loiseau, Jean, Abraham Cowley: sa vie, son œuvre. Paris, 1931.

———— Abraham Cowley's Reputation in England. Paris, 1931.

Long, Edgar, "Drayton's Eighth Nymphal," *Studies in Philology,* XIII (July, 1916), 180–83.

Lossing, M. L. S., "Herrick: His Epigrams and Lyrics," *University of Toronto Quarterly,* II (January, 1933), 239–54.

McEuen, Kathryn A., Classical Influence upon the Tribe of Ben. Cedar Rapids, Iowa, 1940.

Marvell, Andrew, The Poems and Letters of Andrew Marvell, edited by H. M. Margoliouth. 2 vols., Oxford, 1927.

—— The Rehearsal Transprosed. The Second Part. London, printed for Nathaniel Ponder, 1673.

Masson, David, The Life of Milton Narrated in Connexion with the History of His Time. 6 vols., London, 1858–80.

Milton, John, The Student's Milton, edited by Frank A. Patterson. New York, 1930.

—— The Works of John Milton, Frank A. Patterson, general editor. 18 vols., New York, 1931–38.

Moore-Smith, G. C., "Aurelian Townshend," *Modern Language Review,* XII (October, 1917), 422–27.

—— "Reviews," *Modern Language Review,* XXIV (January, 1929), 79.

Moorman, Frederic W., Robert Herrick. New York, 1910.

—— William Browne, His Britannia's Pastorals and the Pastoral Poetry of the Elizabethan Age. "Quellen und Forschungen," Strassburg (1897), No. 81.

Nethercot, Arthur H., "Abraham Cowley as Dramatist," *Review of English Studies,* IV, No. 13 (January, 1928), 1–24.

—— "Abraham Cowley's Discourse Concerning Style," *Review of English Studies,* II (October, 1926), 385–404.

—— Abraham Cowley, The Muse's Hannibal. London, 1931.

—— "Milton, Jonson, and the Young Cowley," *Modern Language Notes,* XLIX (March, 1934), 158–62.

—— "Relation of Cowley's Pindariques to Pindar's Odes," *Modern Philology,* XIX (August, 1921), 107–9.

—— Sir William D'Avenant, Poet Laureate and Playwright-Manager. Chicago, 1938.

—— "The Reputation of the 'Metaphysical Poets' during the Seventeenth Century," *Journal of English and Germanic Philology,* XXIII (April, 1924), 173–98.

Nicoll, Allardyce, A History of Restoration Drama: 1600–1700. Cambridge, 1928.

Padelford, F. M., Select Translations from Scaliger's Poetics. "Yale Studies in English," Vol. XXVI, New York, 1905.

Parker, W. R., "Chronology of Milton's Early Poems," *Review of English Studies,* XI (July, 1935), 276–83.

Parker, W. R. (*Cont.*) "On Milton's Early Literary Program," *Modern Philology*, XXXIII (August, 1935), 49–53.

——— "The Trinity Manuscript and Milton's Plans for a Tragedy," *Journal of English and Germanic Philology*, XXXIV (April, 1935), 225–32.

Powell, C. L., "New Material on Thomas Carew," *Modern Language Review*, XI (1916), 285–97.

Scaliger, Iulii Caesaris, Poetices libri septem. [Heidelberg?] apud P. Santandrearum, 1594.

Schelling, F. E., "Ben Jonson and the Classical School," PMLA, XIII (1898), 222–49.

Shafer, Robert, The English Ode to 1660. Princeton, 1918.

Shillinglaw, A. T., "New Light on Ben Jonson's Discoveries," *Englische Studien*, LXXI (1936–37), 356–59.

Smith, G. Gregory, Ben Jonson. London, 1919.

Spencer, Theodore, and Mark Van Doren, Studies in Metaphysical Poetry. New York, 1939.

Spingarn, Joel E., Critical Essays of the Seventeenth Century. 3 vols., Oxford, 1908.

——— Literary Criticism in the Renaissance. New York, 1899.

Swinburne, A. C., A Study of Ben Jonson. London, 1899.

Symonds, J. A., Ben Jonson. New York, 1886.

Symons, A., John Donne, from "The Library of Literary Criticism" by Charles W. Moulton, Buffalo, 1901.

Thompson, E. N. S., "Mysticism in Seventeenth Century English Literature," *Studies in Philology*, XVIII (April, 1921), 170–231.

Thompson, G. A., Elizabethan Criticism of Poetry. Menasha, Wisconsin, 1914.

Tillyard, E. M. W., "Milton and the English Epic Tradition," Seventeenth Century Studies Presented to Sir Herbert Grierson, pp. 211–34. Oxford, 1938.

Van Doren, Mark, The Poetry of John Dryden. New York, Harcourt, 1920.

Vaughan, Henry, The Works of Henry Vaughan, edited by L. C. Martin. 2 vols., Oxford, 1914.

Warren, Austin, "Crashaw's Epigrammata Sacra," *Journal of English and Germanic Philology*, XXXIII (April, 1934), 233–39.

Wells, Henry W., "Ben Jonson, Patriarch of Speech Study," *Shakespeare Association Bulletin*, XIII (January, 1938), 54–62.

Wendell, Barrett, The Temper of the Seventeenth Century in Literature. New York, 1904.

Whitaker, Lemuel, "Michael Drayton as a Dramatist," PMLA, XVIII, No. 3 (September, 1903), 378–411. (New Series Volume XL, No. 3.)

White, Helen C., The Metaphysical Poets; a Study in Religious Experience. New York, 1936.

Willey, Basil, The Seventeenth Century Background. London, 1934.

Williamson, George, The Donne Tradition. Cambridge, 1930.

———— "The Restoration Revolt against Enthusiasm," *Studies in Philology*, XXX (October, 1933), 571–603.

Wilson, John D., "Giles Fletcher and 'The Faerie Queene,'" *Modern Language Review*, V (October, 1910), 493–94.

Wither, George, The History of the Pestilence (1625), edited with notes and introduction by J. M. French. Cambridge, 1932.

———— Works of George Wither. Manchester Publications of the Spenser Society, 41 vols., 1872–1885.

Woledge, Geoffrey, "St. Amand, Fairfax and Marvell," *Modern Language Review*, XXV (October, 1930), 481–83.

INDEX